YOUR KEY TO CREATIVE THINKING

ALSO BY SAMM S. BAKER:

CASEBOOK OF SUCCESSFUL IDEAS

HOW TO BE A SELF-STARTER

ONE TOUCH OF BLOOD

MURDER VERY DRY

HOW TO BE AN OPTIMIST—AND MAKE IT PAY

MIRACLE GARDENING ENCYCLOPEDIA

SAMM S. BAKER

YOUR KEY TO CREATIVE THINKING

HOW TO GET MORE AND BETTER IDEAS

HARPER & ROW, PUBLISHERS
NEW YORK AND EVANSTON

FIRST EDITION

I-M

LIBRARY OF CONGRESS CATALOG CARD NUMBER: 62-15738

This book is dedicated to your more creative, more productive and more successful future . . . where you're going to spend the rest of your life.

CONTENTS

YOUR KEY TO CREATIVE THINKING

1

HOW THIS BOOK CAN MAKE YOU MORE CREATIVE

A man's mind, stretched by a new idea, can never go back to its original dimension.
OLIVER WENDELL HOLMES

You are about to enjoy one of life's greatest experiences—the stretching of your mind, by yourself. You will become a more creative individual, thinking more alertly and effectively, producing profitable and rewarding creative ideas.

The six-step creative method in this book will lead you to learn exactly how. It will take you beyond your current "original dimension," to teach, stimulate, stretch and enlarge your capacities and your abilities.

Becoming more creative can be one of the most exciting and gratifying accomplishments of your life. An educator states that "virtually every person has more creative ability than he is actually putting to use."

You don't have to start as a natural creative "genius." Very few people do. If you read and practice, you'll become more creative. It has been proved many times over. As a leading professor of psychology stated, "The capacity to create . . . is not limited to the highly gifted person, but is the birthright of every person of average talent."

Another wrote, "Creativity (latent or expressed) is in each and every one of us."

We're not concerned here with creativity in art, music or literature, but primarily with basic creative thought, action and problem-solving in everyday living. A novelist affirmed that "everybody has imagination"—but you must learn how to use it most productively.

This volume aims to make it relatively quick and easy, as well as challenging fun, to develop your mental muscles and become a more productive and successful creative person.

As a simple example of creative thinking, note this blank circle, which here represents a creative challenge:

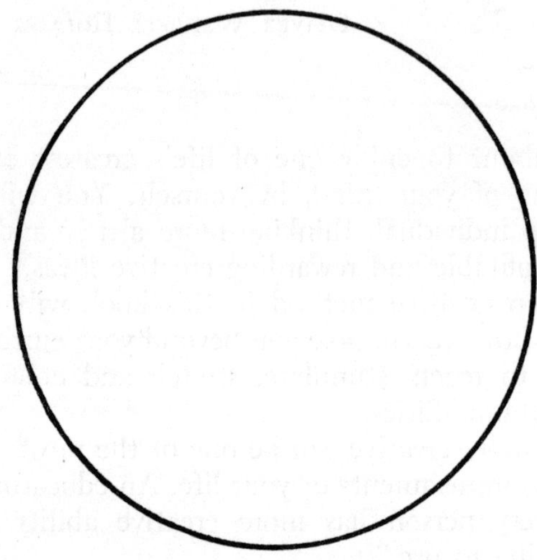

You'll find intriguing and entertaining practice puzzlers like this one throughout these pages. They'll help you develop your mental muscles for clearer, quicker, more effective creative thinking. You'll agree with the scientist who described a big part of creativity as "a sort of solving of puzzles."

Consider the circle problem: By using four straight lines, into how many parts can you divide the circle?

Don't disparage this problem and other puzzlers as child's play. Famed mathematicians use this and other puzzlers to help develop and open the highly trained and able minds of advanced students. A university professor who used such puzzles in teaching noted that "Many go back centuries, to Greek and Roman and medieval days, for their derivations."

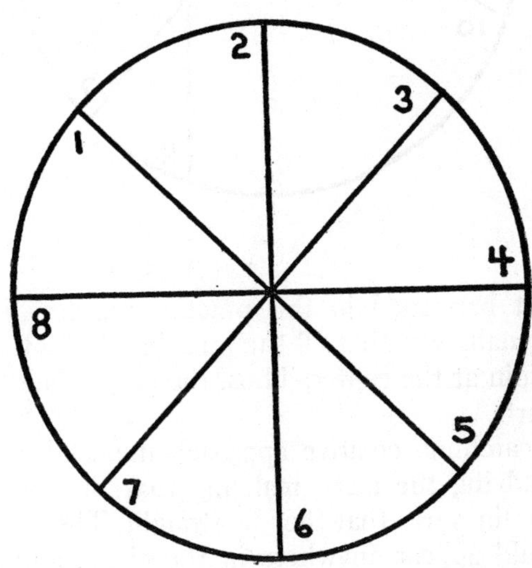

Here you see how most people "solve" this problem. They draw the four straight lines as shown here. They give the answer, "You can divide the circle into eight parts."

That's the obvious approach and answer, but an unimaginative one. When you learn to put your mental muscles to work most efficiently, you'll find that you can manipulate those four straight lines to increase the number of parts in that circle by over thirty-five percent in this way:

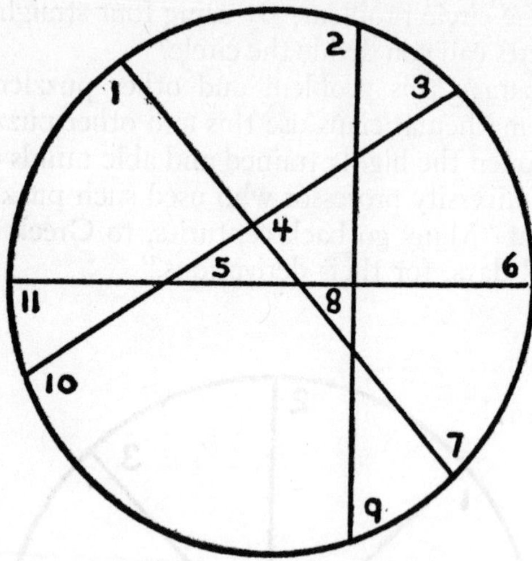

Note what happened in this practice puzzler. The obvious reaction originally was that all the lines had to be the same size, and had to join at the center. Thus, the circle could be cut only into eight parts.

But the searching, creative approach included analyzing the problem, studying the facts, realizing that the only restriction regarding the lines was that they be straight. They could be long or short, could appear anywhere in the circle, and could cross each other at any point. You could produce eleven segments.

This creative approach would thus have increased your productivity over thirty-five percent in this case.

Apply that kind of extra productivity to your business, social or personal activities. It becomes clear that you can profit enormously by learning how to be more creative—and using your new ability accordingly. The invention of pills, for example, was a scientific triumph; putting sugar-coating on them was creative.

You'll learn here how to look beyond the obvious, to resist and reject the first solution, at least until you've considered, checked and rechecked. You'll know just how to approach and solve many daily problems in order to reach the answer with the greatest potential gain.

You'll profit greatly too as you feed and develop the tremendous creative need that is within you, as it is in most of us. You'll grow as you utilize all your creative abilities, many of them hidden because they are underdeveloped.

We have this need in us from our earliest beginnings. A child's need to play is creative. An adult's striving to improve is a creative need, in whole or part. And the accomplishment is a constant and renewing deep personal gain.

Efficiency in living is not enough. A leading educator has pointed out, "The wonderful efficiency of the oyster succeeds only in producing more oysters." Being actively creative satisfies your urge to inquire, to invent, to produce more. It has been said, "Doing nothing is the most tiresome job in the world, because you can't stop and rest."

What Is Creativity?

The dictionary defines "create" as "to cause to come into existence; bring into being; make; originate; to produce as a new construction out of existing materials."

Here are other definitions of creativity advanced by recognized educators, psychologists, creative experts:

"The process of bringing something new into birth."

"Bringing into birth some new reality." (Plato.)

"Bringing into being something new and novel."

"Involving an original concept or idea and a beneficial result."

"Involving new and beneficial ideas put into action."

"Bringing about notable changes in things, thoughts, social structures, through action."

"A process of planning, experiencing, acting and interacting."

"That process which results in a novel work that is accepted as tenable or useful or satisfying by a significant group at some point in time."

"Thinking which results in a solution not previously known to us."

So we move forward, with this general, accepted premise: Creative thinking is the kind of thinking which aims to produce something new and useful, something better than before, which may be carried through to a valuable, beneficial, productive result.

Proof That You Can Be More Creative

The best proof that you have the basic element needed to be more creative is that you're reading these words right now. The act of opening this book and studying the method in it forms an all-important first move toward producing valuable creative ideas.

As you go from page to page, you'll gain confidence in your ability to think creatively. You'll give up any notion you might have had that one must be "born creative." Many research projects have proved that the great majority of people can learn to be more creative.

In tests at a prominent university, students who took courses in creative thinking and action averaged over ninety percent better than comparable persons at the same school who had not taken such studies. Proved—the capacity to practically double the ability and power of varied individuals to produce useful, valuable creative ideas!

But such results are not confined to long courses at universities. Excellent advances have been scored by courses in creativity that are as short as ten hours. These are given by industrial firms, varied businesses and after-hours training organizations to hundreds of thousands of persons, men and women, from many areas of life. In repeated instances, these people have more than doubled their output of worthwhile creative ideas.

C.Q. Versus I.Q.

There is increasing regard for the C.Q. (creative quotient) as compared with the I.Q. (intelligence quotient). A highly rated newsletter reports that: "Psychologists have found that standard I.Q. tests are scandalously inept at discovering many kinds of innate intelligence. Testers found that only thirty percent of outstandingly creative children have outstanding I.Q. ratings, even though they perform well in school. A study made of Air Force scientists shows that there is little correlation between high I.Q. and outstanding scientific (creative) performance."

Also, tests at a leading university show that I.Q. tests reveal little about creative talent. A researcher states that: "If selection is based on I.Q. alone, we will miss at least two out of three of those persons best fitted to be our scientific leaders of the future." It appears clear that while a high I.Q. is certainly not a hindrance to creative attainment, it is not essential in becoming a productive creative thinker.

There is endless proof also that age is no limitation to creativity. A friend remarked to me, "Anyone who thinks teen-agers can't be creative has never seen one build a sandwich."

The patent office is flooded more each year with inventions based on creative thinking, produced by men and women of all ages. The list of creative accomplishments by persons over seventy would fill many pages.

Don't be concerned that you may be too old or too young, too set in your ways or too unknowing to be creative. The time to start and to benefit is now.

Your Participation Is the Essential Element

Your alert and active participation is absolutely necessary to gain the most from these pages. This book is not a lecture, not a general essay or discussion about how to think and act creatively. It provides a specific six-step creative method that will produce for you when you use it.

It took over a thousand years to formulate this method. My own studies, added to many others, covering thought, knowledge, accomplishments, concepts and writings about creativity, going back over a thousand years, have contributed.

Consider that you've joined a workshop course where you'll apply interesting and productive techniques. Don't feel hesitant or uncertain because of a lack of previous training or knowledge. It may be true that talent is a gift, but most everyone can develop the ability to be functionally creative.

But you must apply yourself industriously to learning the method. You may have seen the sign tacked up on an office wall which warns: "Look out for those promises of something for nothing. They don't put that cheese in the trap just because they love mice."

Take heart and energy from this statement by one of the greatest creative geniuses in all history, Professor Albert Einstein:

"Imagination is more important than knowledge. Knowledge is limited, imagination embraces the world, stimulating progress, giving birth to evolution."

The six-step method will show you exactly how to use your imagination to produce valuable creative thinking and ideas. This method is not restrictive. It provides a foundation for your thinking, and teaches you how to build on such a base. Then *you* do the building. What you construct is limited only by the extent of your application and exertion.

Following this method might be compared to gardening. A book can tell you exactly how to go about planning a garden, selecting the right seeds and plants, then planting and tending the growth for best possible results. Without this knowledge, you can't have the finest garden. But, then, what you plant is up to you. How beautifully your garden grows depends on how accurately and energetically you followed directions and used your own imagination in planning.

You can grow good creative ideas just as surely as you can grow glorious plants. But keep in mind a quotation from Kipling, noted in another volume I wrote, the *Miracle Gardening Encyclopedia,* which stated:

> . . . gardens are not made
> By singing:—"Oh, how beautiful!"
> and sitting in the shade.

You can't just "sit in the shade;" you must dig in. You must learn and work to produce vigorous ideas.

Beware of Negative Thinking

Many people have prevented themselves from reaching possible goals, and have limited their abilities, only because they *thought* they were limited. Medical reports reveal astounding facts about man's unconscious processes in limiting himself. For example: under hypnosis, athletes have broken their records by as much as twenty-five percent improvement in performance!

Was it hypnosis which increased the athletes' abilities? Of course not. But, under hypnosis, the subject would be released from limitations he had imposed on himself. If he believed he had reached his maximum performance, he just couldn't do any better. Without any such negative block, he exceeded all his past performances.

You have the capacity. The six-step creative method will teach you how to use and apply it. Approach this opportunity with a free, optimistic attitude. Push away any negative feeling of personal limitation or inadequacy.

Profit in Many Ways

Whether you're a businessman, housewife, white- or blue-collar worker, professional man or woman, student, artist, writer, actor, or in some other category, you can benefit greatly from becoming more actively creative.

You can make gains in business, socially, or in whatever areas concern you most. You can give more to living, to yourself and those about you. And you can get more out of life. Creative thinking can become a natural part of your processes and daily progress, starting now and benefiting you through all the years ahead.

As you become more creative, you'll also gain in self-confidence. With improved ability, you'll be more likely to take the initiative in approaching and solving everyday problems. You'll be leading more, and others will be pleased to follow you.

Whatever your abilities, you will function better and become more productive when you apply them creatively. The very essence of creativity is "to see, to be aware, to respond" and to produce.

The World Needs Creative Thinking and Ideas

In the business world, in community and global problems, even in your daily activities, there's a growing demand for creative effort, abilities and ideas. You benefit when you can supply valuable ideas.

A leading psychologist states, "The coming of the space age is another force contributing to the upsurge of interest in creativity. Conditions call for increasingly imaginative solutions. . . . The needs for creativity are enormous."

The business world pays generously for ideas, for productive creative thinking. In school studies, in your home life and community or other activities, direct or indirect profit is just as certain to result when you make a practical creative contribution that advances the effort or project.

A leading magazine reports that companies in the United States alone are paying out over twenty million dollars each year just for employees' suggestions. And this is a very small part of the amount being paid for fresh and useful creative ideas.

An executive of one of the largest industrial firms in the world is quoted as saying that no big company can stay alive and forward-moving without a constant supply and flow of bright creative thinking and ideas.

International figures have said that the future of the world depends in good part on the quality of creative thinking, and on the creative ideas developed and proposed by mankind for every facet of living.

Rewards Are Great and Personal

In addition to the obvious and tangible rewards in money and prestige, the greatest benefits you get from developing a creative outlook and ability are the gains within yourself. This applies not only in the area of achieving success but also in an exciting inner feeling of happiness.

Being creative is like opening a door to a wonderful new house. With each creative step and attainment, you open the door to a new room, to another inviting aspect of living. You gain new insight and a new thrill and enjoyment from living.

My aim is to make every page of this book instructive, helpful and inspiring. I have carefully planned, researched and written this volume to aid people in every walk of life to live more creative, and therefore more productive and fulfilling, lives. This includes men engaged in almost any activity; women in business, in the home or in other pursuits and students of all ages.

The methods are here. The learning, the practice and the application are up to you, requiring your alert and energetic follow-through. The more effort you apply, the more you gain. Your creative powers will increase as you move ahead with the first set of mental-exercise puzzlers and problems!

You are about to embark on an exciting, rewarding new phase of what Mr. Justice Holmes called "the adventure of the human mind."

First Practice Session

You can exercise and build up your mental muscles. This is just about as certain as the fact that you can strengthen your physical muscles by exercise. You can strengthen your mental muscles by solving the specific puzzlers scattered throughout this book. Tackle these problems alertly and energetically.

Don't skip back to the solutions after a brief glance; you won't get the exercise benefits so helpful in improving your creative abilities. These puzzlers provide a mental warmup for you.

"Exercise your mental muscles" is not just a catch phrase. With the aid of these puzzlers, and by applying yourself seriously to each step of the six-step method, your mental muscles must grow, function and produce for you creatively as never before.

This first set of puzzlers, like the earlier circle problem, helps train your mind to avoid the obvious. You seek and find an extra creative dimension, even if it's only a slight imaginative step beyond the obvious answer. Don't be discouraged if the solutions don't come easily at first. By the time you finish this volume, you'll be able to solve mental-exercise puzzlers and problems more readily and speedily, as you learn the creative approach.

Now tackle the first five puzzlers before you start learning each step of the six-step method. There'll be many more problems, of varying types and approaches, just as there are many differing physical exercises for differing purposes. Remember primarily in working to solve this set: *Avoid the obvious approach or solution.*

Avoid-the-Obvious Mental-Exercise Puzzlers

(Solutions begin on page 229.)

1. ONE-LINE PUZZLER. This famous problem challenges your creative ingenuity. You are to begin by placing a pencil point on the star in the diagram below. Without lifting the pencil from the paper, you must draw a continuous line which crosses each line in the diagram just once, ending at the black dot. You are not permitted to cross any line more than once.

It can be done, crossing each line only once in each box with your continuous pencil mark—but the solution is a challenge to your creative insight and cleverness. A little study of the instructions and the problem will unlock the solution, which is not an obvious one.

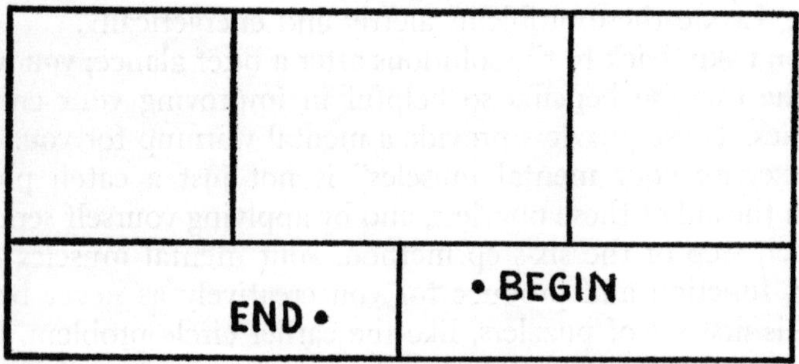

2. TANTALIZING-TOOTHPICKS PUZZLER. Your problem is a simple but tantalizing one. Arrange a batch of toothpicks in the formation shown here, to form nine squares. Now, remove eight of the toothpicks so that only two squares are left.

As in many creative problems, aim to figure out the basic clue to the revealing solution. Don't restrict your imagination in working on this ingenious challenge.

3. DIVIDE-AND-CONQUER PUZZLER. Match your creative thinking ability against this intriguing match problem. Place sixteen matches in a shape as shown here. The challenge is to add eight matches in such a way as to divide the figure into four parts that are of equal size.

When your mental muscles have been trained, you'll be able to solve a puzzler like this in a few minutes. But without the fundamental clear insight regarding the problem, it may seem insoluble—until you gain added knowledge about unlocking such a challenge.

Here's a tip: Study the shape itself carefully before you proceed to set the eight additional matches into place.

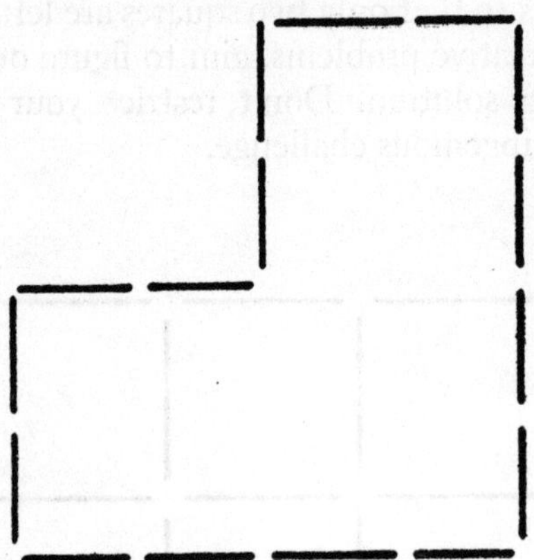

4. MATCH-MANEUVER PUZZLER. Your problem is to manipulate six ordinary wooden kitchen matches so that each one touches every other one firmly. This is more of a challenge than you may think at first consideration.

If you try to touch the heads or ends of the matches at the center, arranged as the spokes of a wheel, the thickness of the extremities won't permit such a solution. Yet, if you get by one usual barrier, the solution is surprisingly simple. Remember, don't let your thinking be confined to the obvious in tackling this match-maneuver puzzler.

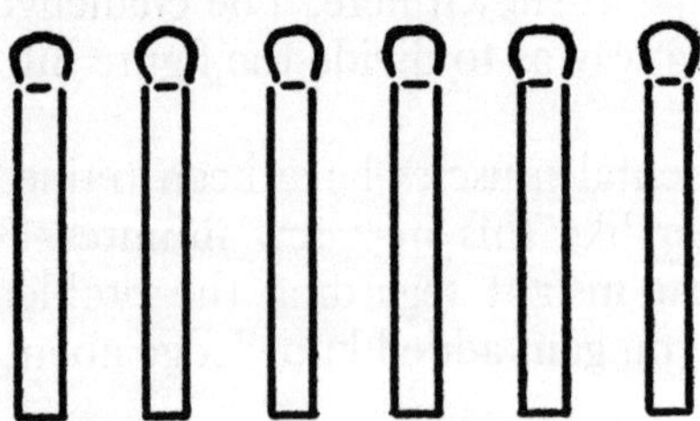

5. Identify-the-Shape Puzzler. I saw this intriguing problem first put into use at a business meeting where five executives were apparently getting nowhere in trying to solve a difficult production problem.

Finally, to ease the tension, the chairman said, "Here's a little puzzle I'd like you all to try." He drew the shapes here on a sheet of paper.

"Now," he went on, "I want each of you to draw the top view of that shape. If you'll loosen up an approach this puzzle with an open mind, you should be able to draw the correct top view within two minutes by the clock. Go!"

You try it. Take a pencil and draw the top view of the shape. You already have the correct front and side view.

Keep in mind the title of this batch of puzzlers: "Avoid-the-Obvious."

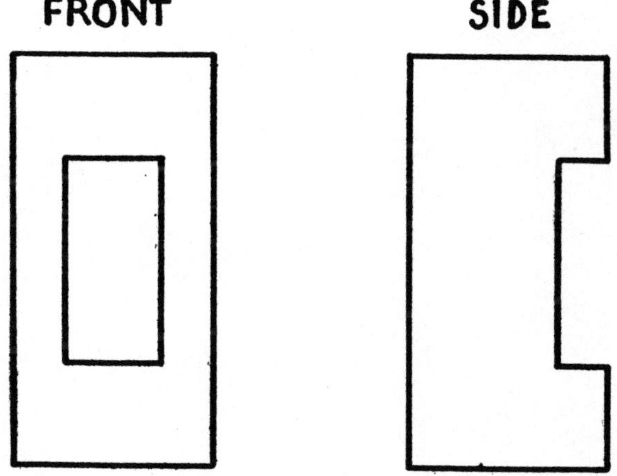

These puzzlers, and the other challenging problems to come, are important as they relate to improving your productive thinking in your everyday living.

Dr. Robert Hutchins, former president and chancellor of the University of Chicago, was quoted as stating, "The biggest enemy of human progress is mental indolence. As Aristotle said, 'Learning is accompanied by pain.' Too many people won't go through that pain."

Instead of thinking of any "pain" in learning, realize instead that it can be a joy forever to learn to produce excellent ideas through practiced creative thinking. The six-step creative method that follows will show you how.

2

HOW TO RECOGNIZE PROBLEMS AS A CREATIVE CHALLENGE

Before you proceed to learn the six-step creative method, you must realize that almost any problem presents a creative challenge.

For example, as a business executive, how can you increase sales in your department? You might take the obvious approach of adding more salesmen. Or, you could act creatively to boost the effectiveness of your present salesmen and distributors.

As an employee who wants a raise, you might simply ask for an increase, and get a little more money or none at all. Or, you could develop some creative ideas that would show the company how to make more profit through your services, and win a sizable raise in pay. A personnel counselor recommends, "To get a job or get an advance, first get an idea."

If you're a housewife, there are many creative challenges all about you, waiting to be solved for the convenience and enjoyment of your family. Consider something as simple as a clothes closet. You can permit a messy situation to develop, as in so many homes, where everything tumbles to the floor whenever the door is opened—the way it happens in television comedy skits. Or, you can plan creatively so that everything has a clean, orderly place in the closet, saving time and temper for everyone in the family, and winning praise for yourself. And there are unlimited creative decorating and other opportunities in every home.

In essence, the necessary approach is for you to regard and tackle almost every problem as a creative challenge. And you must develop and firmly establish the conviction in your own thinking that you're a potentially creative person. A famed psychologist affirms that a wife, mother and homemaker is creative when she produces ingenious and inventive ideas and methods in her home, and he writes, "To originate a first-rate soup is more creative than daubing a second-rate painting."

Once you say with complete assurance to yourself, "I produce useful ideas," you've made important headway toward being truly and continually creative.

There's Creative Machinery in Your Cranium

Here's one way I've convinced others to realize that they do possess latent creative ability. I tell them to study the following diagram which I draw roughly on any handy sheet of paper:

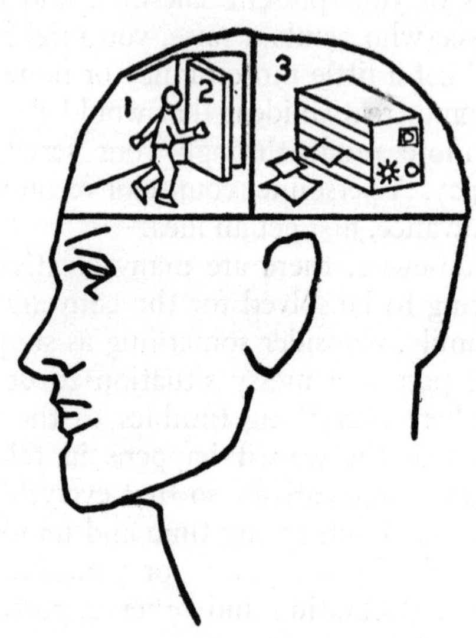

Here's how to utilize this picture. With almost every problem that comes up, consider that the top of your head is divided into compartments as in the drawing. You're standing in position (1) in the front room of your brain. Behind the door (2) is your idea factory, (3) a manufacturing plant of ideas. In order to reach the idea factory and start the thinking machinery to produce ideas, you must first unlock the combination on the door to your "manufacturing plant."

You Must Start the Machinery Going

You'll find that picturing those little rooms up in your head, time after time, closing your eyes and visualizing this diagram, will help you to approach each problem as a creative challenge.

When you're faced with a problem in business or at home, or wherever and whenever it may occur, the natural tendency so often is to become baffled or bewildered and say, "It can't be done!" In effect, at that point, you're standing in the little front room of your mind, staring at the problem, and deciding that you can't do a thing about it.

Instead, make yourself open the door to the idea factory behind it. You know that you possess that manufacturing plant in your head, because you've learned from the facts stated on previous pages that you're potentially creative. Remember that the act of opening this book and turning from page to page is, in effect, creative procedure.

Don't just give in when you're face to face with many problems—as you may have done too often in the past. Don't frown and insist that you're "stumped." Decide instead that you'll use the steps of the creative method you'll learn here as a combination to unlock the door and put the thinking machinery into operation.

You'll find that, once you adopt the creative approach, you're going to greet almost every problem, each day, as a creative challenge. You'll be able to solve more problems than you ever thought possible. The six-step method will become part of your natural, active thinking and action. Your production of helpful creative ideas and solutions will multiply astonishingly, to your continuous gratification and gain.

Creative thinking and the resultant productive ideas often seem surprisingly simple, once you put your mind to them.

Simple Problem and Creative Solution

For example, consider this problem: You want to know whether a child over three years old, who still cannot read, can actually see clearly the various letters on a chart fifteen feet away, such as this:

With normal eyesight, the child could tell you the letters. Yet, the child can't read, and you don't know whether his eyesight is average or worse.

You probably know the answer to this challenge from personal experience. But it's very much worth your consideration as an illustration of the importance of putting the creative process to work on a very elementary problem. Here's one basic example of the necessity for further action rather than quick surrender.

In this case, you might normally stay in the anteroom in front of your brain and say, "Well, there's no way to solve this problem. The child can't read; therefore he can't say whether he can see the letters or not, since he can't identify them in any case. We'll have to wait until he's older."

Instead of being flatly negative, take the positive approach: You unlock the door to the inner room and set your thinking machinery into motion. You start asking a very simple series of questions in respect to solving this very easy problem creatively—easy once you put your creative processes and abilities to work.

The direct questions proceed in obvious relationships; let's progress in very elementary fashion:

Q: Can the child recognize the letters on the chart?
A: No, the child can't read.
Q: Can he describe the letters on the chart by form or shape?
A: Not clearly enough so you can be sure of what he means; there'd always be some confusion and resultant uncertainty.
Q: What simple objects *can* the child recognize on sight?
A: Quite a few, but he can't read letters yet.
Q: Can you draw some objects the child is familiar with?
A: Of course. He could name a flower, a pear, a bird, a tree.
Q: Now the creative solution is clear, isn't it?
A: Yes, indeed. Instead of having letters on the chart that the child can't read or describe, draw some objects that he can recognize and identify, like this chart:

It seems so simple when you know how. But the key to the combination here was to recognize the problem as a creative challenge. The next move was to unlock the door to your thinking machinery and to create the practicable answer.

Without that first decision to try to solve the problem creatively, the special eye chart for children, now in use all over the world, would never have been devised. Someone had to recognize that this problem was a creative challenge, which could be solved by creative thinking, leading to a useful and valuable idea.

Once you make this conscious creative attitude a natural part of your approach—as you should, starting right now—you'll find that you'll be able to produce a flow of creative ideas, large and small, utilizing the six-step method.

Six Words That Say It All

A very able and successful man suggested that a great impetus and way to creative thinking and ideas might be embodied in these six words: "Find a need and fill it." This is an excellent challenge and thought-starter, as far as it goes. But, in a way, it's like telling you, "Get in an airplane alone and fly."

You can get into an airplane even more easily than you can "find a need." But once in the pilot's seat, you can't fly until you know how. Nor is it readily possible to guide your thought processes to find ideas to "fill the need" until you learn how.

You will learn by the method in the following chapters. Also, the truly creative person finds new answers to needs that were previously nonexistent. For example, people didn't think they "needed" a telephone or a phonograph before they were invented. Your creative approach therefore will include problem-seeking and problem-solving.

Right now, exercise your mental muscles with the following practice problems. In each case, a need was filled in actual daily living. You probably know most of the answers—they're embodied in products you can find in stores, or already in your house or featured on the pages of magazines.

Go over the following list fast, jotting down the answers on a sheet of paper. Then compare your solutions to those on the corresponding solution pages later. But do it speedily ("speed is what you put down a hot plate with").

This is excellent exercise for your mind, plus important clarification of the big point you should learn from this chapter: Approach problems as creative challenges.

Fill-the-Need Practice Problems

(Solutions begin on page 235.)

1. CHALLENGE: How did refrigerator makers solve the need to provide more storage space for food in the cold interior?

2. CHALLENGE: Makers of white bed sheets needed to increase demand; how did they do it?

3. CHALLENGE: The family needs a change from just plain vegetables for dinner; what to serve?

4. CHALLENGE: A couple in a one-room apartment needs a desk and a serving table, yet hasn't room for both; how to fill their need?

5. CHALLENGE: Many homes with metal cabinets installed needed more hooks on interior shelves on which to hang cups. Yet hooks couldn't be screwed into the metal as into wood; how to fill the need?

6. CHALLENGE: Women complained that their work gloves became dirty and messy too fast when used in the kitchen, garden and elsewhere involving contact with dirt and grease; how to fill their need for something better and less costly?

7. CHALLENGE: Many women asked for something better than the old-fashioned metal vegetable grater, because peelings scattered over the dish or bowl onto the table surface; how to fill the need?

8. CHALLENGE: A woman wanted to read all the latest books, and liked owning books. Yet she felt she couldn't afford to buy them all, and didn't like waiting her turn for weeks and months at the local library; how did she fill her need?

9. CHALLENGE: Leading manufacturers of macaroni products realized the need to make them more attractive to children so that women with large families would serve macaroni more often; how did they add special appeal to children?

10. CHALLENGE: Producers of vitamins realized that, beyond making people know the benefits of vitamin capsules for the family, it was necessary to remind people to use them daily at one or more meals; how did they solve this need?

11. CHALLENGE: A creative manufacturer developed a mending tape with a remarkable adhesive on the back. Applied to many different types of fabrics, the tape would mend a crack, hole or tear instantly. But the big problem became: how to present so commonplace an item as mending tape so it would catch special attention and attract many purchasers?

12. CHALLENGE: Women wanted lipsticks in many shades. But an alert manufacturer challenged himself this way. "How can I make sure women will buy my lipsticks in all the shades?"

Where to Find the Challenges

I found all these creative challenges and solutions right on the pages of just one issue of a leading national home magazine.

An excellent exercise for you, week after week, is to go through the pages of your favorite newspapers and magazines carefully. Check the helpful editorial features and advertisements. See how so many creative-minded businesses and individuals looked for a need, found it, then filled it and profited accordingly.

You'll profit too when you learn how to find a need and fill it. Face your own problems, recognize each as confronting you with a challenge or need, and then apply the six-step method to help arrive at the best creative solution.

Expose Yourself to Alert, Creative Minds

You will definitely benefit by being constantly on the lookout for problems and the creative solutions. And, just as surely, you can help keep your creative potential at top activity by exposing yourself as much as possible to other alert, creative people.

You'll find that you can be more creative when your mind is prodded and activated by other creative-minded individuals. Surely you can recall the few or many occasions when you've come from a gathering or meeting with bright, alert persons and commented, "I feel so 'alive' after the interesting discussion tonight. My mind is jumping with ideas!"

Much of the beneficial mental exercise you can get from contact with others can be your own doing. Take the lead. Challenge others at a social gathering, or after a business meeting, with some of the brain teasers you learn in this book.

Bright individuals will come back with other puzzlers and you'll find your mind "jumping" with interest and enthusiasm. You'll enjoy a more stimulating time, and others will enjoy you more.

Exercise Increases Creative Power

You'll find proof as you become more skillful in solving puzzlers, for example, that the more creative you try to be in finding the solution, the more adept you'll become. Your creative power increases as you exercise and use it.

One of the most successful sales executives I know always spends at least ten minutes going over his sales presentation in his mind thoroughly before facing his prospect. He does this not just to refresh his memory, but primarily to activate his thinking processes.

He told me, "I always take that short warmup period to exercise my mental muscles. I find that my mind is then fresh and alert when I face the other fellow. When he throws his problems at me, my brain is already in high gear to produce creative solutions. The more I exercise my mind beforehand, the more quickly and surely ideas come popping out."

Mental-Exercise Sessions Furnish Proof

Carefully regulated tests have proved that mental exercise works remarkably well even in respect to physical effort. As one instance, the members of a team of basketball players were required to sit on a bench and *think* about throwing the ball into the basket from the foul line. Without a single physical action employed, that thinking session lasted over fifteen minutes.

On the occasions when these athletes simply "thought" in a concentrated way beforehand about making those foul-line shots, they scored more than twenty percent higher than when they went out to take the shots without preliminary thinking.

Some might label this kind of pre-thinking as self-hypnosis. But whatever anyone calls it, concentrated thinking is mental exercise that will prove its value in whatever you undertake. That's true of business or home activity, or even physical exertion.

Checklist of Mental Elements That Make Up the Creative Person

From a review of many case histories, studies and conclusions by psychologists, executives, educators and writers, the following ten-point checklist has been produced. The points cover the basic mental elements that are essential in continual creative thinking and resultant ideas.

How many of these mental elements do you think you possess right now? Jot down these elements on a sheet of paper and write "have" or "have not" opposite each.

1. DESIRE. To supply the spark that moves you to utilize all other elements and attack each problem, you must possess and

develop the desire to make things better. That volition to improve the status quo is the basis for all creative thinking, activity and the production of creative ideas that will make things better. A friend tells me that a common statement among chess players is, "When you find the *perfect* move, look for a better one."

2. ALERTNESS. Being alive, awake, "wide open" to note everything that happens to you and around you.

3. INTEREST. Not only aware of what goes on, but also definitely interested in digging below the surface.

4. CURIOSITY. A spirit of inquiry so that you not only want to dig below the surface but you also think of and ask questions on all aspects of a problem, situation, item or person.

5. THOUGHTFULNESS. The desire to view all aspects, not just fleetingly or temporarily, but to devote considerable thought to understanding exactly what forms the entity.

6. CONCENTRATION. The ability to focus your interest and thought, and keep it focused, so that you can think about and understand details and aspects in depth.

7. APPLICATION. This includes effort, industriousness, the application of energy and hard work constantly and repeatedly. Edison said, "Genius is two percent inspiration and ninety-eight percent perspiration."

8. PATIENCE. The tenacity to keep coming back to the problem or situation, time after time, until you're thoroughly satisfied with the solution. The impatient person tends to grasp the first answer and run with it, or deserts the situation entirely in short order.

9. OPTIMISM. This embodies self-confidence and enthusiasm, in a combined viewpoint of reasonable, positive assurance. You

feel that you will find the wanted solutions, rather than regarding the chances pessimistically and negatively.

10. CO-OPERATION. This is the desire and willingness to share your creative ideas with others, to help develop them to the fullest with a co-operative attitude. You consider reasonably the reactions of others, with the view of accepting and applying suggestions and even modifications which will make your ideas most practicable and productive.

How Did You Score?

Add up the check marks and see how you scored, without fooling yourself. If you scored "have" on eight or more of the elements, you rate high and you're well started toward full development as a creative person.

If you scored "have" on only seven or fewer of the categories, you'd better go to work on yourself to develop those qualities. You certainly can if you want to. It will pay you to keep rechecking that list and rerating yourself every week or two.

There are a number of other elements that contribute to the makeup of the creative person, but these ten are fundamental and essential.

Ten Key Creative Mental Elements

Desire	Concentration
Alertness	Application
Interest	Patience
Curiosity	Optimism
Thoughtfulness	Co-operation

In past teaching, I have urged others to write down those ten qualities (as above) on a small slip of paper—just the key leading word in each—and carry the listing. Then they check up on the list each day whenever possible, perhaps at lunch, on a bus or train. They review their attitudes and reactions during the day and realize where they have fallen down in regard to any of them, and try to correct the failures in the future.

This system has worked wonders for those who use it, in developing these ten basic mental elements that make up the creative person. I urge you also to carry such a checklist. Compare your actions each day against the ten points. Act consciously to develop and apply those characteristics. You'll then be able to check them all as "have" on your personal list in a surprisingly short time. You'll soon be far better qualified to see and approach almost every problem as a creative challenge, and then solve it by the six-step method.

Now Face the Challenge!

At this point, you should realize the worth, importance and necessity of reminding yourself to face your problems as creative challenges.

You have checked the list of mental elements that make up the creative person, and you either possess these elements already or you'll develop them and make them part of your normal attitude and approach.

Push aside any negatives or feelings of inadequacy, if present. Creative activity is only fearful to those who regard it so. All you have to do actually is to utilize the mental abilities that you naturally own right now and will develop to the utmost in the future. Then you'll find that daily creative thinking is not difficult but exciting and stimulating. Give yourself fully to learning and practicing the six-step method that follows.

Involve yourself emotionally as well as intellectually, and you'll savor the full rewards and joy of being an effective creative person. You'll inevitably profit from your own thrilling and productive creative ideas.

H. G. Wells wrote, "Human history is in essence a history of ideas." You can make your own more successful history—if you will!

3

THE SIX-STEP CREATIVE METHOD

Now you're all set for your great "adventure of the mind"—to study and assimilate the six-step creative method. With repeated application, you'll make it a natural part of your thinking and action from now on. You'll be able to step up your creative thinking and production of ideas far higher than ever before.

It's worth repeating that this six-step method is no strange magical formula compounded of mysterious "instant wizardry." This sound and sensible procedure is a distillation of wisdom and practical usage, employed by brilliant and successful creative thinkers over the centuries.

The ultimate six-step method, as I have created, taught and used it, is synthesized and projected here for easiest understanding, adaptation and usage by you. It will serve you for the rest of your life.

Five Concentration Puzzlers

(Solutions begin on page 238.)

To obtain greatest benefit from study of the six steps of the method, you should *concentrate* on the first listing of the steps. Fix your mind on the few simple words that name each step, and try to fasten them in your consciousness. You'll automatically learn them well as you read the details later.

To help you limber up your mind now, try to solve the five mental-exercise puzzlers that follow.

Fair warning: These problems are tricky. To solve them requires concentrating on the stated details. It's vital that you should not overlook key facts or insert any elements yourself that don't actually exist in each challenge.

Concentrate on noting and absorbing the details of each puzzler simply and clearly. This exercise helps prepare your mind for complete understanding of the statements made later in this Chapter that describe each of the six steps.

1. THE ELEVATOR MYSTERY. This puzzler may seem absolutely crazy, yet the solution is obvious—once you get it. Try it on your friends later. You'll be amused at how many people are baffled by it.

Suppose you're an elevator operator who has worked for twelve years in a twenty-two story building. On the average, you're on the job eight hours a day. Now, when you start at the basement, making a complete trip to the top, and stopping only at every other floor, the trip takes exactly four minutes and thirty seconds.

What is the elevator operator's first name?

2. THE SECRET OF DRIVING. Whether you can drive a car, or have only ridden in an auto as a passenger, you have the ability to solve this puzzler—but you must concentrate, or you'll fail.

What is the first thing you do in order to operate an automobile after you get into the car?

3. PENETRATE THE SMOKE SCREEN. Reading very late at home one night, a heavy smoker ran out of cigarettes. All the stores were closed and he was most anxious to keep smoking while he kept reading. What to do?

He gathered all his ashtrays and found thirty-six cigarette butts. Very cleverly he found that he could put each six butts together to make one whole cigarette (you'll have to take this procedure for granted as being possible).

How many cigarettes in all could he smoke during the balance of that night?

4. Uncork Your Thinking. Solving this little mathematical problem requires keen concentration. For, simple as it seems, most people come up with the wrong solution because they don't focus on the facts with complete clarity.

You buy a bottle and a cork for $1.10. When you ask the seller how he breaks down the cost of each, he tells you merely that the bottle costs a dollar more than the cork.

How much does the cork alone cost?

5. A Matter of Correct Timing. Here's another example that helps teach people not to jump to obvious conclusions, but to take time to concentrate long enough to absorb all the elements of a problem.

It takes a clock thirty seconds to strike six o'clock. How long does it take the clock to strike twelve?

Six-Step Creative Method

I urge you to concentrate fully on the wording of each step of the creative method, especially as you read it the first time.

Eventually, your mind will approach, grasp and follow through with each step just as readily as a person swims, for example. At first, when one is learning to swim, each action seems impossible to comprehend or accomplish. You thrash about in the water. Your instructor tries to teach you how to move one arm and then the other arm. You must be aware of the position of your hand, wrist, elbow and upper arm at each stroke. You must co-ordinate the movements of one arm with the other arm. Your head must be down, not held high—or you'll sink.

Then your torso must be balanced properly or you'll tend to sink down toward the bottom like a rock. You must kick one leg a certain correct way, not in an awkward, ineffectual motion. Then you must manage the other leg similarly.

How can you possibly co-ordinate all this? You wonder. How parallel the rhythm of each leg with the other, and then with the motions of your arms? Oh, no, you despair, I can't possibly learn how to swim, even though so many others have accomplished it.

And then—a seeming miracle—by learning the essentials and practicing sufficiently, suddenly you're swimming. You're moving awkwardly, but making headway. And then, magically, you become more graceful; you swim faster, easier. And you'll know how to swim as long as you live; you'll never completely forget how.

So it is with learning to think creatively and to produce valuable creative ideas. First, concentrate on the following basic words that define the six steps. You'll drive them into your consciousness best if you memorize them.

Copy the compact listing that follows, so you can study the fundamental six steps when you have a moment on a train or bus or waiting for an appointment. Concentrate on the key capitalized words.

When these six steps have become a natural part of your thought and action processes, you'll be a more creative person.

SIX-STEP CREATIVE METHOD

1. Develop the Creative ATTITUDE.

2. Analyze, to Focus on the Wanted SOLUTION.

3. Seek Out and Fill Your Mind with FACTS.

4. Write Down IDEAS, Sensible and Seemingly Wild.

5. Let Facts and Ideas SIMMER in Your Mind.

6. Evaluate, Recheck, Settle on the CREATIVE IDEAS.

4

STEP ONE: DEVELOP THE CREATIVE ATTITUDE

If you look for it, you can find excitement and the hard core from which to strike creative sparks—even in the commonplace.

The late, great comedian, F. Chase Taylor, whom you may remember as radio and television's unique wit, Colonel Lemuel Q. Stoopnagle, used to tell a zany story about how to select the winning horse before the race started.

He would say very seriously, "Just look through your binoculars at all the horses at the starting gate. Then, to pick the winner, all you have to do is focus your glasses on the right horse. . . ."

First you have to look. Centuries ago, a philosopher wrote, "You'll never find the unexpected unless you're looking for it."

As a warmup to understanding and absorbing step one, try the following practice puzzlers. They're planned particularly to help "open the pores" of your mind—a prime essential of the creative approach. You must be wide awake to solve these tricky little challenges. They'll stimulate and test your alertness and ingenuity. They'll help you learn how to look—and see—creatively.

Five Wake-Up Practice Puzzlers

(Solutions begin on page 240.)

1. Name the City. What large and well-known city in the United States is half golden and half silver?

2. The "Nothing" Problem. Giving some thought to "slanguage" can help you solve this unusual puzzler. Arrange four matches as illustrated here. By adding two more matches in a certain way, you can produce the desired solution which is—nothing.

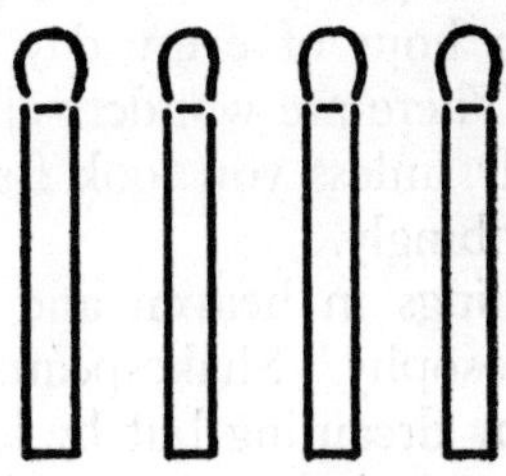

3. Detect the Device. As a person interested in developing your creativity, you're probably familiar with many of the latest inventions. See whether you know the answer to this one. What's the name of the device which is used to help people see through brick walls?

4. Problem of Gravity. The scientific mind is a creative mind in that it is always searching for answers. However, scientific knowledge is not essential in solving this puzzle, although a scientific creative approach will help. Your challenge is to tell what is the center of gravity, and to confine your answer to no more than three words.

5. A Question of Dollars. This puzzler is not easy to answer, for it involves one major obstacle—you have to possess a dollar bill. Once you pass that hurdle, your challenge is to find —right on that dollar bill, in no more than three minutes—a description of a delicate, secluded type of woman. Don't overlook the possibilities in breaking words apart and even considering slang.

How to Look and "See"

"There is none so blind as those that won't see." This expression written hundreds of years ago, is urgently recommended to you as the key to absorbing step one—developing the creative attitude.

Decide that you *will* open your mind, as well as your eyes, and see—every waking hour of every day and night—see with your mind's eye, too. There are wonders all about you, but you will not see them fully unless you look for them and at them consciously, alertly, probingly.

"There are more things in heaven and earth . . . than are dreamt of in your philosophy," Shakespeare wrote. And you will see those things, not by dreaming but by looking. You can and you will if you put your mind to it, starting right now, adopt an attitude of "openness to experience."

Approach this first step without preconceived notions or prejudices, and without fear of ridicule from anyone at any time. This is the starting point; as with a simple broad jump, even a great and soaring leap of the imagination begins at an ordinary jumping-off place.

A noted professor of psychology named as a prime element of the creative attitude "the capacity to be puzzled." A famed French mathematician referred similarly to "the capacity to be surprised." A creative executive urged, "Let yourself get excited, or elated, or enthused . . . sizzle, or steam, or bristle." In other words—feel alive.

The imaginative, searching attitude will not only help make you a creative person but will make all of living more exciting for you. It will tend to keep you young "forever."

Check your memory and you realize that interest and excitement are prime attributes of all the fascinating, young-minded creative people you know. They may be old in years, but they're young in enthusiasm and in the striving for accomplishment—just as you can be.

Whatever you are, you can be better at it with a creative viewpoint and approach. If you're a shoe clerk, you can be more successful as a creative shoe clerk. And that's true for the executive, housewife, student, whatever you may be or want to be.

An Example of Seeing and Not-Seeing

The following example has proved more effective in getting across this vital point than any other means I've ever encountered. I developed this device while teaching an advanced creative writing course at New York University. This simple dramatization was used to reveal to students the importance of alertness, excitement and interest in making the most of the everyday things of living. Please note it well.

At an early point during an evening in each term, I'd walk about the classroom as I lectured. Casually, I'd stop at a window, glance out and say lightly, "The moon's out."

There'd be no notable reaction from the students. Hardly a flicker of interest. I'd go on talking about whatever subject was under immediate discussion.

Toward the end of the class period, I'd casually stop at the window again. This time I'd look out and say, "What a moon out there! It brings to my mind the stirring words of Walt Whitman when he wrote:

> Lo, the moon ascending,
> Up from the East, the silvery round moon,
> Beautiful over the house-tops, ghastly, phantom moon,
> Immense and silent moon.

"What a beautiful moon," I'd repeat.

This time, everyone in the room would be alert and interested. The students nearest the window would pop from their seats and peep out eagerly to see the "ghastly, phantom moon." They'd exclaim, "It's lovely!" "How beautiful!" "What a thrilling sight!"

Then I'd point out to the class the significant lesson in this incident. Actually there was nothing extraordinary about the moon on this evening over any other night. And when I'd mentioned it the first time, no one had been aroused or impressed in the slightest degree.

But when I endowed the normal moon with the excitement, color and creative drama of Walt Whitman's magnificent lines, it became a magical moon, an object of ecstasy and glory, giving exceptional pleasure to all.

In exactly that way—alert, lively creative thinking can be far more effective than an inert, commonplace, "average" attitude. Here's just one illustration of only one element of the specific factors that you should make part of your own character and attitude. By recognizing and developing these points within you, as delineated further in this chapter, you'll possess and use the creative approach.

This knowledge, and your actions accordingly, will accomplish "miracles" in making you a creative thinker—and will multiply enormously your production of useful, profitable creative ideas.

How Ideas Grow from the Creative Attitude

Here are three specific and actual examples of how successful ideas have started because the problems were approached from the enthusiastic, searching creative attitude—and not from the viewpoint of commonplace, unseeing acceptance. Note them carefully.

What's a Girdle Made Of, Made Of?

Mention the word "girdle" or "corset" in a television comedy routine and immediately there's a snicker from the audience. But there's nothing funny about it to a manufacturer of girdles when his problem is to sell them.

Sit down now with a group of us who were gathered about a table on which a designer had placed her newest girdle creation, Style 323. Our problem was to work out a plan to sell the garment.

The sales manager picked up the girdle, glared at it, then dropped it back on the table. "Well," he grumbled pessimistically, "it sure doesn't look like anything special, particularly at a ten-dollar selling price. So, we'll just add it to the line and see what we can do with it."

The manufacturer commented, "It's a nice garment. It does a good molding job on the figure. We ought to get the average sales out of it."

Advertising Style 323 was my responsibility in this case. I asked the designer, "What can you tell us about this girdle?"

She said defensively, "It's a well-designed garment. It fits and it holds. It's a good girdle."

"That's not good enough to sell it," I persisted. "The trouble is that we're all looking at this new offering, but we're not really *seeing* it at all."

I picked up the item and asked, "This band at the top is a little wider than on other styles. Why? And how come this front seam has so many tiny stitches instead of wide-spaced stitching?" I went on like that, detail by detail.

As the designer explained each point, interest and excitement was gradually reflected in the eyes of those around the table. Finally I said enthusiastically, pointing to a sheet of notes I'd jotted down, "Look—I've added up nine different points of superiority. This girdle is nine ways wonderful!"

The energized sales manager picked up the garment again and examined it intently. "That's right," he agreed happily, "this baby *is* nine ways wonderful, and I never even realized it."

"None of us did," the manufacturer admitted, "because we didn't bother to really see it."

Illuminated by the creative approach, we coined a name for the "nine ways wonderful" girdle. In due course, it scored an exceptional sales success. But if no one had really "seen" it, there wouldn't have been any recognition of its particular superiorities. It would have remained just average-selling Style 323 in the maker's offerings.

An alert, searching creative attitude made all the difference, as it can with so many of the everyday problems you encounter.

The Case of the Scratchproof Plastic

I was involved in selling an excellent new plastic covering material which embodied an outstanding creative idea in its manufacture. Most such plastics are permeated with color throughout the sheeting. But this material had the color sprayed on the back, showing beautifully through the clear, transparent sheet.

As a result of this brilliant concept, the color on the back couldn't be marred on the surface of the material, because the color was shielded by the plastic sheeting.

In spite of this remarkable superiority, the product wasn't selling any better than other materials in its field. I traveled with a salesman on his calls to try to find out why. On each call, the salesman ably explained the merits of the product, but didn't make much of an impression.

When we stopped for lunch, I stepped into a variety store and made a purchase. On our next call, the salesman told his story again about the way the product was made, as he showed a piece of the material for examination.

The prospective customer looked at the material and said, "Well, it looks like any other plastic, and I have enough such material in stock. Try me next time."

I pulled out of my pocket a ten-cent nail file that I'd bought at the variety store. I said to the prospect courteously, "You know, you're looking at this material, but you're not seeing how much better it is than any other plastic sheeting you've known."

The man appeared surprised. He retorted, "I don't get your point."

I handed him the nail file and said, "Here—please scratch the surface of this material with the nail file. Scrape it, gouge it—but you can't mar the color."

The prospect grinned. He scraped away energetically at the material with the tough strip of rough metal.

"See for yourself," I urged. "It's like trying to scratch off color that's painted on the back of a pane of glass by scraping the top of the glass. You can't do it. And it's the same with the color applied to the bottom of this strong transparent plastic sheeting—you can't scrape it off, rub it off or wear it off from the top."

"Now I *see* the big difference," the merchant agreed. After more detailed discussion, he gave the salesman a sizable order.

Following this incident, each salesman carried a swatch of material and a nail file, both attached to a small card. Many thousands of "nail file test" cards were distributed. They helped produce sales totaling millions of dollars.

Here's further definite proof for you of the vital difference scored by "seeing" something, as compared with merely "looking" at it.

As Thoreau stated it, "I see beyond the range of sight." You can do the same by taking the first step in adopting the creative attitude and seeing beyond the range of common sight—if you will.

The Gourmet Cook's Secret

A trip took us to a city where I phoned an old friend whom I hadn't seen for many years. He insisted that we come out to his home for dinner, although his wife warned us that she was serving leftovers.

The main course, a turkey casserole, turned out to be one of the most delicious dishes we'd ever enjoyed. The hostess thanked us for our sincere compliments but maintained that she'd simply used "yesterday's turkey."

Her husband affirmed that this was true. He explained, "Miriam is famous for her recipes, and it's primarily because she's a creative cook."

"What do you mean by a creative cook?" my companion asked.

"Well," our host answered, "her biggest kick is to create a masterpiece out of the commonplace. Another woman will look at yesterday's turkey and see nothing but leftovers. But Miriam looks at that cold bird and sees a steaming casserole, fragrant with herbs and spices and other delectable ingredients."

"It's very simple, really," our hostess commented. "For instance, leftover turkey is either a cold, uninviting carcass, or a bubbling, luscious casserole—it's all in the way you look at it."

As I was saying, the first step in the creative method is "in the way *you* look at it."

Elements of the Creative Attitude

To make step one, the Creative Attitude, part of your personal makeup, start now to develop the elements in the following listing:

1. *Keep your mind open—look and see.* You've noted on the preceding pages how essential it is that you not only look with your eyes, but also see with your mind's eye. In other words, a prime essential is that you should establish and maintain a *conscious creative attitude*—a constant creative frame of mind. Clarence Darrow advised, "The pursuit of truth shall set you free—even if you never catch up with it."

Make it a habit to keep your mind open and your senses alert and receptive, for you never quite know where an idea will come from or when it will come. Every seasoned creative thinker you've ever known or admired will affirm this as a most dependable fact.

An open mind means a wide-open door to that creative machinery in your head, as diagramed previously. Keep seeking and asking. As Charles Steinmetz stated, "No man really becomes a fool until he stops asking questions."

2. *First make a start—then expand.* It's trite but nonetheless as true today as when John Heywood wrote it some four hundred years ago: "Rome was not built in one day." Realize that a journey of a thousand miles begins with a single step. So concentrate on the first step, not on the thousand miles ahead.

Resolve to go forward step by step, and I guarantee that each successive time the journey to the creation of a worthy idea will seem a little easier for you. Keep before you as a resolution the four words, "I'll make it better!"

When I first started writing creatively, a story of a thousand words loomed as a tremendous challenge, almost an insurmountable one. Then a five-thousand-word story seemed a little less difficult but still practically impossible.

From there I proceeded to twenty-thousand-word stories and articles. Then I moved on obstinately, spilling the well-known blood, sweat and tears, to a sixty-thousand-word book, then another, another and still another.

When I recently finished writing an instructive gardening encyclopedia of close to a hundred-thousand-words, I realized that—while it was arduous and difficult—I had approached it with far more confidence and less trepidation than my first thousand-word story.

Try this system of percentages when you tackle a problem and begin your creative thinking, as I do in creating a book. Don't look toward your objective and worry, "Gosh, it's so far away!" My system in approaching a four-hundred-page book is to concentrate on the first page, not to worry about the last.

I set out to write the first page, as you should approach the first step in creative thinking. When I finish that single page, I tell myself happily, "Great—I've made a start—I've finished the first page." Then I move ahead, my sights on page 51, and when I finish that, I note, "One-eighth of the pages done already"—not, "Still seven-eighths of the way to go."

At page 101, I remark eagerly, "Over one-fourth finished." At page 201, I say triumphantly, "I'm past the half-way mark, I've topped the summit of the mountain—from now on, it's all downhill, comparatively easy going."

I urge you to adopt this attitude. Concentrate optimistically on the amount of ground you've covered, rather than the distance you still have to go. You'll find that making a start and then moving on step by step, concentrating just on the one next step at a time, will be a big step forward for you in becoming proficient at productive creative thinking.

There's a tremendous difference in the approach and your ultimate success when you say, "Wonderful, I'm twenty-percent finished with the project," rather than, "How will I ever manage—I still have eighty-percent to do." You'll have more impetus when you accent the positive and minimize the negative.

Also, don't try to rush your progress. Be content to move forward one step at a time. Don't seek perfection at each step. You'll be able to refine your activities and ideas better at a later time.

3. *Provide time periods for creative thinking.* Each person's mind operates on a different time-efficiency basis. Select the time periods when you naturally would be most likely to produce ideas. Some people are most energetic early in the morning, but lose mental pep and energy rapidly toward evening. Others know that they don't get rolling well until hours after arising, attaining their greatest effectiveness in the evening.

Analyze yourself in this aspect, and concentrate most of your thinking accordingly, even though you're certainly not going to limit your creative thinking exclusively to those hours.

For example, when I was at college, I found that my mind operated most alertly and efficiently for creative thinking and work at a certain time each day for a period of two or three hours, no matter how long my mental energy stayed at a peak. At that time, I'd lock my door and refuse to answer any visitors or phone calls. Soon my friends learned that I couldn't be reached during that period.

I found that I'd accomplish more during that daily "creative time period" than in twice the hours at any other time of day or night. You'll discover the same gratifying result once you establish your own creative time periods and maintain your schedule as much as is practicable for you.

Currently, with my hours more crowded, my system of allotting myself specific creative time periods is regarded with amusement by some friends. I take a train from suburb to city and back each weekday morning and evening. I walk between home and railroad station, fifteen minutes each day; then from station to office, fifteen minutes more.

During those four quarter hours when I'm walking and have complete privacy, I concentrate my thinking on problems that require solving. I even pause on the sidewalk to make notes of ideas on a small scratch pad when necessary. Those brief creative time periods have proved to be of great value because I've made it a point to use them as a regular part of my daily creative thinking schedule.

Give some thought to your own best time periods right now. Jot down the times you consider might be most effective for yourself.

You may change your daily creative time periods as you go along, year by year, just as I have done. And you must allow for variation, of course. But you'll find it extremely helpful to set aside particular concentration times. In addition, you'll be alert and wide open to ideas whenever you have an opportunity during your waking hours.

4. *Specify places for creative thinking.* One of today's best-selling authors was very busy raising a family in a small apartment while writing her first novel. She told me that she became accustomed to writing at a little white enamel table in her kitchen.

"Every chance I'd get," she said, "I'd sit down at that table and start writing on a ruled yellow pad I kept handy there. That was my 'writing place.' It became almost automatic for me to set down words when I settled on the hard kitchen chair at that table."

A noted songwriter penned his popular verses at a high music stand in his library at home. "I always seemed to find my best inspirations," he stated, "pacing the book-lined room and then stopping at the scarred music stand."

A very successful creative businessman commented to me that he produced his best ideas when he retired each evening for an hour after dinner to a room he'd fitted up over his garage. Thus he combined the best time and the right place for his outstanding production of creative ideas.

Perhaps your most effective "creative thinking place" would be your favorite easy chair in the living room, a hammock in the garden, the little desk in your bedroom, the rocker in your guest room or the porch.

Or it could be an outdoors place particularly congenial to you.

For example, a high-school teacher I know told me that his best creative thinking is done several afternoons a week when he walks to the shore of his seaside town and sits on the huge rocks facing the water.

Oddly enough, one of my best creative thinking places now is on the commuting train during the forty-minute ride to and from the city. I settle into my seat, pull out a pencil and pad, concentrate on a problem, and soon I'm jotting down notes. (A friend suggested that I'd produce many more books, articles and ideas if I simply rode back and forth between suburb and city on the train all day.)

Perhaps you might be able to concentrate best on a bus—but don't miss your stop!

One of the top creative executives in a big business commutes on the train two hours each day, morning and evening. He uses that time for creative work, arranging his plans, instructions and daily work schedules. He insists, "If I didn't have those four hours of privacy each day, I'd never get my important thinking and daily programing done." He has nine children, somewhat limiting his privacy at home.

Make a start now by writing down what might be your best places for daily creative thinking.

Here again, you certainly will not limit your creative thinking to one or a few specific places. In addition to the train, some of my favorite spots are a chair in my back yard alongside the garden, a drawing table in the little "office" next to my bedroom and a reception room whenever I'm waiting for an appointment.

You'll find it a great aid to your own productive creative thinking to select and specify the places that are most effective for you.

5. *Cultivate a constant creative atmosphere.* You've read earlier in this chapter about the importance and value of becoming excited about things. By maintaining an air of interest (no, not frenzy), you see details which provide a springboard to creative thinking.

As a creative gardener, for example, you start with the premise (stated specifically in my best-selling book, *Miracle Gardening*) that a "single blade of grass growing from the earth is a miracle." You regard that blade of grass as an opportunity, not as a chore. Then, in all your gardening work, your attitude is to improve your lawn, your gardens and all your landscaping. You will have established an atmosphere of constantly enhancing the beauty of your property with every gardening task you tackle.

You'll find that many "miracles" spring from a creative atmosphere. For instance, the appearance of mold on a laboratory dish, noted by a scientist who was creatively aware became a vital clue in the development of penicillin. If the doctor had not worked in an alert creative environment, he might have missed one of the most valuable medical contributions of all time.

Keep Exercising Your Mind

You exercise your mind very simply by consciously using most of your time productively rather than just skimming along haphazardly from minute to minute. Be as aware of brain-stretching as you are of stretching your muscles.

Consider the time that you spend with your daily newspaper, for example. Instead of just scanning the news, make it a point to ask, "How? Why? What can I gather from these items? How can I use what's printed on these pages to make things better for myself, for my associates, for my family, for others?"

Exercise your mind in this area with me right now. I've opened this morning's newspaper for the first time, as I sit in the yard on a sunny Sunday morning in spring. Look at the paper with me, consciously seeking out items that might be approached creatively for personal benefit.

Here's the radio program listing. Look—an excellent record concert you'd like to hear. Get the portable radio and enjoy the background music while you read the newspaper. Or, if there's no battery-operated radio available, why not rig up a radio here with a long extension cord plugged in through the nearby window? There's a little creative spark that contributes to happier living.

Turn the page. Note the want ads—"Home Furnishings

Wanted, Highest Prices Paid." You've been thinking about getting rid of that old dining-room set that's been cluttering up the attic. Why not make some phone calls, get a few dollars for that dust-collecting furniture? And (your mind moves on energetically) use the money to get a portable radio so that I can hear music or the ball game or the news out here in the back yard.

Look farther. Here's an interesting suggestion on the home page to decorate a youngster's room with a large map of the world. There's a good thought. Instead of repapering the room because of the ink splotches over the desk, put up a colorful map there. It'll brighten the room, help Junior with his studies and stimulate his imagination to roam to far countries. That's a creative, money-saving solution to what was a nagging wall-papering problem.

It's all right there in today's newspaper, a batch of provocative and useful idea-starters—just one common, everyday instance of what you can gain by exercising your mind.

Hobbies Spark Creative Thinking

Hobbies, too, offer fine possibilities for keeping your mind more alert and active, through woodworking, painting, gardening, cooking, decorating, stamp collecting—you name it.

Even puzzle-solving and games provide excellent exercise, as you'll find from tackling the puzzlers and problems in this book. Perhaps you'll go on from there to more complicated challenges such as intricate crossword puzzles, double-crostics, involved mathematical problems.

A friend of Albert Einstein's observed that he had a corner of his bookshelves filled with special collections of mathematical puzzles and games. He pointed out that the interest of exceptionally brainy men in such "play" is in the same direction as the kind of thinking that has often led to monumental scientific discovery.

Realize this: Even the most complicated scientific effort is often systematic application aimed at producing new and better answers to puzzles offered by nature and by various phases of living. Similarly, challenging hobbies provide problems; you work out the answers by intermittent or sustained thinking and effort.

Seek hobbies that appeal very much to you particularly. They help you to channel your natural instincts, interests and abilities into pursuits that produce not only pleasure but also solid results for you. After applying yourself to an absorbing hobby, even just for an hour or two at a time, you find your creative approach alerted and energized.

Expose Yourself to Creative People

An extremely wise man, Walter Pater, constantly reiterated that "we need some imaginative stimulus," a most important element of the creative approach.

As pointed out earlier, you become more alert when you're in the company of wide-awake people, as you react to the stimulus provided by their bright mentalities. And, by prodding yourself with their company, your own interest is aroused and your abilities improved.

Take a tip from another Pater statement: "To know when one's self is interested, is the first condition of interesting other people."

An integral part of becoming more creative is that you become more interested, and more interesting. Thus, in both directions of your creative development—your gains from other people, and your contributions to others—it's most helpful to seek out and expose yourself to creative persons, study and events.

And, by listening and discussing problems with others, you'll become far better able to solve them for yourself—creatively.

6. *Develop the ten creative mental elements.* Remember the integral building blocks used in erecting the structure of your new creative attitude. Study again the details in Chapter 2 regarding the "ten basic mental elements of the creative person" in this checklist:

1. DESIRE to make things better.
2. ALERTNESS—"wide open" to everything.

3. INTEREST in digging below the surface.
4. CURIOSITY—constant spirit of inquiry.
5. THOUGHTFULNESS leading to thorough understanding.
6. CONCENTRATION to penetrate matters in depth.
7. APPLICATION of energy and effort.
8. PATIENCE to solve problems in detail.
9. OPTIMISM, combining enthusiasm and self-confidence.
10. CO-OPERATION—working productively with others.

It will pay you to apply constant awareness and effort to making all these elements part of your character and personality. This will go far to build the most productive creative approach within yourself.

Try to "loosen up" your thinking so that ideas won't be blocked out by preconceived notions or conclusions in your mind. An example: the leg of a low chair breaks and two men in a small cabin seek to prop it up immediately. Both of them look for a stick the right size, but there is nothing around except a hammer.

One man sees the hammer and forgets it, because in his mind a hammer is for hammering, and for nothing else. The other man looks with an open creative attitude; he picks up the hammer, which is exactly the right length, and uses it as a chair leg. He by-passed the mental block which limited the uses of the hammer.

This point was illustrated clearly by a series of research experiments. First an experimenter waved before a group of adults a card containing a splash of red paint. Asked what they saw, they all replied that they'd seen red.

But when he turned the card over and waved at them the side with a similar red spot in the shape of the ace of spades, some said brown, some pruple, some gray. Their preconceived conclusions that an ace of spades is black prevented them from identifying the spot as red.

Remember, the next time you approach a problem, to keep your outlook from becoming fixed and tight.

Review

It's very much worthwhile reviewing here again the phases that make up step one of the six-step Creative Method—developing the creative attitude:

1. Keep your mind open—look and see.
2. First make a start—then expand.
3. Provide time periods for creative thinking.
4. Specify places for creative thinking.
5. Cultivate a constant creative atmosphere.
6. Develop the ten creative mental elements.
7. Avoid mental blocks and preconceived conclusions.

Let the Lessons Penetrate

I recommend to you that you apply the ten creative mental elements to making step one a part of your thinking processes, in this way:

Sharpen your desire to absorb this first step on the way to developing your creative thinking and production of ideas.

Open your awareness to every nuance of the step, as expressed in the preceding pages.

Whet your interest in digging deeply into every detail.

If you don't feel that you understand any point fully, go back over it in a spirit of searching inquiry.

Think about each point so that you do in fact understand every aspect thoroughly. Washington Irving said, "Great minds have purposes, others only have wishes."

Concentrate on each phase of this step in turn, so that you penetrate to the core of each point in depth.

Apply all your mental energy to digging into point after point of the explanations and suggestions. It's true that "the best way to get rid of work is to do it."

Patiently go over each phase again and again if required to absorb it fully and clearly. Josh Billings advised, "Consider the postage stamp . . . it secures success through its ability to stick to one thing until it get there."

Proceed optimistically, with full enthusiasm and confidence that you will be able to master this initial step and those that will follow. Disraeli, aiming high, said that "every production of genius must be the production of enthusiasm."

Co-operate fully with the instructions here, in taking each suggestion along the way, not only in the preceding material, but also in the pages that are ahead.

Patience Will Pay Off

There's a potent and very useful lesson to learn in an old Chinese story. The Emperor had heard many glowing tales about an aged couple who lived deep in the country. It was remarkable that both man and wife were close to a hundred years old and that they had recently celebrated their eightieth wedding anniversary.

But most extraordinary was the fact that the couple was reputed never to have had a serious quarrel. They raised many children, who had stayed amicably close to home. Apparently there had been no disrupting family friction.

The Emperor summoned the old man from afar. He sat him in a beautiful room alone, at a table bearing paper, pen and ink.

"Start writing, old one," the Emperor ordered. "I want you to write down the secret of your wondrously successful marriage and family life, so that I may read it all when I return here at the end of the afternoon." The old man picked up the pen and immediately started writing.

When the Emperor returned hours later, the old man was still writing. At once he put down the pen and handed over many sheets of paper.

On each sheet, the old man had written hundreds of times just one word: "Patience."

Similarly, I urge your patience and sincere application to all the suggestions along the way on these pages, even if some of the material may appear repetitive at times. I assure you that the repetition is purposeful and necessary to help drive essential elements deep into your consciousness now, for your most productive activity in the future.

Rarely is one able to hit a nail on its head with a single blow and drive it in fully. The effective way to drive that nail in straight and firm is through repeated blows, none too vigorous and none too weak.

So it is in learning how to develop creative thinking and the resultant production of valuable and usable ideas. It will pay you to proceed as instructed, for your personal gain. Reflect on the wise statement in the Bible, "Let patience have her perfect work."

Don't expect perfection at first. By proceeding methodically here from page to page, step to step, you'll learn and you'll profit eventually and unquestionably. It is said that "life is hard by the yard, but by the inch it's a cinch." You must apply yourself assiduously to absorbing this material. Realize that food may be full of vitamins, but you can't absorb these vitamins and the benefits from them unless you eat the food.

You can have confidence that you'll get better at getting ideas by using this method. Just as surely as you improve your aim by throwing darts at a target, the more you throw "thoughts," the more ideas you'll hit upon.

You must make a start, then follow through. Rembrandt might have kept all those masterful, magnificent paintings of his inside his head. Only after he picked up the brush and applied paint to canvas did his creative genius take on form and enduring life.

You have so much to gain from developing your creative thinking deeply. As essayist Richard Jefferies wrote some hundred years ago: "Let me exhort everyone . . . to think outside and beyond our present circle of ideas. For every idea gained is a hundred years of slavery remitted."

5

STEP TWO: ANALYZE EACH PROBLEM TO FOCUS ON THE WANTED CREATIVE SOLUTION

One of the most important steps in the creative process is to make sure that you're focusing on the wanted solution. Here is where many people lose out completely in being creative. By not sighting the right goal, they head in different directions, in wrong directions. Thus, they fail miserably in striving to create usable, valuable ideas or in reaching successful creative solutions.

The point is just as clear as this: Imagine that you're heading toward a specific city which is located on the road to the right, yet you follow the left fork by mistake. No matter how long or how ably you drive along that road to the left, you'll never arrive at your destination.

In fact, the more powerful your car is, and the faster you drive, the farther you move away from your goal. You'll miss as surely as a football player running with the ball to the wrong goal line.

This seems very elementary, doesn't it? Yet it's an apt illustration because it makes the point so clearly. No matter how fast and far and efficiently you travel toward a wanted creative idea or solution, you'll never reach it if you're going in the wrong direction. Oliver Wendell Holmes said, "I find that the great thing in the world is not only where we stand, but also in what direction we are moving."

Let's say that you have developed the alert, eager, enthusiastic and energetic creative attitude, as delineated in step one. Now you must be sure you're moving in the right direction, that you're focused on the right target.

This can be very tricky. You may think you're taking the correct approach to accomplish your desire. Yet you may be misleading yourself, because you haven't thought through and focused on the real goal.

As one brilliant executive stated it in a leading magazine, "You can't come up with the right answers unless you know the objectives."

Analyze . . . for an Accurate Creative Result

This is an extremely valuable point in respect to all creative thinking; if you are to progress through to the right creative idea that will really solve the problem concerned, you must understand the real problem first. As a doctor put it, with a smile, "No use trying to figure out scientifically what's causing a man's headaches, if the real reason is that his shirt collars are too tight."

An excellent way to analyze the problem clearly is to cut it up into pieces. A specific method for you to follow in breaking down a problem is suggested by the "goal chart" that you'll find on succeeding pages in this chapter. Check the exact examples as to how you can work this procedure—and how the procedure works for you.

Here's a common instance to show how wrong you can be if you don't break the problem apart and get into it deeply. You might think of buying a company's stock because some exceptionally big new promotions are in preparation, larger than ever before. Your analysis might be, "They're really being progressive now; they're going places—and I'm climbing aboard."

Yet you could be completely wrong. The reason for the extra promotional push might be, for example, because sales are falling and something drastic must be done. So you'd better analyze deeply first, lest you reach an entirely wrong conclusion.

Surface appearances can definitely, although not necessarily, be deceiving. In order not to fool yourself about your personal creative problems, you must take nothing for granted. You must probe step by step toward the correct goal for a successful creative result.

In short, breaking a problem apart for clearer analysis usually adds up to a far more productive solution. For instance, in advising young men about choosing a college, a leading educator pointed out that the problem had to be analyzed not as a whole but in its particulars. He emphasized that the problem should be considered not as a total question, "What's the best college?" Rather, it should be subjected to detailed analysis as to "What's the best college for *me?*"

By accurately defining the problem itself, you help to spotlight the correct objective. For example, consider the following case.

The Case of the Murderous Moles

A typical gardener (you can multiply this actual case by millions) was outraged over the damage that moles were causing in his lawn. They were digging holes and trenches deep under the grass, murdering its growth and beauty.

It wasn't bad enough, he raged, that his grass was weak looking and sickly green anyhow. Why, he could reach down and peel off strips of grass as you lift and peel carpeting from a floor.

But at least he was working to improve the grass, watering and fertilizing it heavily. And now those murderous moles!

So he set his objective—to trap and kill those moles. But they were canny. He'd trap and kill one, then others would appear. They learned to avoid the traps and the poisonous bait.

The man was going out of his mind, and telling everybody about it, when I happened to meet him at a friend's home. When he learned that I'd written some gardening books, he pleaded with me for help.

"You'll never win, the way you're going at it," I advised him.

"Now, think a minute. What are you really trying to do? What's your real objective?"

"I'm trying to kill the moles," he answered impatiently.

"You'll never succeed," I stated flatly. "More moles will keep coming along. Anyhow, your objective isn't really to kill moles."

Puzzled, he asked, "What do *you* think I want to do?"

"You want to grow a good lawn," I said.

"Sure," he agreed, "but first I have to get rid of the moles."

"No," I contradicted him. "First you must concentrate on growing a good lawn. Once you do that, you'll get rid of the moles without any further effort at all."

"I don't get it," he sighed.

"Here's how simple it is," I explained. "First, focus on the real problem. You want a good lawn, but the grass is weak and sickly—you can rip it up easily by the handful. Your actual problem is to find out first what's causing that undesirable condition. Once you focus on that clearly, the solution becomes clear."

He started to nod understandingly. "I suppose there's a disease or something in my lawn," he said thoughtfully.

"That's right," I agreed. "That condition is caused by underground grubs eating at the grass roots. And the moles feed on the grubs—that's why they dig into your lawn, and not in your neighbors' yards."

His eyes brightened. "That's true," he said eagerly. "My lawn is the only one in the neighborhood that attracts the moles. If I can get rid of the grubs, I won't be afflicted by those murderous moles."

"Sure," I told him. "Treat your lawn with a chlordane product made specifically to get rid of grubs. Your grass will be safe for years. You'll be on your way to having a thick, green lawn."

Obviously, that man could have gone on for years, unhappily and ineffectually, trying to kill moles. Yet he could easily have sighted his objective and asked: "Why is my grass so sickly? Why do moles invade my property and not my neighbors'?"

The answers would have headed him toward the simple and successful course of action. That's an all-important part of the creative procedure—to sight the objective correctly, focus on it and then work toward the effective solution and activity.

Tune up your mind with the short "mystery practice puzzlers" that follow. You can solve them by sighting the objective in each case. But you'll never reach the solution if you permit yourself to become confused and pointed in the wrong direction.

Five Mystery Practice Puzzlers

(Solutions begin on page 242.)

1. The Case of the Threatening Dagger. Carl Blake and Oscar Lamb were close friends but were competing for the title of vice-president in the bank where they worked. It was generally conceded that Carl would be appointed within a week.

One evening, Carl was home sick, sipping slowly from a glass of water. He had been sipping water repeatedly all day. Suddenly he looked up and saw Oscar threatening him with a sharp, daggerlike letter opener. He threw up his arm and knocked the weapon out of Oscar's hand, as his wife watched from the doorway. Oscar spoke hurriedly, and Carl calmed down immediately.

The next night, as Oscar was visiting him again, Carl died suddenly. The wife told police about the attack with the sharp "dagger." They seized Oscar and questioned him immediately about his suspicious, threatening actions.

What explanation could Oscar give that would keep him from arrest due to the sudden death of his rival? (All the clues have been stated to help you focus right on the clear solution.)

2. The Case of the Scot-Free Shoplifter. A man was caught red-handed as he was shoplifting a valuable mink cape in a large department store. Soon he was released because of a particular, unusual physical condition. He admitted the theft and repeatedly challenged the police to put him in jail, but they couldn't. He even said that they couldn't jail him if he were a murderer. Why not?

3. The Case of the Inefficient Operator. A switchboard operator in an office complained to her brother, who was a detective, that she had been fired without reason. "My employer warned me that I was too talkative and would be fired if I asked any unnecessary questions during the course of phone conversations. But after he overheard a very businesslike conversation, he fired me immediately. I feel like murdering him!"

She repeated the conversation word for word. The detective said, "I can't intervene with your employer, since he was right. You'd better forget about wanting to kill him."

You are to give your solution after noting the precise conversation, as follows:

Operator: "Good morning; Hottentot Company."
Caller: "This is Mr. Brown. Please connect me with Mr. Hottentot."
Operator: "What name? Please spell it."
Caller: "Brown—B for Bratwurst, R for rhinoceros, O for osculation—"
Operator: "What's that—O for what?"
Caller: "O for osculation, W for whiffenproof, N for nitwit."
Operator: "Thank you, Mr. Brown. Here's Mr. Hottentot."

Exactly what excess words did the operator use that caused her to be discharged?

4. The Case of the Mysterious Letter. The postmaster in a small town found a letter in his mailbox with only three words on the front, as follows:

WOOD
JOHN
MASS

As he was examining the envelope, which was properly stamped but had no return address, he noticed that the police chief had entered the post office. He told the chief that he didn't know where to deliver the letter.

The shrewd police official examined the envelope for a minute, then told the postmaster where to send the letter. Sure enough, the letter reached its correct destination.

What were the right name, city and state?

5. The Case of the Dastardly Dream. A faithful employee for over ten years, Frank Boggs arrived at the home of his boss at eight o'clock on Tuesday morning to drive him to the airport. He was supposed to be there at eight on his way home from work, and was exactly on time.

Driving to the airport, Frank said to his employer, "I'm very much disturbed by a horrible dream I had last night. It seems that you came out to the factory and I didn't recognize you, but thought you were a thief. I shot you in the stomach and you were bleeding terribly. I recognized you then and tried to stop the blood, but couldn't. I held you dying in my arms but I couldn't do anything and felt just awful."

"What happened then?" the boss asked.

"I was screaming for help—then I woke up," Frank concluded. As they arrived at the airport, he added, "I sure felt terrible."

His boss jumped out of the car and said, "You're going to feel even more terrible, I'm afraid. You're fired!"

You have all the clues. Why did the boss fire faithful Frank?

Look for the "Hidden" Goal

The vital lesson of step two is for you to learn how to find the actual destination you want to reach. Usually you must be taught how to discern the real "want," or goal, so that the idea or solution you create will be most useful and effective.

In many cases, probably in most, the goal is "hidden" from yourself by yourself, or by circumstances, or by deeply-imbedded, preconditioned attitudes on your part. Thus, as in the mystery puzzlers, if you go off in the wrong direction, heading toward a misdirected goal, you'll never reach the right target or solution.

Remember that the goal is too often hidden, as in this puzzle teaser:

Problem: A teacher in mathematics said he wanted to find out which student was fastest at figures, and at figuring out accurate solutions most speedily. He asked how much dirt there was in a rectangular hole measuring three by three by four feet. He pressed the trigger of his stop watch. Within five seconds, the student with the highest grade popped up his hand and said, "Thirty-six cubic feet." What's your answer?

SOLUTION: The student with the highest grades was all wrong with his quick answer. The correct solution is, "No dirt." There is no dirt in a hole.

Note in this very simple example how you can go off completely, and never reach the correct solution, if you start toward the wrong goal. The "hidden" goal here was to find out how much dirt was in a *hole,* not the obvious target which appeared to be the necessity of figuring out a mathematical solution.

Now let's see exactly how this same misdirection applies to problems and solutions in real life. Study these examples carefully; they illuminate significant points that you can apply to your own development of essential accuracy in your creative thinking and production of ideas.

The Mother's Feeding Problem

A mother told a wise friend that she was having a terrible problem trying to get her child to eat spinach. "I have to plead, bribe and finally force Johnny to eat his spinach," she complained, "and it's driving me crazy. You're so clever, can you give me some tips on how to get him to eat his spinach?"

"Well," the friend mused, "you might disguise the spinach with bread crumbs and herbs so that it's different and delicious. But I don't think that's your problem at all."

"I ought to know," the mother insisted, "and I must find a solution."

"Let's dig into it," the friend suggested. "Why do you want Johnny to eat spinach?"

"Because it's good for him," said the mother. "It's loaded with iron and vitamins, and lots of nutrition—"

"Stop right there," the friend interrupted. "You want to give Johnny lots of nutrition, so he'll grow strong and healthy, right?"

"Of course," the mother retorted. "And, as I was saying—"

"You were saying," said the friend, "that you want to feed Johnny spinach. But what you *really* want is to keep him healthy.

So your problem is not 'feeding spinach,' but providing proper nutrition."

"Of course," the mother agreed, "that's exactly what I want, so—"

"So forget about the spinach," the friend advised. "Instead, find out what healthful foods he does like, and feed him those, in tempting recipes. And ask your doctor what good-tasting vitamin and mineral products he recommends. Remember that your goal is to promote Johnny's good health—and to heck with the spinach!"

The lesson seems so clear now, doesn't it? Yet the mother hadn't been able to work toward her actual target, as the "spinach angle" had hidden the goal from her. Similarly, and just as surprisingly, the goal you want is frequently hidden from you until you learn to focus on it.

New Job or New Interest?

In big decisions and strivings, as well as in small things, misdirection in seeking a solution can be very serious as well as ineffectual.

Consider this actual case of a man I'll call Harry Dewar. As a friend, he came to me for help. "I've been trying to do some creative thinking about myself and my future life," he told me, "because I've almost come to a big and crucial decision. I've about decided to give up my job and try some other work."

I was surprised and somewhat shocked. Henry had been with his company for nine years, had advanced steadily with them, and was in line for further promotion. I asked, "Why have you decided to leave?"

"I feel hemmed in," he answered. "There are creative feelings within me that can't seem to get out. I need to express myself."

"In what way?" I wanted to know.

"Well"—he dug for an explanation—"I think I have some artistic abilities. But they have no outlet in this job. Perhaps I can find other work which would provide an outlet for such expression."

I took another tack and asked, "Do you hate your job?"

"Oh, no," he hastened to assure me. "I like the people, and the work itself is interesting—but it's limiting, too."

"I think that you don't understand your problem accurately," I told him. "What you really want is to express yourself artistically and creatively. Just changing jobs won't accomplish that. Another job probably would just set you back years in earning power."

"I suppose that's true," said Henry thoughtfully. "But how can I express myself, then?"

"Instead of seeking another job, why not first look for an outlet for whatever artistic talents you may have?" I suggested. "Join an evening art class. Become a weekend artist. It may give you just the outlet you need. If not, you can take other steps. But don't throw over your job because you feel repressed artistically. Your goal right now is to express yourself, so take positive action in that direction—that's the right creative step. I don't think you'll find a positive solution in the negative action of chucking your job."

The solution worked out well for Henry Dewar. His new artistic striving made him happier in his living, and better at his work. He had been fortunate in moving toward the goal he really wanted, but it had been "hidden" from him before the clarifying step in creative thinking had illuminated it vividly.

Think about it: Haven't you often hit out at A, when your discontent had actually been caused by B? Yet, if you'd thought about it, instead of striking out impetuously, you'd have realized that B was really your tormentor. Thus, doing something about B should have been your goal, although it had been hidden from you—by yourself, and by lack of clear thinking and sighting.

How to Sight the Correct Goal

As proved in usage by others, you'll find the following series of simple, basic questions very useful in helping you to drive right through toward the wanted creative solution. I use these questions to help analyze each problem, as part of the effective creative thinking process.

To clarify the process further, consider sighting the correct goal by use of the following "goal chart":

GOAL CHART

AIM: ______

1. WHY?

2. OTHER WAY TO ACCOMPLISH THIS?

3. STILL ANOTHER WAY, OR WAYS?

4. WOULD ANY OF THESE WAYS ACCOMPLISH THE PURPOSE BETTER?

GOAL: ______

How to Use the Goal Chart

By subjecting your aim or purpose—that is, what you think it is at the start—to the successive questions on the chart, you'll usually focus on the wanted creative solution. Thus, you'll accomplish step two of the creative method and progress further to step three.

See for yourself how this chart progression works in clarifying the problem and leading to the wanted solution. Let's apply the test to the two problems covered earlier in this chapter.

THE MOTHER'S FEEDING PROBLEM

Aim: How to feed the child spinach.

1. *Why?* Make child strong and healthy.

2. *Other way to accomplish this?* Feed him other helpful foods.

3. *Still another way, or ways?* Prepare spinach more deliciously in variegated recipes. See doctor and get advice on tasty vitamin preparations.

4. *Would any of these ways accomplish the purpose better?* Yes, other, more inviting foods would overcome child's objections. Adding vitamins to diet would improve nutritive value of meals.

Goal: Make the child strong and healthy, rather than persist in trying to feed child spinach in the diet.

Just as the logical progression of questions and resultant answers focuses on the "hidden" solution here, you'll find that it works on bigger and more complicated problems by breaking down covering or confusing obstacles. From this point, you can progress confidently and directly toward the wanted solution.

NEW JOB OR NEW INTEREST?

Aim: Give up job, get other work.

1. *Why?* Need to express myself. This job doesn't accomplish that.

2. *Other way to accomplish this?* Interested in art, take classes nights.

3. *Still another way, or ways?* Become a weekend painter. Visit art exhibits. Read books, acquire greater understanding of art.

4. *Would any of these ways accomplish the purpose better?*

Possibly; could try before taking drastic step of quitting good job.

Goal: Think creatively toward expressing myself best artistically.

Note how far removed is the original aim from the actual determined goal. In this instance, if you were the subject concerned, you might have made a tragic error in focusing your creative thinking on quitting your job rather than seeing first whether some specific creative expression (painting, in this instance) might not be your wanted but hitherto hidden solution.

The Gardening Hobby Problem

As further practice in learning step two of the six-step method, let's examine another actual case. A woman was determined to interest her husband in gardening. She asked for my help.

"I'm determined to get Steve to spend some hours working in the garden evenings and weekends," Alice told me tensely. "He's so wound up when he gets home from the office that he just can't relax. If he'd just get out among the flowers and shrubs, get his fingers into the earth and enjoy the delights of checking the new growing things each day, I know he'd be easier and happier. Have you any ideas about how I can accomplish this?"

I suggested to Alice that she apply the steps of the creative thinking method to this problem. Her concern may appear rather insignificant on the surface, but it involved the basic health and well-being of her husband and his future. Certainly a creative idea that would apply here would be of enormous value to this family.

Using the goal chart, step two in her creative thinking process developed simply and logically. Here's how Alice figured out her "goal" in this instance:

Aim: To interest Steve in gardening.

1. *Why?* To help him relax from overbearing business tensions.

2. *Other way to accomplish this?* Interest him in something else which would take his mind off business, evenings and weekends.

3. *Still another way, or ways?* Urge him to take up some other hobby or pursuit, such as carpentry, bridge, golf.

4. *Would any of these ways accomplish the purpose better?* Perhaps, except for pursuits that would take him away from his home, from which he derives great interest and pride.

Goal: To provide Steve with special interest and relaxation, and to accomplish this by seeking out a hobby, in gardening or other directions, which would encompass home activity.

Going beyond step two in this case, here's what evolved from following through progressively with the creative thinking method. Alice explored and gathered details and facts about a number of hobbies, in and out of the gardening area, which she thought might interest her husband.

She arrived eventually at this bright idea. Since Steve was a gourmet who sought out and enjoyed exceptional foods, he'd probably be fascinated by the possibilities in growing a special herb garden.

As Steve became involved in growing many delicious and exotic varieties of herbs, his active mind expanded the possibilities. From growing herbs, and then using them creatively in cooking, he took to packing them in attractive little jars with printed labels reading "Steve's Special Spices." He delighted his friends and business acquaintances with gifts of his own home-grown spices.

If he had been so minded, he might even have gone further and developed a business in herbs and spices (as happened with a bright, creative woman I know who enriched her life and her bank account in this way). As it was, the goal was reached most fruitfully as Steve achieved relaxation and greater happiness with his new creative hobby, arrived at creatively by his wife.

The Ambitious but Overburdened Young Man

The son of a good friend approached me with a problem that pressed on him heavily because its solution would influence his business future. He was seeking a creative solution and was stumped.

As practice, decide how you would proceed to help advance a solution through step two, in sighting the correct objective. Here are the facts.

The young man, Ralph, had finished college and obtained a position with a sizable advertising agency, just exactly the kind of firm he wanted to join. As part of the system, he had to serve his apprenticeship for six months on pickup and delivery around the extensive offices. This meant that he made the rounds of all the offices six times a day, delivering mail, memos and other material, then picking up and sorting the various papers, and redelivering.

This kind of apprenticeship made very good sense for the firm and for the young man, even though the work might seem unchallenging and even tedious. Day after day, Ralph came in contact with every division of the agency, so that he absorbed the atmosphere and a surface knowledge of the general and interlocking procedures.

Meanwhile, the supervisor could watch Ralph and the other young men doing similar work. He noted their interests and aptitudes and judged their personalities and abilities in their daily contacts with hundreds of other people in the offices. At the end of the trial period, he could move them forward into other departments.

After a few weeks of this work, Ralph told me that he was afraid he couldn't handle the job, even though he wanted to. He was a short, rather frail young man, and he was finding it physically difficult to handle the loads of mail, memos, booklets and other material on his rounds.

"I gather an armload like the other fellows," he explained to me, "and soon I can't hold it all securely. Stuff keeps slipping out of my grip. At least a couple of times a day I dump a load of memos on the floor of some office—and is my face red!"

"What are you going to do about it?" I asked.

"That's why I've come to you," he answered. "The only solution I can see is to go to the supervisor and ask to be transferred to some other job. That'll probably mean they'll let me go because I can't handle even this simple routine work. And," he added, "there are lots of fellows who'd like to have my opportunity with this firm. Is there anything you can suggest?"

To the qualified creative mind, the solution here is obvious, so apparent that it's amazing that none of the young men (or the firm) had thought of it over the years.

Here's how Ralph was guided to proceed from what he *thought* was his aim to what actually was his wanted goal.

Aim: To win a transfer to some other job in the same firm.

1. *Why?* So he could stay with the company and advance in this business which interested him so much for his future.

2. *Other way to accomplish this?* (As soon as you see this answer you realize that it's the obvious move, yet it was hidden just as obscurely as the answers to any of the tricky practice puzzlers). Devise some way to handle the present work.

3. *Still another way, or ways?* Figure out convincing reasons why it would be better for the firm to use your services in another department right away.

4. *Would any of these ways accomplish the purpose better?* If some way could be worked out to enable Ralph to handle his present job, that would undoubtedly be the best solution. It wouldn't disrupt the organization plan or involve any special pleas to the supervisor.

Goal: Create a means to handle the job as well as or better than anyone else.

Here's exactly what happened, a capsule triumph which reveals the specific value of thinking efficiently and producing a solid, effective creative idea.

Focusing right on his goal—a means to handle the job—Ralph followed through with the procedures of the six-step method, as delineated for you later. He devised a collapsible and expandable carrier made of light aluminum mesh, with a strong canvas strap handle.

With this ingenious "invention" he could carry a load of material without spilling or disarrangement. He found that he could complete his rounds more swiftly, smoothly and efficiently than anyone else.

As a result, the clever solution drew the notice and comments of people throughout the company. The supervisor complimented him. The president of the firm, meeting him in the hallway, noted the interesting contraption he was carrying. He invited Ralph into his office for an explanation and discussion.

Ralph's "invention" was duplicated for all the others doing the same work. Within a few weeks there was an opening in another department and he was moved up, with an increase in salary, months before his apprentice period was due to end.

Great Are the Gains from a Bright Creative Idea

Another point worth noting here is that it often pays to discuss the problem with someone who's not familiar with it. Being completely objective about it, a bright individual can often see the correct goal which you've been missing because you've been too close to it and too enmeshed in confusing details.

Use the Goal Chart

Eventually you'll be able to breeze right through step two, to help focus on your correct goal or objective so you won't go off in the wrong direction in producing effective creative ideas.

Meanwhile, use the goal chart, even though it might seem to be an elementary crutch. Actually, it's a valuable tool. It will help you make step two a natural part of your personal creative thinking processes.

"Practice is the best of all instructors," is a maxim attributed to the philosopher Publius, back about 42 B.C. It makes just as good sense today. I suggest that you practice step two now by setting down a half-dozen or more of your personal or other problems, and then going down the ladder of the goal chart with them, answering point by point.

Read, Reread and Three-Read

When you use the goal chart, you are automatically analyzing the problem and setting down details which advance you toward seeing the clear, true objective. Another aid is to write down the problem as I have done with those delineated in this chapter.

Then, after you've written down the outline, I advise you to read it slowly, reread and three-read. You'll be gratified by how often a third reading will illuminate details that you missed previously.

Try it with the practice puzzlers, for example. A rereading and three-reading will frequently reveal the decisive clue that you passed over the first time. By leaping to conclusions hastily, you may well be heading for a bad fall. You owe it to yourself to follow the carefully worked-out and proved procedures set down here.

Spinoza stated it this way: "He who would distinguish the true from the false must have an adequate idea of what is true and false."

It's just good sense, isn't it? Unless you sight your objective clearly, and aim your creative efforts right at the center of your target, you're not likely to hit the bull's-eye.

By following the precepts in this chapter, linked to the preceding one, you can't help but improve your accuracy and step up your creative thinking ability, as you move on to step three.

6

STEP THREE: SEEK OUT AND FILL YOUR MIND WITH FACTS

"First I fill my mind with facts." That's the statement of one of the most successful creative business executives I've ever met, a man with a top position in one of the world's largest commercial organizations.

He was speaking with three of us at lunch, explaining how he tackles most every problem. He went on for emphasis, "I just cram my head full of facts—and something worthwhile always comes out."

Proceeding with the six-step creative method, you've learned —and, I hope, already adopted and put into daily application— the wide-open, searching creative attitude.

Secondly, you're seeking to analyze each problem, first to isolate and then concentrate on the correct objective. Without achieving that, whatever you do on a problem from now on could be moving in the wrong direction, or at any rate not toward the most effective solution.

And now you arrive at step three, where you seek out and fill your mind with facts. You will be following here the creative process of Edison, whose habit, it is reported, was to compile all available facts and ideas on a subject, and then seek previously unknown or unrecognized relationships among them. Even going back hundreds of years, Sir Isaac Newton talked of searching for knowledge by compiling facts "like children who pick up pebbles on the beach."

To help tune up your capabilities in seeking out the facts, I suggest that you first warm up with the following special puzzlers. They're aimed to help you focus on the facts.

Five Fact-Finding Puzzlers

(Solutions begin on page 244.)

1. The Baffled Nonworker. Herman Walters worked steadily at his job week in and week out, yet he hadn't been given a raise by his domineering boss for several years. Finally, prodded by his angry wife, Herman asked for a raise.

"You want a raise?" his employer exploded. "Why, I shouldn't be paying you at all. Let's look at the actual statistics. You're supposed to be working 8 hours a day. You'll admit that's only one-third of each day. So, even in a year of 366 days, that means only 122 days of work. Right?

"Now, follow my figures," he proceeded. "You didn't work Saturdays or Sundays. Considering 2 days for every 52 weeks, we deduct 104 days from 122 days, leaving only 18 days of work. From that we take off your 2 weeks of vacation, and 4 holidays, a total of 18 days.

"That winds up with a big fat zero," the boss emphasized. "So you don't really work at all. Yet you have the nerve to ask me for a raise!" He told Herman, "You'd better get back to your job and not bother me with any nonsense about increased wages."

Herman gazed at his work-hardened hands in bewilderment, and wondered how all his hours of labor added up to zero. Can you figure it out for him?

2. Chained to a Dilemma. Charlie Bennett was in trouble. He wouldn't receive his monthly allowance from his father for another week. Meanwhile he had to pay his boardinghouse landlady for the next seven days or she'd boot him out. When he explained the situation to her, she said she'd settle for a small chain he owned, made of seven precious links.

But Charlie didn't trust the landlady. To be sure that she'd serve him meals properly all week, he offered to give her one link a day for the seven days. She agreed, but said she'd allow him to cut away only one link of the chain altogether.

You must figure out the facts. Charlie did, so that he was able to solve his dilemma and give his landlady one link for each day by the end of the seven days. Study the chain and link your mind to the solution.

3. How Far Flies the Hummingbird? In this thoroughly improbable problem, you are to accept the "facts" as correct, as the solution lies in figuring out the facts, not in any sleight-of-mind.

Consider that two motorcycles travel from Hometown to Bigcity, which are 50 miles apart. They travel directly toward each other until they meet. One motorcycle goes 30 miles an hour, and the other speeds only 20 miles an hour.

As the motorcycles start from each place simultaneously, toward each other, a super-muscled hummingbird, which has been sitting on the handlebars of one motorcycle, takes off and flies toward the other motorcycle at a speed of 100 miles an hour.

As soon as the energetic hummingbird reaches the other motorcycle, he turns around and flies back to the first one. Then he takes off immediately again, shuttling back and forth from one to the other until the two motorcycles meet.

After you catch your breath, you're to figure out how far the hummingbird flies during this hectic proceeding. If you focus on the facts, you can solve this seemingly complicated puzzler in less than a minute.

4. THE CHICKEN AND THE CHICKEN-EATING DOG. A farmer found himself in quite a stew. There he was on one side of a river with a very small rowboat, and he had to get to the other side of the river in order to deliver a fat, sassy chicken, a bushel of corn and a large chicken-eating dog, all of which he had sold to a customer across the river and down the road a piece.

Since the boat was so small, he could only carry one of the three burdens in the boat at a time, along with himself. But if he took over the bushel of corn and left the chicken and the chicken-eating dog, he'd lose the chicken. If he left the chicken and the corn, the chicken would eat the corn and he'd lose that money from the sale. However, the dog was anti-vegetarian and had no interest in eating corn.

How did the farmer solve his problem, or did he give up the sale and head back to the farmhouse without completing the delivery?

5. PROFIT AND LOSS PUZZLER. You needn't be money mad to go mad over this confusing money problem. Here are the facts. Pete owed Wilbur $20 and had promised to pay him on Friday, which was today. There was just one hitch, a considerable one. Pete only had $14 to settle the debt, and he was ashamed to offer Wilbur part payment.

Finally, Pete figured out a plan whereby he could multiply his money, and he decided that nobody would lose. He went to a pawnshop where he gave the proprietor a $10 bill and obtained an $8 loan on it with no trouble at all. He then sought out his friend Ernest and sold him the ticket covering $10 in currency, for $8. Now Pete had the $4 left over from his original $14, plus the $8 he'd obtained from the pawnbroker, and the $8 he'd received from Ernest.

Thus, by his complicated maneuvering, Pete had $20 total, which he gave to Wilbur to pay off the debt, as promised.

That looked like a clear profit of $6 for Pete. Did anyone lose on the transaction, and if so, how much?

In the case of all these puzzlers, a clear and complete assembling of the facts is the prime requisite in arriving at the correct solutions. With the facts before you comprehensively, the answers are arrived at quite simply and easily.

But unless you assemble the facts, these problems often seem incredibly complicated. As a canny but confused creative thinker put it, "*Cherchez la* fact."

A Tip From Dickens: "Facts and Figures! Put 'em Down!"

Facts are the basic raw materials from which many creative ideas grow. When you tackle any subject that concerns you, about which research is possible, make it a positive action to seek out and note down any facts, theories, suppositions, propositions. Collect anything related directly and remotely to the subject.

The story is told about the great attorney Clarence Darrow, who must certainly be included high on the list of creative men in law. Cross-examining a very able doctor during a trial, Darrow had torn apart his testimony as he trotted out an amazing array of medical facts and knowledge.

After the trial, the noted lawyer was asked, "Where did you learn medicine and get your M.D.?"

Darrow replied with a twinkle, "In my study last night, from midnight to 3 A.M."

Think of facts as fuel for your mental furnace. In this step, you shovel the facts into the receptacle—your mind. Then, in steps four, five and six, you'll learn how the thinking room in the back of your head will burn up those facts through productive creative thinking to produce the bright ideas you want.

The famous inventor Alexander Graham Bell said that "the successful businessman is the one who has observed, remembered and compared the *facts* of business. And all the achievements of science have come from doing those three things." He advised repeatedly that ideas grow from facts.

Set Down the Facts

Make it a habit to carry a notebook or scrap of paper, or whatever is convenient for you, so you can set down facts or thoughts wherever and whenever there is a need and an opportunity.

I don't feel dressed unless I have a notebook in my jacket pocket, with a pencil attached, or a slip of paper in the pocket of my shirt in case I'm not wearing a jacket, and frequently a thin pad in the hip pocket of my trousers or sports shorts if I'm wearing a T-shirt.

I make notes immediately upon finding any facts or coming upon a thought worth remembering. Note that phrase "worth remembering," because just "wanting" to remember isn't enough. Phychological tests have proved conclusively that most people forget 25 percent of what they've learned—even what they want to remember—within the first twenty-four hours. And, within a week, 85 percent is forgotten.

Remember that "of all liars, the smoothest and most convincing is memory." But if you've written it down correctly, there's no chance of remembering it wrong.

So, unless you're willing to forget, or distort, what you've learned, you'd better write it down. Another worthy slant is that you relieve your mind of the necessity of remembering, once you've jotted down the fact or item. That, in turn, releases your mind more freely for creative thinking rather than subjecting your brain to the strain and necessity of remembering all such details.

For example, if you need ideas regarding office procedure, note the facts about what goes on—write them down in a notebook. Once you've written down the details, you can go on to other matters, handle interruptions, take care of your current chores. Then, later, you can come back to your notes and act to transform them into original ideas, as suggested in step four.

Set a Time Limit

An extremely able researcher of my acquaintance never achieved more than moderate success, for one primary reason. He didn't know when to stop. He'd go on collecting facts, and then adding more facts, until the head of his department had to tell him emphatically on one job after another, "Give me your report by close of work tomorrow—or else!"

I can't give you any set time limits or quotas regarding how many hours, days, weeks and even months or longer you should give to fact-finding. I can't tell you exactly how many facts you should seek. That obviously depends on the extent of the problem and the amount of material available.

You'll have to learn to say "when" to fact-filling, just as you must know the limit when pouring liquor into a tall glass. You must determine and know your own needs and capacities. And you'll find that setting the time and quota limit comes naturally, after you proceed in your fact seeking and absorption many times.

Just as you've learned what your nutritional requirements are, you'll acquire facility at measuring the amount of brain food you need and can digest and absorb.

Beware of False Facts

Walter Lippmann, acknowledged to be one of the great journalists of all time, stressed the necessity for clear, correct seeking of facts in this way: "A good reporter should have endless curiosity plus equanimity. I mean curiosity without the desire to use facts differently from what they happen to be."

Similarly, you should note down the fact first for what it is, not what you want it to be or wish it were. Shaping facts into ideas comes in the next step. But gathering facts is the harvest time. The transformation of facts into ideas, just like making the wheat into bread and other foods, comes later.

Many noted thinkers have said, "Facts are stubborn things." You must be just as stubborn in seeing them for what they are, as differentiated from what they are not, so that you may later strike vital, electric, usable sparks from them.

Make it a point to check a fact whenever it seems fuzzy or possibly fake. In double-checking, you'll usually come upon more reliable material that can be useful. If you fake the facts, you'll wind up fooling yourself. It has been said that "a half truth is generally the worst half."

Fixing your thinking upon a surface impression can be very misleading, as proved by optical illusions like the following:

Which of these lines is longer, A or B?

Now measure with a ruler. "Checking the fact" by measurement proves that both lines are the same length. The formations of the ends seem to shorten one and lengthen the other. Yet if you hadn't checked, you might have gone right ahead with the wrong "solution" that B was a longer line. Any procedures and conclusions thereafter would have been wrong.

Are A and B of equal length here? Don't trust your eyes. Measure and find out surely.

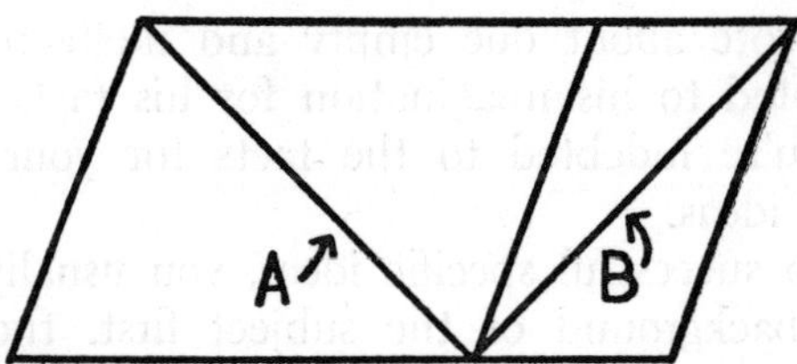

Is the high hat taller than the brim is wide? Measure and then know. Don't be fooled by the fact that a vertical line usually looks longer than a horizontal line.

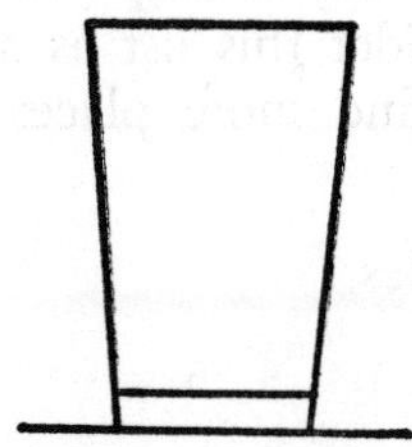

Which circle is bigger, A or B? Measure for yourself. Realize that the environment or conditions surrounding an apparent "fact" may be misleading—unless you double-check.

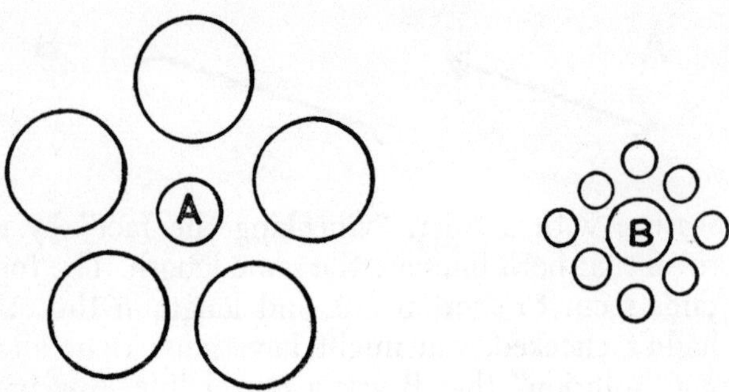

Remember these instructive optical illusions, as a lesson to remind you to guard against "mental illusions" in gathering and writing down facts. If you twist a false "fact," you're likely to come up with a wrong or ineffectual idea.

Freneau wrote about one empty and ineffectual character, "He is indebted to his imagination for his facts." Rather, be sure that you're indebted to the facts for your imaginative, solid, creative ideas.

To develop successful specific ideas, you usually must study the general background of the subject first, thoroughly and honestly. The true facts help illuminate the real needs and directions for the development of brilliant new ideas.

Checklist of Sources for Facts

Here's a reminder listing to help you check all the possible sources for facts. Consider this list as a basic beginning from which you go on to find more places from which to mine valuable facts:

Library reference files
Books

Magazines
Newspapers
Trade publications
Pamphlets
Other printed literature
Local, state and national government files and printings
Schools and universities
Experts and authorities in each field
Observation
Interviews
Conversation

Research the Facts in Depth

Here's a suggested procedure for getting the facts, all the facts, and nothing but the facts:

1. When studying printed matter, make detailed notes of pertinent and related points as you go along. Your aim here is to pile up your own reference facts from the material at hand.
2. Reread the material, checking your notes as you go page by page, this time also seeking—and then writing down—the big over-all points that the writer is making.
3. Go over your own original notes this time. Check each point for clarity. If anything seems fuzzy, confused or incorrect, refer again to the literature to clear up any question in your notes.
4. Rearrange your notes now for utmost efficiency in respect to further usage, as preparation for the next step in the six-step creative method.
5. Now, from this rearrangement of your notes, sort out and isolate the key facts. Thus, you spotlight the essential facts which will form a springboard to further aid your effective creative thinking.
6. Seek a personal interview with an expert in the field, or plan other personal interrogation. You'll probably have only one chance to write down the notes. Do so as accurately as pos-

sible. Then, at your first opportunity after the interview, go over your notes and rearrange them, as suggested in points three, four and five in the preceding.

Although these repeated procedures may seem irksome at times, and even unnecessary to you, I urge you to persist as directed. This method has been proved many times. The point-by-point progression helps to convey the facts into your thinking room in an orderly, practical manner. You gain the necessary knowledge in depth, leading to much easier and surer development of valuable creative ideas.

It pays to dig in deep lest you become one of those people "who read just enough to be thoroughly misinformed."

Always keep your notes. Don't throw them away. Instead, file them where you can get at them again quickly, easily and repeatedly, for further reference and usage time after time. Your work on this step is often of enduring as well as immediate value. Don't take any chances of losing it.

Fact-Finding Questioning

When you're digging for facts in printed matter, or particularly in a personal interview, it helps to list general questions beforehand. You can make up your own list, depending on the aspects of the particular problem. Also, use the following checklist as an aid.

This listing has worked very effectively many hundreds of times for me, and for others. I suggest that you copy the list on a separate sheet or card to carry with you on an interview. Also, take it along as a guide in getting the answers out of printed material in your hunt for facts and comprehensive information.

Checklist

1. What are the three basic foundation points about this matter? (Or one, two, six, twelve or whatever number of points seems reasonable and sensible in respect to this particular problem, depending on its size, depth and scope.)
2. How is it similar to others?

3. How does it differ from others?
4. How far back does it go?
5. How did it start?
6. How did it develop?
7. What are the outstanding developments?
8. What are its primary functions?
9. What are its principal merits?
10. What are its faults, if any?
11. What is it related to, past and now?
12. What are the latest facts, theories, advances in the field?
13. How does it serve or perform best, in respect to competitive comparisons, if any?
14. What are opposing opinions, if any?
15. What does its future appear to be?
16. Have you any suggestions in respect to further investigative possibilities on the matter?

In my experience, I've proved convincingly to myself that these basic questions usually get the answers and the facts needed. Other questions are likely to spring from them as you proceed. And other facts present themselves in printed matter or personal interviews, as the questions bring to light unexpected, helpful material in most cases.

In effect, such questioning acts to break apart a problem into many parts and subdivisions. You'll find that this will help you in accumulating detailed material on each part of a problem. It all adds up to a greater sum of facts, more grist for your creative-thinking mill.

Ask almost any successful creative person, and he'll tell you that a thorough breakdown and examination of all the parts of a problem is usually essential as a preliminary to producing effective and usable creative ideas. Never forget it: facts are the prelude to ideas.

A Tip from a Tip Sheet

Here's one example showing how even the most unusual and unlikely reference material may function for you. This is based on a true though rather unusual case illustrating how this fact-finding step operates.

An acquaintance named Jerry, who works for a large paint company, stopped by to see me. He explained that the advertising department in his outfit had started a contest among all employees. The firm would pay sizable cash prizes for the best names for the colors in a new line of paints.

He told me, "The contest information urges that the names be different, imaginative and dramatic, but I don't know how to get started. Could you advise me?"

I discussed step three with him, and suggested that he go to every possible listing of names he could find, in almost any category. I included library reference files and other sources that I've noted for you in this chapter.

"By listing and studying the colorful names for almost anything," I said, "you'll accumulate a reference file for your brain to work on. You shouldn't copy the names exactly and offer them as your personal suggestions, of course. But such lists will stir and activate your imagination so you can come up with bright creations of your own."

A few weeks later, Jerry came by again, grinning broadly. He told me excitedly and gratefully that he'd won several cash prizes, and much praise, for the names he'd submitted. "You gave me good advice," he explained, "telling me to look up other listings."

I was very pleased, and asked, "What reference material did you find most helpful?"

He hesitated, flushed and then blurted out, "Well, I have a hobby—I bet on the horses. And I found the most dramatic, colorful and inspiring names in my horse-racing tip sheets."

You never know. It pays to dig everywhere.

The "Soda Pop System" of Filling Up

In explaining to young associates how to go about filling up the mind best with facts, I've found that I get the point across most effectively (for them) by calling this procedure the "soda pop system." Here it is.

Go slowly in absorbing facts, filling your mind gradually, rather than overwhelming it with a flood of facts that it can't hold and study properly. Think of the process of fact-absorption as though you're filling a glass with highly charged soda pop.

Take a ten-ounce bottle of cold soda and a ten-ounce glass. If you pour fast and freely, all at one time, the fluid swells and flows over the top of the glass so that much of it is lost and wasted. The glass simply won't hold all the substance by this sudden pouring method.

But pour in slowly and carefully. Then pause as the bubbles rise dangerously close to overflowing the top of the glass. Pause until the liquid is settled. Then pour again slowly, repeating the pauses and the pouring.

By this method, you can fill a ten-ounce glass with ten ounces of highly charged soda without wasting a single bubble. So, use this system to absorb facts properly in your mind. As you pour in the facts, let them settle. Wait a bit before you pour in more. Your mind will thus absorb all the facts it can possibly hold and use. It won't be filled to overflowing with a lot of empty bubbles.

Hard Work Pays Out

Realize that some extremely successful people have spent months and even years in gathering the facts and researching the subject, as an essential part of producing brilliant ideas that have paid off in tremendous rewards of every kind. As noted earlier, you don't have to spend years; you may limit your researches to a few hours, days or weeks. It depends on the extent of the problem and the time limit imposed upon you, if any.

But it's true that the more work you put in, within reason, the more will come out in useful ideas. All experts in this field agree that the mind must be provided with facts and the work of gathering and absorbing the facts is absolutely necessary in practically every case. Aldous Huxley wrote that "facts do not cease to exist because they are ignored." Someone will find them, use them and capitalize on the opportunity they represent. Why not you?

Most great creative scientific discoveries, as you know, have developed from studies of the available proved facts, and from research about opposing and opposite theories. Remember number 14 of your checklist of fact-finding questions, "What are opposing opinions, if any?" You gain from examining many viewpoints.

It pays in many cumulative ways to find out everything about the problem first. You'll often discover things other than the things you're looking for, illuminating new facts that may well become new revelations. They can lead to fresh, productive new ideas, as delineated on later pages. For as you proceed, fact by fact, you're automatically turning the problem around like a many-faceted crystal, seeing new ideas and aspects of it.

Those "sudden flashes" of million-dollar ideas that seemed to happen to the unrealistic heroes in the movies years ago—they just aren't so. Such flashes, as you'll find out, do come—but only following preparatory digging, cogitating, trying, after your mind has been filled with material relevant to the problem.

Even if you find the digging for facts unpleasant and seemingly unproductive, keep going. The rewards will be more than worthwhile. As Thomas Carlyle wrote about the greatest creative thinkers, even those few in the genius category, "Genius . . . is the transcendent capacity for taking trouble first of all."

If it becomes tedious and tiresome, renew your energy with the realization that you are preparing your mind to produce the brilliant, profitable solutions.

If you're sports-minded, you might compare this preparatory stage to that of the seasoned fighter who first feels out (researches) the facts about his opponent's style and abilities, by jabbing, blocking and testing. Thus, he's gathering material about the problem. And then, from knowledge gained, he attacks and strikes where and how it counts the most.

If you just lash out without preparation, figuring that "inspiration will strike," you're more likely to find yourself flat on your back, in effect, instead of being cheered as a creative champ.

Own a "Magical Jug" of Facts

Proceed optimistically with this fact-finding step.

Think of it this way: As you fill your mind with facts, propositions, questions, sidelights and other reference materials pertinent to the problem under consideration, it's just as though you're filling a "magical jug" with priceless, life-giving liquid.

With this magical jug, no matter how often you drink from it, the contents are not diminished; they remain; the jug is never emptied. The reference material remains intact for you to use from now on, and to go back to for refreshment time after time. Here is an ever energizing source and inspiration for creating new ideas and variations of valuable ideas.

It will pay you to follow step three thoroughly, to: Look, Listen, List and Learn.

7

STEP FOUR: WRITE DOWN IDEAS, SENSIBLE AND SEEMINGLY WILD

After the fact-finding of step three, you're now ready to write down a good number of creative ideas on whatever problem or challenge is facing you. In effect, then, in this phase of the six-step method, your action is to study, use, re-form and spring off from the facts you've gathered in step three. Then you'll produce the creative solutions to the problem.

A novelist described this process very specifically as he told about a creative scientist who worked up his ideas by digging into his research, and noted that "it was pleasant to see every hour eat its way into the mass of facts."

Most appropriately, since you'll be matching and initiating creative solutions to problems, I suggest that you warm up your mind by solving some ingenious match puzzles that follow. In these, the matches and the details of the puzzles are your "facts." You'll probably have to make a number of attempts in different directions, just as you'll later set down many different ideas until you arrive at the clear and successful solution.

Match-the-Facts Practice Puzzlers

(Solutions begin on page 248.)

1. Four-Square Problem. The facts of this puzzler are the five squares that you see formed here. Duplicate this formation with matches.

Now, by shifting just 2 of the matches, form four squares instead of five.

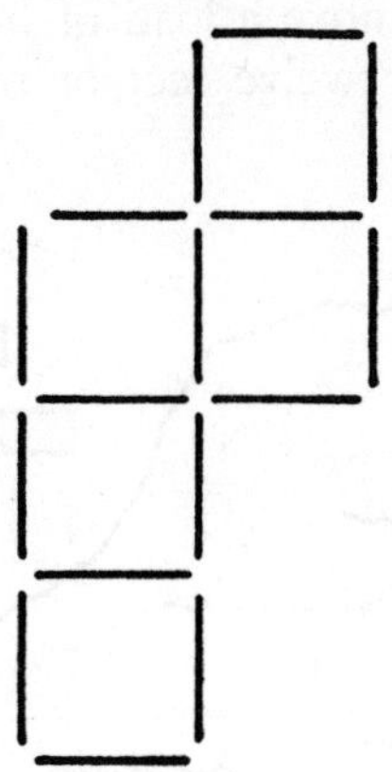

2. Form-a-Square Puzzler. Here's a tricky problem that requires a little study and ingenuity to unlock it.

Place four matches exactly in the position shown in the diagram.

Now, form a square by moving only one match.

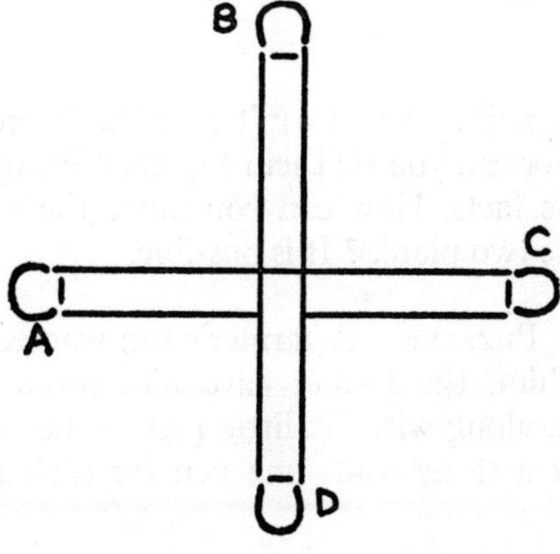

3. Reach-the-Island Problem. You must match the solution to the facts in this case, by imagining that each of two matches you'll use is a ten-foot-long plank.

Your problem is to move a load of bricks on a wheelbarrow to the island which is twelve feet or more from the shore at every point.

You have no nails, so you can't nail the boards together to extend them. Nor can you tie them together by any other means.

Those are the facts. How can you move the wheelbarrow to the island on the two planks? It is possible.

4. The Pigpen Puzzler. A farmer's son wanted to raise pigs. To encourage him, the farmer gave him seven wooden walls made of boards, along with six little pigs, so he could construct six pens against a stone wall—one pen for each pig—according to this plan:

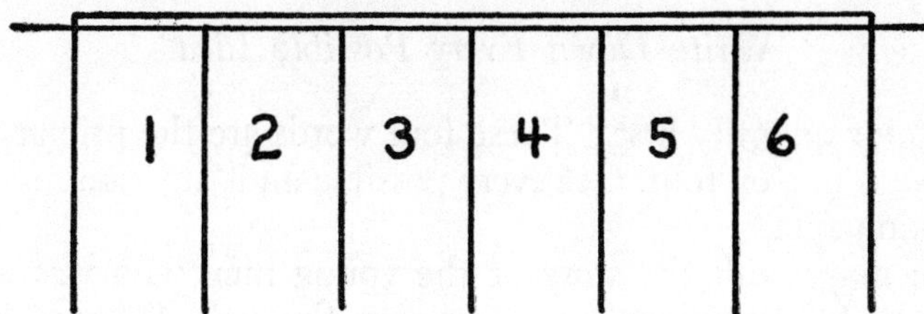

But the night before the young fellow could build the six pigpens, someone stole one of the walls. The farmer's son knew he couldn't get any more walls from his father, yet he'd have to forfeit the pigs if he couldn't provide a separate pen for each.

The sad fact remained that he had only six wooden walls at his command. Here's your challenge, based on these facts: Using six matches instead of wooden walls, see whether you can solve the youngster's problem for him.

5. Nine-Into-Three Transformation. Place the matches in the simple formation shown here.

Now, remove just eight of the matches and leave three squares.

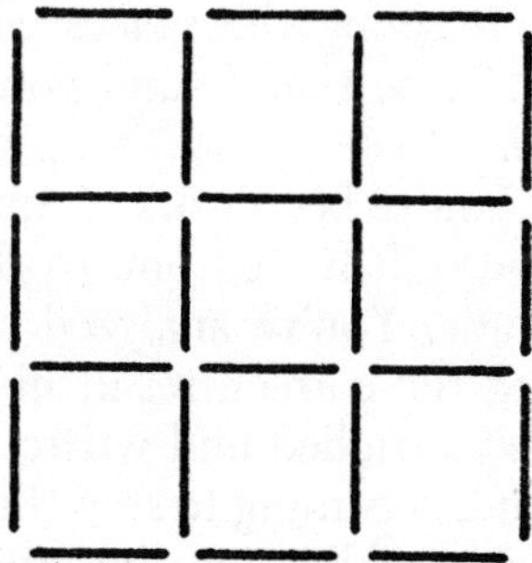

You'll have to fiddle around quite a bit with the "facts" to solve this one. (Here's a softhearted clue: One of the squares is smaller than the other two.)

Write Down Every Possible Idea

"Go for quantity first." These four words are the primary key to success in step four. Get every possible and "impossible" idea down on paper.

You may recall the story of the young man who was asked what was his technique for impressing the girls. He explained, "As soon as I meet a girl whom I find attractive, I ask her for a kiss."

The questioner was shocked, and demanded, "Don't you often get your face slapped?"

"Yes," the young man said blithely, "but you'd be surprised how often I get kissed!"

Once you start setting down every idea, seemingly sensible or wild, you'll be surprised (and delighted) by how often you score with a good, usable idea.

Go for quantity first. You'll apply selectivity later to arrive at quality of ideas eventually, as you'll learn in step six.

Start Filling the Spaces

My personal procedure is to take a long, ruled yellow pad at this point and to start filling the spaces with ideas, line after line, page after page. Note that I—and you—have advanced to this stage step by step.

Now consider that you've been working on an actual problem. You have attuned yourself in step one to the wide-open, alert, seeking creative attitude. You've analyzed the problem so that you're working toward the correct, resultful wanted solution, as in step two. And you've studied and written down all the facts you've been able to find, according to step three.

Now you will set down ideas, on line after line. First, you'll reach into your mind and into the fact file. Then you'll apply the systems suggested on following pages for step four.

Don't be satisfied with one or two or a half-dozen ideas. Keep digging for *dozens*. You'll find that quantity piles up almost automatically with the Creative Quiz System of sixteen key questions listed later.

Samuel Johnson stressed the desirability of having an open mind for many ideas when he commented about one uncreative individual, "That fellow seems to me to possess but one idea, and that is a wrong one."

A noted psychologist affirms this point when he emphasizes that he never asks a person, in the course of teaching creatively, "What is the best use for a brick?" Instead, he'll phrase the question, "How many uses can you think of for a brick?" The aim here too is to spur ideas in quantity.

Keep trying and you'll keep listing. I've drawn inspiration, when I feel I'm almost hopelessly blocked, from an anecdote about the historic creative leader, David Ben-Gurion, a prime builder of Israel.

A *Lesson from a Nation-Builder*

In working to improve a problem area in that pioneering land, Ben-Gurion was told that a vital desert section was absolutely unusable. Even piping in large quantities of water wouldn't help, he was informed.

"Who says so?" he asked.

His adviser explained, "Our experts, who have been studying this problem for many months, report agreement that the situation can't be solved. There's just nothing to do."

"Yes, there is," the determined leader stated flatly. "Let's get another set of experts."

The work went on. The problem was solved.

Remember that lesson, as I do, when you think you're blocked, that you can't find any more ideas, that "there's just nothing to do."

Keep writing. Keep listing ideas, simple or complicated. As the work goes on, the problem will be solved.

I find further sustenance in the story illustrating the persistence that helped Albert Skira of Switzerland to become one of the greatest of art book publishers. He decided that he had to publish a book with illustrations of the work of the artist Picasso. This would help greatly to advance his business and position in the publishing world.

It is reported that Skira called Picasso's phone number without success. Unable to get through to the artist, the persistent publisher phoned every day for a year. Finally he reached Picasso himself, managed to arrange a meeting and eventually published a notable volume.

By comparison, it makes your job of setting down general ideas seem quite easy, doesn't it? As Sinclair Lewis (and many other creative people) has been quoted as saying, a primary part of creativity is "the application of the seat of the pants to the seat of the chair."

Then you simply pick up a pencil and apply your ideas to paper, spurred by the idea-starters that follow.

Creative Quiz-System Checklist

Here's a checklist of sixteen questions to answer, to help you produce many ideas for each problem you tackle. You may have heard students wailing, "I know all the answers—it's the *questions* I don't understand." These questions are very easy to understand. The answers, leading to ideas, will come with a little personal mental prodding.

Write your problem at the top of a ruled pad.

Then answer each of these questions that makes sense on this problem, filling in one or more of the ruled lines. Some of the questions may not apply to each problem, but most will function to bring a few or many answers.

Sixteen Idea-Starter Questions

Remember, you start from the facts you have amassed as a background and which provide a "mine" of information. Now you'll set down ideas that will be inspired by these questions:

1. Break down problem into smaller parts, and list ideas for each segment?

2. Adapt and apply ideas from similar problems or products?
3. Adapt and apply ideas from dissimilar problems or products, in related or unrelated categories?
4. List faults: how correct these?
5. List good features: how expand, increase or improve these further?
6. How simplify it?
7. What can be added or increased to improve?
8. What can be removed beneficially?
9. What extra and new uses and applications?
10. What complete changes can be made?
11. Substitute something else entirely?
12. How about reversing, starting backward, inside-out, reshaping, doing exactly the opposite?
13. How vary the problem and applications?
14. How combine various aspects?
15. Review: how can it be done or handled better?
16. What *more* can be done?

Use Idea-Starter Questions as a Springboard

You'll be turning back to the list of sixteen idea-starter questions again and again, now and for weeks, years and quite possibly for the rest of your life. This listing provides a format, a routine, a springboard for your creative thinking and production. Once you put pencil to paper, the ideas start to flow.

If you don't get another thing out of this book, you'll still find this basic creative quiz system invaluable. Whenever you're stuck for an idea or a solution to a problem, turn to this list of questions, start answering them, start writing.

The great Alexandre Dumas was known to force himself to fill a certain number of pages every day. He wouldn't stop until he completed that set number of pages. I have read that he started filling the blank pages by spurring himself with questions, such as, "What would happen next? What would the character do? Would somebody new walk in? How would he react to changes in the current set of circumstances?"

Debate with Yourself

The self-questioning system is not uncommon with writers, to get oneself started filling the blank, staring, challenging new page. You have the springboard questions laid out for you here. Tackle them to answer them, and you must and will pile up ideas as a result. Keep trying, keep probing—above all, keep writing.

One self-starter method is to "debate" with yourself about the problem. First take one side, and then the opposite. This tug of war, of arguments for and against any particular viewpoint, frequently operates to produce salient new slants that may grow into ideas.

Don't be concerned or blocked by any feeling of a lack of originality in the ideas or answers you set down at this step. You are an individual, and as such, you're different from all others. Your answers too will be different, and therefore must have some element of originality, just as your fingerprints are individual, personal, original, even though everyone else has fingerprints too.

Action, a piling up of ideas, that's what's important at this stage. Start answering and you'll start amassing elements, answers, ideas.

Questions Give Birth to More Questions

The very essence of creative thinking is that questions you ask yourself bring up more questions to probe and answer. Let's see how this applies by studying the idea-starter questions in more detail.

1. *Break down problem into smaller parts and list ideas for each segment?*

This is the divide-and-conquer method, as indicated in puzzlers in an earlier chapter, and expanded later.

You'll recall that with those puzzlers, the basis of finding solutions was to divide the questions first into segments and then produce the answers from an analysis of the parts. Often it's finding the comparatively simple small answers that leads to the tougher, big answer.

For example, if you're aiming to improve a household appliance, your best approach may well be to take it apart, then first work to improve each part as a preliminary to a better whole. Apply the questions to each part. Could that small wheel be made of a tougher material so it wouldn't break? The answer might revolutionize the efficiency of the whole appliance.

You'll see exactly how to apply all these questions, as shown by many specific examples of usage in various problems and areas.

2. *Adapt and apply ideas from similar problems or products?* This related-problem approach is one of the most practical and effective. If it's a personnel problem, could the idea I used in handling Tom in the shipping department work with Helen in bookkeeping?

Scientists, you know, are constantly checking—would the effective element in Product A apply in improving Product B? Would the idea the P.T.A. committee used so successfully in organizing hobby groups be effective in boosting efficiency in the school cafeteria?

Consider and set down similar problems, and see whether you can adapt the productive answers to your current problem. Here's a practically infallible thought-starter for producing a list of ideas.

3. *Adapt and apply ideas from dissimilar problems or products, in related or unrelated categories?*

For example, there doesn't seem to be any clear systematic connection between the running of your home and office. Yet, could the method you used for arranging the tools and setup around your workbench in the basement be applied to the filing and storing routines in your office?

Has an apple falling from a tree any relationship to a revolutionary concept of gravity? It did in Newton's case.

Seeking to create a new toy, an alert individual who was interested in the workings of human anatomy questioned, "Would youngsters also be intrigued?" The answer was "yes"—and a very successful product was created, a transparent put-together-yourself replica of the human figure.

Needing an inexpensive container for samples of spices for cooking, I questioned myself about packages used in completely unrelated fields. Answering by listing all the little containers in my home, I came across a small plastic pill bottle. It proved to be perfect for our purpose. It was used to sell many thousands of spice samples, with no package change at all.

So many ideas can be adapted or copied from unrelated fields, and the creative originality here is in the conversion and usage.

4. *List faults: how correct these?*

One of the best starters is the listing of inadequacies or faults of a problem or product; this point also is expanded later.

Creative people concerned with improving the telephone have proved this over and over again. If you were applying this question to the telephone of just a few years ago, for example, you might have noted: Wire kinks up. Unattractive in the room. Takes up too much space on desk or table. Takes too long to get the operator. Too cumbersome in many rooms.

The questioning process led to answers and creative improvements in this idea that have scored increases worth millions upon millions of dollars: non-kink wire, attractive phones in decorator colors, beautiful flat instruments instead of tall monstrosities, speedy dial operation. And now you can get phones that clamp on, hang or hide and fit in almost anywhere, thanks to productive creative thinking exactly as suggested here.

Your first move in answering this question is actually to list the faults. The results are "instant ideas," as you list how to correct the faults.

5. *List good features: how expand, increase or improve these further?*

This is another sure spur to new ideas. First, you list the excellent features, then you improve on them.

If the design of a product is a good feature, perhaps you can beautify it further by adding color. If your problem is to help a child, the special feature of his active imagination can be expanded to lead toward developing his artistic prowess and thus increasing his lifelong happiness. If a portable machine has an easy-to-carry feature, it might be made even better by providing a more comfortable grip on the handle.

You'll find that once you list the good angles, the positive characteristics of those features lead readily to even better developments with them.

6. *How simplify it?*

Thoreau wrote, "Our life is frittered away by detail. . . . Simplify, simplify." And we might go on from there to state so truly that too many problems are encumbered and obscured by detail. So many solutions and ideas spring from the process of clarification and the act of simplifying.

What could be a simpler idea than the bent piece of metal that is the safety pin, a simplification of complicated, cumbersome clamps and clasps? What more effective idea than the one which strips away all confusion and unnecessary detail, and reveals true, basic meaning?

How often have you tried to solve a problem, then had some keen, creative person point out the solution, as you gasp, "But that's so simple!" Referring to the telephone again, a big step forward was that of combining mouthpiece and earpiece into one part, a vivid example of creative simplification.

You'll find that when you aim to answer this question, number 6, and set down ways to simplify, you'll be well on your way to sound creative ideas and solutions.

7. *What can be added or increased to improve?*

Here is an example of how you can apply even more questions on top of these sixteen basic questions. Ask such applicable questions, according to the case, as: Can it be made bigger? stronger? wider? higher? deeper? heavier? expanded?

A creative idea that helped boost a magazine's popularity tremendously was to make all color pages "bigger" in effect by carrying the color out to the edges instead of leaving a white margin all around. Yet this expansion method had been passed by for years by people previously associated with the publication and competitive magazines.

Can it be doubled? tripled? quadrupled? multiplied even more? A creative person profited by adding a double set of oarlocks to a rowboat so that two people could row, for greater speed with less effort. A creative motion-picture-theater executive increased his profits by being the first to start double features. In many mechanical gadgets, you can multiply the power many times over by doubling or tripling the size of the motor.

Two slices of bread make a delicious sandwich? The first restaurateur to offer triple-decker sandwiches profited handsomely from his creative idea, as many others have since.

My next-door neighbor has fourteen children and insists that his blessings have multiplied far out of proportion to the actual numbers from this literal creativity. Whether you agree or not, it does pay to consider the question of multiplication in producing creative ideas and solutions.

8. *What can be removed beneficially?*

Ask yourself additional sub-questions in this phase: Can it be made smaller? diminished? stripped? weaker? narrower? shorter? shallower? lighter? contracted?

A creative designer who worked primarily with wood produced a beautiful and successful line of bowls for table use. Asking directly whether something shallower could be developed, he designed attractive flat, square, small slabs of wood which became very popular as coasters for glasses. Similarly, large brandy glasses were duplicated in tiny shape to produce fast-selling little novelty cordial glasses.

Economy in small cars was obtained by using aluminum materials for the motor. Suitcases were made more practicable by manufacturing lighter frames and materials—easier to carry. Soda bottles were improved and sales increased by producing "shorties" that take up less space in the refrigerator than common long-necked versions.

Can lightness, smallness, reduction of the number of parts

improve a product that's your concern? Ask the questions of yourself. You be the one to come up with the ideas and solve the problems accordingly. Don't wait until you're the one who says, "Now, why didn't I think of that?" Ask yourself the questions, set down the quick solutions, and you'll come up with the right, successful, ultimate answers.

As amusing applications of the diminishing and expanding measures, I submit two "stoopefying Stoopnagle inventions." One was an alarm clock with only half a bell, so that if two people were sleeping in the same room and only one had to get up, the half bell would awaken only one of them.

The expanded invention was a twenty-foot pole, for use in not touching two people that you wouldn't touch with a ten-foot pole.

9. *What extra and new uses and applications?*

Start setting down new uses, extra applications, regardless of those three murderous words "Can't be done." They're sure death to new ideas. For example, someone might have said about the smaller transistor radios, "Improve them? Can't be done. They're small, attractive, functional—that's the end of it."

But a bright creative mind applied a number of extra applications that boosted sales—added a long strap to hang from the shoulder or even a nearby tree, welded on a clamp so the radio clipped in a second onto a golf cart, auto door or baby buggy, included a loop so the set could hang on a wall or door.

"Can't be improved?" Whoever says that about anything is incredibly obstinate or just plain unimaginative and completely uncreative.

Go ahead, make your own list. I'll bet you can write down at least three further improvements for transistor radios right now. It's excellent practice to step up your own creative abilities by listing new uses for some established item. Then set down the extra uses and applications in respect to your own challenges.

10. *What complete changes can be made?*

Remember that you're to write down even fantastic exaggerations and radical departures at this point. It's gratifying that so many unprecedented and even seemingly impossible directions can be explored rewardingly.

Creative auto designers scored notably successful advances when they departed from standard auto design to produce small, streamlined sports cars and then more compact family models. Horizontal freezers were changed completely by some brilliant engineers who aimed to produce successful upright models. Wonderful progress was instituted by broad-minded men who changed from just canning goods to freezing them also, a complete departure.

A creative woman changed her home and life entirely and happily. She took stock of how she could utilize her particular abilities to change and improve her status. Then, working with her co-operative and creative husband, she transformed her basement into a studio. She started giving arts-and-crafts lessons that brought her family a fine income and extra conveniences.

Another mother with a flair for decorating decided to capitalize on her talent and interest. She changed her living room into a showroom for upholstery and drapes, materials, wallpapers and related items. She built a successful decorating business right at home.

List complete changes? Of course you can. Open any magazine and see what successes have been gained solidly by changing completely. Here's evidence in just one issue before me: A heavy woman noted that her problem was, "How can I become attractive?" She sought out a diet, stuck to it, trimmed down from 190 pounds to 130 pounds, attracted a husband and raves about the "complete transformation that transformed my life."

Look—page after page of advertisements on instant coffee, certainly a radical departure from regular cans and bags of coffee brewed in a variety of pots. A change for more sales, if not for a better beverage.

Tubeless tires—somebody's bright and radical idea that "couldn't be done." A fast-selling tool—combination hoe, rake and digger—a complete change from the conventional rake.

A poet praised "the enchanting miracles of change"—just as you will as you improve your creative abilities and gains. Change is the essence of progress. Work toward it as suggested here.

11. *Substitute something else partially or entirely?*

This is often the key to new and revealing creative departures. Very often people overlook a solution that's possible through some slight or sizable substitution. Your answers to question number 11 will help reveal such provocative flaws or errors.

Are you seeking a more efficient work method? Perhaps the answer lies in substituting other materials and procedures rather than making entirely different arrangements.

Want to improve the looks of a room? Consider re-covering, refinishing and rearranging your furniture rather than discarding and getting new pieces.

Take a tip from a creative food packer who substituted eight different vegetable juices for straight tomato juice to produce an additional best seller.

Remember that substitution is a helpful tool for providing new inspiration and success. Try it.

12. *How about reversing, starting backward, inside-out, reshaping, doing exactly the opposite?*

As a very simple example, perhaps you're seeking a way to persuade a committee to adopt a plan you have in mind. Instead of pursuing a forceful, high pressure course, you might succeed by reversing your approach and doing exactly the opposite—trying soft, flattering persuasion.

If you're trying to invent some gadget, you might fail in drilling through a surface, but succeed in fastening a clamp around the outside instead.

A creative genius produced a better bandage by switching from the usual aim of making it stickier. Instead, he took the opposite tack. He devised a bandage that was sticky but wouldn't cling so firmly that it would hurt the skin when being removed. This was an enormous success.

Smart merchandisers of whisky did a turnabout from the viewpoint that a brand should be flavorful and full-bodied. When they offered a lighter, milder drink instead, their sales zoomed.

Many problems in business are solved by reversing the attack and aiming to show people how economical a product is, rather than how luxurious. For instance, a coffee blender who charged more for his brand scored a notable success by promising better coffee from fewer spoonfuls per pot.

A maker of a skin foundation liquid decided to take the opposite viewpoint. He increased his business by creating a longer-lasting, more flattering, dry cake makeup.

A valuable plant hormone became even more important when creative scientists sought out its opposite potency as a weed-killer.

Remember that you can often benefit by elongating the truism "opposites attract" to "opposites attract better ideas."

13. *How vary the problem and applications?*

It is valuable and effective to question how a shift in the facts and applications may make a big and profitable creative difference. For example, a manufacturer of filing cabinets decided that he could increase his market by making decorative styles for the home, as a variation of his regular business line. The smaller cabinets, in attractive and decorative wood finishes which went well with other furniture in the room, were an immediate and continuing success.

Thus, a variation of the same basic product proved to be the effective new creative approach. Similarly, a carpenter who conducted his business from home set out to apply creative variations to the shelving he made for homes. In addition to the usual shelf cabinets, and shelves clamped to walls, he designed and built a wide variety of ingenious new types of shelves. Some were hinged; others "floated" from the ceiling on firm wires. Other removable, adjustable shelves could be slipped in and out of decorative wall grooves in seconds. In effect, his creations were all answers to question number 13—how to vary the applications on his particular problem.

You'll find that this question provides a valuable spur to setting down many ideas and approaches on the problem that concerns you.

14. *How combine various aspects?*

Very often, borrowing or combining different parts or aspects relating to your problem will produce exciting and effective ideas and solutions. As one example, a creative engineer combined features of electric irons with those of steam irons. The result was the production of electric steam irons which have proved a boon to housewives (and manufacturers).

In solving an office problem for a particular department, I've found it very effective to combine operational features of three or more other departments and apply them successfully in a plan to improve this one.

A deodorant manufacturer scored a sensational success by combining the meritorious aspects of a lotion with the benefits of a handy applicator. Result—the very popular roll-on products.

Once you start digging into the possibilities, and answering question number 14, you'll find that you can create bright new slants for your business, home and other activities.

Originality may well derive from borrowing and combining several unoriginal aspects from other sources. The resulting combination can be, as proved many times, both "new" and very successful.

15. *Review: how can it be done or handled better?*

After you've gone through the fourteen previous categories of questions, and written your first set of answers, go back and review them carefully. As you check one answer after the other, keep asking: How can it be made better?

You'll usually find questions coming up that haven't appeared in this listing, even though it's a comprehensive basic set. Write down those new questions on another sheet of paper. List answers to them, and add the answers to your previous list.

Remind yourself that there's nothing made that can't be produced a little better, nothing done that cannot be accomplished a little more effectively. While there is eventually a time to stop and say, "This is the best I can do"—right now, at this stage, aim for betterment. You're seeking quantity at this point, so search out more answers that are just a little better than what you have already. Then write them down.

16. *What more can be done?*

This question may seem like an extension of number 15, but actually it's a further and additional approach to piling up the largest possible quantity of ideas. I've found it very effective, and so have others who've tried this method, not to write "finis" to the listing yet.

I set myself a quota usually of three more answers to each question. But even if you determine to seek only one more answer per question, you'll have added over a dozen more creative possibilities. So, set a quota, one or two or three or more, and go down the list, number by number, until you've completed your listing. A job well done, and one that will surely bring you solid rewards.

From No Ideas to Many Ideas

Each time you set down answers to the listing of idea-starter questions, it will be obvious to you that you've already made a great advance in your creative thinking abilities toward the solutions and ideas that will help you so much. You will have proceeded from a blank sheet of paper to a detailed listing, a host of ideas. You may ask yourself in astonishment, as I do so often, "Where did all those ideas come from?"

They came from attacking and following this creative quiz system energetically and with unswerving perseverance. You will have proceeded to that vital next step, from fact-finding to producing ideas. The list you've compiled is concrete evidence of your creativity, of your able, accelerated thinking and productivity.

Divide-and-Conquer System

As I've noted previously about my approach in writing a book, I recommend a similar self-spur to yourself, to keep you going from question to question in this listing, and from answers to answers. It's based on the same divide-and-conquer technique as advanced in question number 1 of the previous listing.

Your enthusiasm is high through the first and second questions. As you approach the third question, you can tell yourself, "I'm one-eighth through the list already." Thus you're dividing your task into segments, and your goal is to finish one at a time rather than all sixteen questions in one gulp.

After finishing the fourth, you may be slowing down, but it helps to realize that you're already past the quarter mark. On you move, with number 8 as your target, because then you'll be half done—you've passed the mountain peak and it should be easier going on the downslope toward number 16. Soon you'll be past number 12, the three-quarters' mark, with only four to go.

By breaking down your progress into segments this way, you'll usually find it helpful and much easier. You'll find it further proof of the value of question number 1, "Break down into smaller parts, and list ideas for each segment?"

And, remember, you need not set down answers to all the questions. Even if you answer only a few, you're already building a list of possible creative ideas.

Alphabet Creative-Spur System

Here's a little creative-spur system that I've always kept as a helpful, small "secret method" for myself. It's a quick aid in sparking creative thinking and rapid results.

This system is simply a matter of running down the alphabet with the key word of your problem and developing ideas in rhyming variations of the word.

For example, I may need a little creative idea for a birthday note to a friend or acquaintance. Instead of writing the usual, unimaginative "Happy birthday," I run down the alphabet.

Using the key problem word, "birthday," I seek words that rhyme with or sound like it. Thus, I come up with a list including: first day, girth day, mirth day, search day, worth day.

By running down the alphabet in your mind silently, you'd come up in seconds with a line such as "May your birthday be a joyous mirth day—and the happiest since your very first day!"

This is the simplest kind of application and result. I've found that the alphabet system has helped me produce ideas worth thousands of dollars to me, and millions of dollars (no exaggeration) to businesses with which I've been associated.

As an actual case history, see exactly how the alphabet rundown method worked on an important business problem which we'll analyze as a specific example later, in much greater detail.

Running a Detergent Down the Alphabet

The problem in this case was to come up with a solid creative idea for a new detergent product. Using step four of the creative method, you'd apply to the problem the sixteen key questions listed previously. In addition, using the alphabet system, I produced the following listing of idea approaches, based on the key word "detergent."

B-tergent. Perhaps an ingredient could be added which would increase the value and appeal of the detergent, just as vitamin B does in various food and drug products. Or, you might be reminded of an element that already exists, which starts with the letter B (or A to Z) and would improve the existing product.

C-tergent. This suggests an extra ingredient again which would improve the product as vitamin C does in foods and juices. Also consider "see-tergent," emphasizing the end result of using the detergent, an idea based on "seeing" the big difference this detergent makes. Perhaps a before-and-after comparison. Maybe apply a scientific test under lights, or through a camera, to help you "see" the difference in cleanliness produced by this detergent, compared with other cleaning products.

Emergent. Feature this as the "emergent detergent"? The point is that you can see how greater cleanliness "emerges" from using this detergent.

Also, as a further alphabet-inspired variation, perhaps there would be a need for an "emergency" detergent which not only cleans usual dirt and stains but also removes the exceptional splashes and deep stains which require emergency action and treatment.

Gee-tergent. Promote this product in sprightly fashion as the "gee-whiz" detergent—"Gee whiz, what a difference it makes in extra cleanliness, extra beauty!"

He-detergent. Consider featuring this one as the "he-man" detergent that has extra muscle to clean out the toughest dirt, grease and grime.

Eye-detergent. Perhaps a series of eye tests, again focusing on a comparison of results from this product and other detergents. "Your eye will show you the difference instantly. You'll agree, 'Aye-aye, this is the one for me!' "

J-detergent, jet-detergent. Consider improving the formula of the detergent with jet speed as the big point. Then feature its extra benefits in cleaning faster, "made especially for quicker results in this speedy jet age."

Key-tergent. Improve and sell this detergent as the one "key" that unlocks all your cleaning problems. Made especially for a large variety of uses and benefits, as the one "key" product you need in the home.

Me-tergent. Personalize the benefits of this product to the user, so that she agrees, "This is the one detergent made especially for *me.* I can see exactly how it solves *my* toughest cleaning problems." Show in detail how the product is custom-tailored to work perfectly on a woman's most difficult cleaning chores.

Knee-tergent. Maybe there's a possibility of using a demonstration on the knee area of a garment, particularly with kids' jeans. The dirt gets imbedded at the knees from kneeling at play. Show with a "knee test" how much faster and better this detergent cleans out the knee grime than other products.

As another slant, perhaps emphasize "no kneeling" when cleaning floors and low areas on walls and furniture. Point out that a simple swish of this detergent cleans perfectly, quickly and easily, no getting down on your knees for arduous rubbing and scrubbing.

Still another alphabet-inspired possibility—neat-tergent. Stress that the product cleans neatly, as well as speedily and easily—no sloppy mess—spray it on, swish it off, neat and clean in seconds.

Oh-tergent. Might be featured as the marvelous new "Oh!" detergent. With the very first trial, you'll exclaim, "Oh, what a wonderful, better detergent!" Perhaps work in a special money-back guarantee, "You must not only be satisfied, but enthusiastic—you must agree, 'Oh, what a wonderful, better detergent!' or you get every penny back."

Pre-tergent. This suggests a preparatory phase built into the product, so that it produces double cleaning action. Special ingredients first "pre-prepare" the surface or material, loosening soil and dirt. Then, other important elements take over so that you quickly and effortlessly wipe all grime away, far more effectively.

Cue-tergent. This product might be promoted as the big "cue" to more complete, cleaner cleaning. A brand made great progress when featured as the "coffee-er coffee." This might be the "cleaner cleaner—your cue to cleaner cleaning."

Re-tergent. This product could have another kind of double cleaning action incorporated through a modern scientific combination of better ingredients. Wipe it on (or drop it in), leave it for a few minutes, and special double action takes place. First, it cleans, then, as you leave it for a moment, double action takes over, so it recleans. "It's the re-tergent that cleans and then recleans, all in one quick, easy, one-step application."

She-tergent. This is the detergent made especially with "her" in mind, made for use by the fastidious woman—a modern "she-tergent." It's extra mild, extra gentle on the skin and hands. Performs the toughest cleaning jobs with miraculous simplicity, leaves skin and hands soft and lovely. Indeed a unique, advanced "she-tergent" for the feminine woman of today.

Spree-detergent. This product would be made and featured to perform its work so speedily and easily that you go on a quick "cleaning spree" whenever you use it. Comparatively, you have a "spree" by swishing through your cleaning work, instead of exerting tough, muscle-binding, back-breaking effort.

Try-tergent. Base the promotion of the product on a dramatic "try-it" idea. Big emphasis would be on fact that "one trial will convince you." Offer money back, or double your money back, or a desirable gift for sending in the label from the first package, or appealing variations of such trial offers.

Might be tied in with "tri or "triple"—referring to the products' being "three times as effective as others."

Use-tergent. This idea would stress the many different uses of the product—"The most useful bottle [or can, box or other package] you ever had in your house."

You-detergent. The detergent made with *you* in mind. Perhaps interview many women regarding what they want in a detergent. Then build, create and promote the product accordingly. "*You* asked for it—made to solve *your* particular cleaning problems, just as *you* expressed them—this is the 'you-detergent,' made with *you* in mind."

V-detergent. Tie the story of the product to a "V for victory" theme—"At last you're victorious, you win the battles against the toughest cleaning problems, using the V-for-victory detergent."

We-detergent. Promote this product as the favorite of the whole family. "*We* go for this new we-detergent—mops up the toughest cleaning tasks for Mom, Dad, Sis and Brother." Relate the product in turn to the different cleaning problems of kids and parents.

Whee-detergent. You'll yell "Whee!" with joy when you discover this wonderful product. You'll whiz through the toughest cleaning problems. And when you see the sparkling results, you'll shout "Whee!" with pride and enthusiasm over your wonderful accomplishments.

X-tergent. Feature the product as containing the marvelous new ingredient "X"—based on a new element incorporated in the formula. Then dramatize with X devices, such as "X marks the spot where you cleaned with ingredient X—see the xtra-wonderful difference, compared with the spot next to it."

Why-tergent. Stress the "why" of the remarkable results obtainable with this product. Perhaps get magnified photos showing the differences in the chemical composition, in the way dirt breaks into smaller particles, how the bubbles are smaller than with other products. Track down variations that can be seen clearly, and then tell convincingly the "why" reasons for better results with this "why-tergent."

Z-tergent. Perhaps expand this to become the A-to-Z detergent that accomplishes the widest possible range of tasks. Expand the use of the alphabet system further by listing categories from A to Z for which this product can be useful—apparel, boat, closets, right through to cleaning the old family zither.

Might expand the Z idea further by telling how the A-to-Z detergent *zooms* through dirt and grime.

That's one example of how the alphabet creative-spur system works in actual practice. Using this method in respect to the challenge of promoting a detergent problem, I developed one of the ideas previously set down here, through steps five and six, so that it scored a big hit. The result helped add hundreds of thousands of dollars worth of business with which I was involved, as detailed later.

Just as surely as alphabet soup, cereal and crackers have proved popular, you'll find that the alphabet creative-spur system will be rewarding for you, if you'll use it.

On quick, simple problems, run the key word through your mind, varying it letter by letter, from A to Z, in rhyming fashion.

In respect to more complicated, weightier problems, work with pencil and paper, or typewriter, setting down letter by letter and filling out accordingly, as I've done here with "detergent."

You'll end up with a list of ideas, which you'll then process through forthcoming steps five and six, to produce the big idea, ultimately.

Like-and-Dislike System

Another elementary creative approach to a problem is to list likes and dislikes, and then spur the production of creative ideas accordingly. This is an elaboration of one of the spur questions.

As an example, you might apply this simple method to the problem of creating ideas again for a detergent product. First, list what you *don't* like about the product or comparable items, as in this case:

DISLIKES:

1. Harsh, unpleasant smell.
2. Takes too long to loosen dirt.
3. Very strong, hard on the hands.
4. Package is hard to open and handle, also gets messy with repeated use.

WOULD LIKE TO HAVE:

1. Pleasing fragrance in use and after using.
2. Speedy, easy action—wipe on product, wipe off dirt.
3. Effectiveness of a hand lotion, to smooth skin and leave it soft.
4. Package that's easy to open and use—non-slip, no drip, tight closure to keep perfectly between uses.

Your listings above are practically a basic catalog for ideas. You suggest ideas that would eliminate the dislikes. And you add suggestions which would both counteract the faults and provide positive attributes that people would like to have in the product.

Being Creative with a Personal Problem

See how this like-and-dislike system applies to other problems —for example, how to get the child to eat more nutritious foods, as touched upon in earlier pages. Make a little list, such as:

DISLIKES:

1. Doesn't want the same old flavors.
2. Doesn't like the monotonous look of the same old things.
3. Hates vegetables.
4. Sick of drinking milk.

LIKES:

1. Enjoys something different in flavor.
2. Wants food to look unusual and tempting.
3. Wants something new, some fun out of eating.
4. Wants sweets, cakes, desserts.

Now, start listing creative ways to solve the dislikes and fulfill the likes. You'll start to set down ideas along the lines of the following:

1. Look up new recipes for the same ingredients.
2. Fix the dishes in "fancy" ways that look different and more tempting.
3. Experiment with flavorful toppings.
4. Prepare the "same old vegetables" in new ways—with sauces, adding melted cheese, in attractive mixtures and combinations.
5. Make milk an appealing "treat" by adding nutritious vitamin-enriched chocolate syrup and flavorings.
6. Glamorize ordinary puddings and fruits by adding syrups and other toppings, a touch of whipped cream, some colorful sprills, chopped nuts or a gleaming red cherry.
7. Ask friends who are especially good cooks for their best recipes and suggestions to appeal to kids' appetites.
8. Add fun to the meals by writing out a "menu" now and then, and handing copies out before the meal. Take a tip from some famous restaurants and name the foods; for instance, an egg salad sandwich becomes more fun when you call it a "Donald Duck Special."

Try the like-and-dislike system to spur your creative thinking and ideas. You'll find that it works wonderfully.

Split-Personality Process

This is a variation of the like-and-dislike system. It's a method that I've employed and taught for a long time with great success, because it's so basic and simple in operation.

You "split your personality" so that you're two people, in effect. You're the "buyer" on the one hand, and the "seller" on the other hand. One part of you demands satisfaction, and the other part aims to supply it.

I usually draw up a mental picture of a store counter. Then I become the customer on one side of the counter telling just what I want, what I like and dislike. I then leap in my imagination to the side behind the counter, where I'm the salesman attempting to provide what the customer wants.

I learned this trick from writing advertising. I'd write the advertisement, then read it aloud as though I were the salesman on one side of the counter addressing the words to me, the customer, on the other side. I'd then be able to decide better whether the words in the advertisement would actually be convincing to the degree of making the sale.

This is a procedure of talking over a problem with yourself, or even debating with yourself, discussing the pros and cons of the subject as though you're two different people or debaters.

The process has the special merit of dramatizing the needs in respect to the problem. As you answer the needs with suggestions that fulfill them, you're started on the act of producing creative ideas spurred by the creative thinking demanded of you in your role as the "salesman."

List those answers and you'll find that you're listing more ideas for development through steps five and six.

Break-It-Down Method

Here, in more detail, is a simple process to try in order to spur your creative thinking and ideas, as stated earlier. You break down the problem into parts and then list ideas that apply to the smaller segments.

Aim to divide or break down the problem into at least three pieces, and preferably more. The smaller the segment, usually the easier it is to produce a thought or idea for it.

For example, considering the problem of the detergent again, we might break down the product problem into (1) physical composition, (2) packaging, (3) usage. Then you list considerations and ideas for each part, rather than for the whole, along these lines:

1. Physical composition. Consider ideas that would improve the texture (liquid, powder, lotion, other forms). Other points to work on—color, fragrance, feel, eye appeal.

2. Packaging. Box, cardboard, clear plastic, cloth sack, jar, bottle, paper, combination plastic window and box, drip-proof top, pouring spout. You can list ideas and features for each.

3. Usage. At home, outdoors, auto, office, business. New uses?

Note that by writing answers to each category, you're expanding your thinking by segmenting and simplifying it. Ultimately you wind up with more ideas, and a combination may then produce the one or few big ideas you seek.

Turn-the-Pages System

Here's another sure-fire method I use during step four to stimulate a flow of many ideas. I pick up a current magazine or newspaper and start turning pages slowly, letting my eyes and mind linger on each page before I go on to the next.

With my current problem foremost in mind, I study each page, whether editorial or advertisement, seeking a possible provocative stimulus for an idea, even the smallest beginning, that will prod my creative thinking. In my hand is a pencil, on a table to my right is a pad.

As I turn the pages, I jot down any idea that comes through. Sometimes the ideas are direct derivations; often they're completely different. Yet all have been inspired by running my eyes and mind over the successive pages turning before me.

Try this fascinating, inciting method yourself, pencil in hand. As an example, let's go through a national magazine right now, considering again the problem of producing creative ideas for a detergent. Not every page will provide a spur to an idea for the product or challenge, but many do. Let's list the subject on the page at left, and the idea at the right, this way:

PAGE SUBJECT	IDEA
Photo of female movie star.	Consider testimonials from housekeepers in movie stars' home. These women tell how the product helps keep everything sparkling bright, at its decorative best.
Ad for barbecue sauce.	Make comparative test showing how much better this product works to clean messy, greasy barbecue grill and utensils.
Ad for product that "protects the breath."	Add a fragrance to the product that will make it more pleasant to use than other brands.
Photo of worn-out politician mopping his brow.	Aim to make the product easiest to use, and prove it. "You don't have to exert any brow-mopping muscle."
Ad for electric clocks.	Develop a timing test, using a stop watch, to prove how much quicker the job is finished with this brand over other products.
Article on new books for children.	Dramatize the faster cleaning with this product in terms of happier living for the whole family. Show how the mother who uses this more efficient brand has extra time to read delightful books to her young children.

Note in this instance how a half-dozen ideas have been added to the list by turning magazine pages and making notes inspired by the printed material. Don't worry about this system making you imitative. Actually the creative-oriented mind develops its own original ideas from each starting point.

The content of the various pages serves merely as a stimulus in this simple, absorbing procedure. The stop watch idea does not copy the electric-clock advertisement. Rather, it deals with the value of time and timing.

Nothing is "stolen" from the article about new books for children. The spark that emerged from the page ignited the idea of showing women the benefit of using a more efficient product in terms of having more leisure to help develop worthy cultural aspects of family life. The application of the original thought is completely original.

Try this turn-the-pages system. See for yourself how it helps you to produce new creative ideas or provides clues to many imaginative additional listings for successful development.

Question-and-Answer-Game Approach

This is another variation of the systems that have been suggested in the preceding pages. In this case, you make a question-and-answer-game of your creative search by enlisting the help of your husband, wife, family or friends and associates.

You can either ask questions about the subject of the other person, and then consider his answers in the light of creating ideas, or prompt the other person to ask you questions about the problem. Then, as you give the answers, you find your mind producing helpful thoughts and ideas.

As you go along with this interesting and often entertaining "game," or immediately afterward, write down the ideas so that they don't get lost.

As a bright creative scientist told me, "My wife has no scientific background or knowledge, yet I frequently discuss my problems with her when I'm up against a stone wall in my thinking. I describe the problem and she asks me questions about it. When I'm finished answering her questions, she says that she still doesn't really understand a word of what I'm talking about. But I usually understand a great deal more than I did when I started the question-and-answer session."

Use Some or All Methods

Now you have a variety of different methods to try as a spur to listing many ideas. You certainly don't have to apply all the processes to every problem. But sooner or later, as you proceed with your creative thinking, try them all. That's the best way to find out which one method or combination of methods will work best for you.

The purpose of all these systems is not to constrict your imagination, or tie you down to any "mechanical" processing. Rather, they aim to stimulate, inspire and expand your thinking. By trying them, you find out which ones operate most effectively for you. Also, they may help you create your own special system for the production of the greatest quantity of creative ideas—the big purpose of step four.

Make Creativity a Round-the-Clock Routine

As you become an increasingly creative person, you'll find that the process of thinking and producing ideas is not limited by a nine-to-five-o'clock schedule. At step four, you'll be thinking in terms of new notes on your problem all through your waking hours, and while sleeping too. (But more later on about utilizing your sleeping time for creative thinking.)

Each new little idea or variation of an idea will suggest new ones. You'll constantly be finding new slants, new shadings and relationships, and using them for new ideas.

The vital tip here is to be sure that your active thinking is matched by your note making. Wherever you are, whatever the time or place, carry a little pad or notebook, or even a folded-up sheet of paper. Write down your ideas as they occur to you. Don't be concerned about appearing unusual or eccentric—the idea's the thing.

Without keeping pencil and paper handy, you're like a hunter walking through the woods without a gun. If you haven't a rifle handy, you're certainly not going to hit your target.

As a further parallel, you must hunt for an idea. You're not likely to stumble over one. Keep seeking and you'll keep creating, and be sure you have the pencil handy for writing down those precious and sometimes fleeting thoughts.

Perhaps your reaction to some of these specific suggestions may be, "I'm doing that already—I've been in the habit of making notes for years." If so, that's excellent. It means that you're already a creative person to a greater or lesser degree. That's usually the case or, as previously mentioned, you probably wouldn't be reading this book. It's a great advantage to have this note-making habit, for example, as a head start.

Don't Analyze at This Step!

Don't stop at this page to assess whether each creative thought or idea is good or poor. Write it down, add it to your list. Don't inhibit yourself by the common negative phrase, "It's an idea, but—"

Chop off the "but" at this point. The "buts" will come later, as you'll find out. Right now, write down the idea first. As you'll discover in later pages, analysis and assessment and evaluation of the merit of the ideas will develop and become specifically productive.

Your function and purpose now is to pile up as many ideas as possible. You'll know when to stop when you start repeating yourself in setting down ideas, even after you've tried all the probing methods and variations for investigation suggested in this chapter.

Then, on to the comparative bliss and enjoyment of fascinating and comparatively easy step five.

8

STEP FIVE: LET THE FACTS AND IDEAS SIMMER IN YOUR MIND

This is probably the most pleasant step of all. And, in some ways, it's the most exciting. This is the step where you let your mind alone. You permit all the work you've done in the preceding four steps to simmer in your mind, without conscious effort on your part.

At this stage, the unconscious or subconscious mind takes over. Various experts use different terms—"subconscious," "unconscious," "nonconscious," or other rather technical terms. Because the "subconscious" terminology is most often used, and most commonly understood, we'll use that.

What does it all mean? What happens at this step?

How Idea-Lightning Strikes

Something like the following has probably happened to you, as to others. Bob was a business associate of mine. He popped into my office one morning, excited and enthused.

"I've got the solution to that problem we've been working on," he spouted eagerly. "I thought we'd never solve it, even after all these weeks of studying and concentration. And then suddenly this morning"—his face reflected sheer wonderment—"as I was shaving, not thinking of a thing but scraping those bristles off my chin, the whole solution popped into my head.

There it was, the big idea we've been looking for, bright and shining, like a newborn babe."

He went on happily, "I dashed into the bedroom, with half the lather dripping from my beard, and wrote it down. It's got some rough edges, has to be worked over and smoothed out, but I'm sure it's the right solution."

He finished, "Boy, what a thrill—an idea coming through like that, just like a lightning bolt out of the blue!"

How to Make It Happen to You

The preceding example is a common phenomenon in the creative process. Let's examine in detail how and why it happens, and how you can help make it occur.

The prime essential is to let your mind alone at this point, in order that you too may be struck by that wonderful mental lightning. Relax and enjoy yourself. Do something other than the current problem, think about something else.

And, as a starter right now, let your mind have some fun occupying itself with twenty-five amusing and lightly challenging puzzlers, before you concentrate on learning step five of the creative-thinking method. Meanwhile, everything you've learned and applied up to now will be simmering in your head.

Twenty-Five Relax-Your-Mind Puzzlers

(Solutions begin on page 252.)

1. It seems fitting by way of relaxed self-entertainment to reach back through memory to one of the oldest and most honored riddles of all. Samuel Johnson might have been challenging acquaintances over a tankard of ale in a tavern with this one:

As I was going to St. Ives,
I met a man with seven wives.
Each wife had seven sacks,
Each sack had seven cats,

Each cat had seven kits:
Kits, cats, sacks, and wives,
How many were there going to St. Ives?

2. What bow is it that not even the strongest man can either tie or untie?

3. For what man is it required that another man should remove his hat?

4. This is a weighty problem. What could you put into a barrel that's full of water, in order to make it lighter?

5. Name a word that has twenty-six letters.

6. A man fell off a ladder fifty feet high. The ladder was standing on hard ground and there was no net, person or object to break his fall. How come he wasn't hurt?

7. What is one thing positively which tigers have that no other animal has or can possibly have?

8. Try not to get charred on this question. Which burns longer, a black candle or a white candle? (Both are the same length and thickness.)

9. It's not absolutely necessary to be an expert on insect anatomy to answer this one: What has eighteen legs and catches flies?

10. Where is it that Friday comes before Thursday each week?

11. What's the word that you can pronounce faster by adding a syllable?

12. What is it that someone else usually has to take before you can get it?

13. A six-foot man can eat three eggs at a sitting. How many eggs can a nine-foot-tall giant eat on an empty stomach?

14. This riddle is for southpaws, folks who may be ambidextrous, and all others. Which side of an apple is the left side?

15. Three heavy ladies walking down the street suddenly crowd under a small umbrella, yet not one of them gets wet. How come? (No, they don't stand on each other's shoulders.)

16. No matter how many tongues you may know, you may not know the answer to this riddle. What can speak every language in the world?

17. Are you a student of history? Can you answer this one: When did California begin with a C and end with an E?

18. What is it you break by naming it?

19. A salon that's jammed with a hundred married people might be likened to an empty room. How come?

20. What is it that you lose every time you arise from a chair and stand erect?

21. Farmer Jukes owns a peacock that is his great pride. If it laid an egg in Farmer Schroeder's yard, who would own the egg?

22. Try to figure this one out without a calendar, watch or sundial. On what day of the year do gossipy women talk the least?

23. What is it that's full of holes and yet holds water?

24. What is the one word that almost everybody usually pronounces wrong?

25. To conclude these relaxing riddles, can you translate the following rhyme?

YYUR
YYUB
ICUR
YY 4 ME

How the Simmering Process Operates for You

You know how a good stew improves its flavors, deepens its delicious tastes and aromas, and finally reaches perfection as it simmers. Something like that happens in the "simmering step," number five in the creative process.

Up to now you've worked at and absorbed one step at a time. You will have applied a good deal of effort and concentration. Now you deliberately take your mind off the problem you've been concerned about.

How long? For an hour, a day, several days, a week or more, depending on how deep, serious and involved the problem is. A scientist, working on a problem of extreme gravity, may turn away from it to other pursuits for months or even a year or more, until he finds his answer. But, with most everyday problems, leaving it for a day or two, or even only overnight if urgency is involved, may well be sufficient.

This stage has been called many things by various experts. It has been referred to as the time of incubation, illumination, regeneration, insight, crystallization.

Whatever it is called, there's universal agreement that this step, leading to the "mental bolt of lightning from the blue," does occur and is an essential stage in the production of creative ideas.

So, make it a point, after you've completed the four previous steps, to take this breathing spell, or thinking spell, and leave your mind alone.

Let Up or Lose Out

Even though you may want to keep working toward your goal without an instant's cause, do ease off the pressure. Otherwise you may fall down and fail in trying to race too fast to the solution.

A vivid illustration of this is the story of the bruised and battered child whose amazed neighbor asked him, "How do you manage to fall down so often?"

"It's easy," the little boy answered. "All I have to do is to run faster than I can run."

Heed my advice, which is the same as that of eminent creative thinkers over the centuries. Take it easy before the strenuous effort you're going to exert in step six, the concluding and most rewarding stage. Don't try to make your mind run faster than it can run.

How to Relax

To take your mind, your conscious mind, off the problem on which you've been concentrating, turn to what you personally like to do most, such as:

Read a good book, not related to the problem subject.

Take a walk or a hike, or go fishing.

Engage in some athletic activity.

Play games with friends—bridge, chess, or whatever you enjoy most.

Go to a movie, play or concert.

Listen to good music at home—classical, jazz, whatever pleases you.

Look at some diverting television.

Read magazines, short stories, nonfiction—whatever interests you most.

Go to a museum or art exhibit and look at paintings.

You can enlarge this list to suit yourself, aiming to please yourself to the greatest degree.

A favorite "relaxicize" of many notable creative people over the years has been the reading of mystery stories and books. The Mystery Writers of America organization informs me that among such mystery fans have been Presidents Franklin D. Roosevelt, John F. Kennedy, Woodrow Wilson and Calvin Coolidge, statesman Winston Churchill, philosopher Bertrand Russell, General George Marshall, designers, writers, actors, artists and many other outstandingly creative people. So you're in very good company when you relax with a mystery.

A friend of Professor Einstein reports that he came upon important ideas in advancing his theory of relativity while taking walks in the street or along a road, and even while wheeling his child in a baby carriage on a sidewalk. Thus, even a child can lead you to a new idea while baby-pushing and making the wheels go round.

Frequently I've stopped after long exertions, as delineated in the first four steps of the creative method, to read a book, watch an absorbing television show or attend an arresting movie. Then, after a sound sleep, I find that my mental batteries have been recharged. The ideas I've been seeking start to flow freely and excitingly.

Recommended Recipe: Daydream

You might also indulge in daydreaming, napping or just observing an hour or more of silence, letting your mind float serenely. A friend of mine who is a successful playwright uses this method, and admits that it causes considerable friction between himself and his wife.

This writer's studio is in a small building separated from his house. Now and then, his wife will enter the studio to deliver a message and ask a question, and will find him on the couch half-dozing or just staring at the ceiling. She'll ask, "Why are you loafing?" He'll reply brusquely, "I'm not loafing, I'm working. My ideas are simmering!"

This very able author has complained to me, "Some people simply cannot understand that the creative mind needs a pause for regeneration. When I'm relaxing that way, my mental motor is actually running—it's simply idling, and is ready to speed ahead at any instant."

The great French statesman General De Gaulle recorded his agreement with this principle thoroughly when he said, "Silence is a necessary preliminary to the ordering of one's thoughts." Of course, dreaming continually is not recommended; as a wit commented, "Some people who think they're dreamers are just sleepers."

Proof That the Subconscious Works

At universities and in scientific laboratories, many experiments have been conducted which prove that your subconscious mind "sees" and absorbs impressions at a far faster rate than your conscious mind.

For example, here's a typical experiment. A man is taken into a room for a chat, just as you might walk into a living room where you've never been before. After five minutes, you're invited into the study of the house. There you're told that an experiment is being conducted, of which you weren't previously aware.

You're asked to write down, without pausing, the objects that you recall seeing while you were in the living room. Perhaps you list twenty items before you put down the pencil.

Then, in scientifically conducted experiments, the subject is hypnotized. Under hypnosis he is asked to sit up, is handed a pencil and paper, and is instructed to write down again the objects he saw while in the living room. In many such tests, the person was then able to list as many as two hundred and more items, instead of the previous twenty.

Here is just one proof that the subconscious or unconscious mind is busy reaching out, gathering and absorbing impressions at an amazingly fast rate, far more speedily than your conscious mind.

Actually it has been proved again and again that you are being bombarded every waking hour with sights, sounds, smells, impressions of all kinds that reach and record on your subconscious mind. But your conscious mind is not aware of these hundreds and even thousands of "hits" which do influence your production of actions, decisions and ideas.

During step five, the "simmering stage," your subconscious impressions tend to combine with your conscious efforts and realizations. The relaxed free association promotes the flow and amalgamation of thoughts and impressions and they come out as useful, wanted creative ideas. Yet the rigidity imposed by conscious effort and pressure might well have blocked and prevented this essential creative loosening and flow.

Give Your Mind a Fresh Start

Another way that I've helped people to understand and apply themselves to step five is to dramatize the need for a fresh mental start, as illustrated here. I'd have you, for example, hold out your hand, with fingers outstretched as in the diagram.

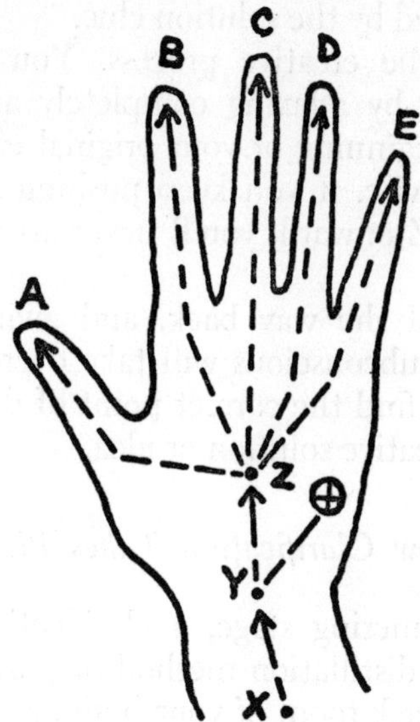

Consider that you have been reading a mystery story, and are seeking to arrive at the solution before the author reveals it —certainly a creative act on the part of you, the reader. You have started your reading at point X. When you have gone some distance to point Z, you feel that you have amassed the essential clues—just as you have gathered the facts in step three of the creative method.

Now, at point Z, you use the clues to arrive at your creative solution. You consider the various suspects, and you work forward to points A, then B, on to C, D and E, trying to pin down which of the characters is the murderer. Usually you're baffled, bewildered and frustrated, and you don't reach the correct solution before the author.

The reason is that you're working forward in your thinking from point Z. But the wily author has actually dropped the main clue midway between X and Z, at point Y, long before you reached Z. Thus, no matter how often you keep stabbing for a solution beyond point Z, you won't reach it, because you've already passed by the solution clue.

Similarly with the creative process. You should give your mind a fresh start by relaxing completely and letting it drift back to the very beginning of your original effort and approach at point X. Otherwise, if you keep pushing and probing without a letup, from Z onward, you'll never arrive at your goal, at the big idea.

But by going all the way back, and giving your conscious mind a rest, your subconscious will take over. You'll then have the opportunity to find the correct point of departure at Y, and will produce the creative solution or idea.

How Clarification Takes Place

During this simmering stage, a clarification process occurs, not too unlike the distillation method of purifying liquids. The inner mind (that back room of your brain, as delineated earlier) is sifting, weighing, gauging and rearranging the facts, ideas and other material you've accumulated during the previous steps of the creative method.

Thus, usually without your consciousness, what has been confused now becomes clarified and understandable. Order is made from the mixture of thoughts, premises and semi-solutions. By this orderly subconscious procedure, the problem is solved, resulting in the idea that comes like a "lightning bolt from the blue."

But, as you can realize from understanding the very practical process that is occurring internally, it's not just a sudden miracle that takes place. Although the resultful, successful idea may seem to emerge newborn and without conscious effort, you know it's another stage in a co-ordinated creative method. And the vital part of your specific procedure at this point is to leave your mind alone, as instructed here.

What you're actually doing is allowing free flow from your conscious to your subconscious, and clearing up the channels for future revealing communication. You're avoiding the blockage of ideas, the long jam in your mind that psychologists call "functional fixedness."

A specific lesson may be gained from this story about Joyce Cary, the distinguished novelist. He told how he had noticed a young woman on a ferryboat. She aroused his curiosity because of the intense emotions reflected in her face, and particularly by a series of wrinkles on her forehead. He wondered, "Why those wrinkles." He felt strongly that he could write a story about her.

Cary spent some time studying her as a subject, but no story structure came through. After reaching a dead end, he put her out of his mind. Three weeks later, in the very early hours of the morning, he was awakened suddenly by the lightning bolt of revelation. He said that the girl had "gone down into my subconscious, and came up again with a full-sized story."

This result applies not to writers alone. Such creative-idea fulfillment can occur for almost everyone. It can and will happen to you.

Don't Be Rigid in Your Relaxation Routines

It isn't "beyond the rules" to let your conscious thoughts touch lightly on your problem now and then during this period. But you shouldn't concentrate on forcing a solution, or you may bury it completely. With few exceptions, the idea you want emerges at a time when you're not fixing your mental spotlight on the problem.

Think, for instance, of the many times when you've tried to remember a person's name but it just doesn't come. You struggle inwardly and blurt in frustration, "It's on the tip of my tongue but I can't remember it!" Then, at a moment when you've released the pressure and are not consciously thinking about it, the name appears bright and clear in your mind and you say, "There it is—I was sure that I knew it—yet I recalled it when I wasn't even thinking about it."

The value of this relaxing process has been proved over the centuries. Long ago, the philosopher Schopenhauer referred to it as a very specific and repeated occurrence which he described as "unconscious rumination."

I discussed this process one day with a shrewd and seasoned fishing guide who was famous for having an almost magical sense about where the fish were biting. He agreed and said, "I do a lot of thinking and then dreaming like that. It's like getting my boat to some place on the lake and drifting around and idling the motor for a while. Then, all of a sudden, my mind has figured out where to go and I rev up the motor and head there fast."

What actually happens in the guide's mind is that all his past experiences, plus the stories and rumors he has heard recently, are sifted in his conscious and subconscious as he "dreams." From this sifting, he finally reaches the determination of where the fishing should be best, and it usually (but not infallibly) is.

It is the same in your pursuits. During this quiet development stage, the mind, under the surface, is actually very busy mulling over, organizing, sorting out and categorizing material which has been absorbed previously. Then the ideas emerge as a result of this inner processing, somewhat in the manner of statistics and computations being rolled out by a computing machine.

Make no mistake nor let anyone confuse you by an intimation that this formula restricts your creative initiative or original flights of imagination. Your results are personal and imaginative, the ideas emerge as a result of your own individual creative thinking.

You follow a six-step method here, but the creative performance is strictly your personal inspiration, production and gain.

You Must Put Material In . . . To Get Ideas Out

This is a basic fact you must understand and fulfill: Your subconscious mind cannot feed ideas out unless you first put the material in, as instructed in the previous steps.

You cannot produce the ideas without providing the fundamental facts first, any more than you can bake a cake merely by reading the recipe. You must put in the facts—in this case the eggs and flour and milk and other ingredients—or the baking pan will be empty.

Unless you work on and co-ordinate the actual elements first, you can't have your cake and eat it too.

You may read fanciful accounts of a scientist who sees a mold form on some old mixture and suddenly exclaims, "Eureka, penicillin!" or the inventor who notes steam arising from a kettle and shouts ecstatically, "I have it—the principle of the locomotive!"

Such renowned creative scientists have usually poured in months and years of research and experimentation before the flash of illumination, of clear recognition and resultant discovery appears.

All the more credit to them—and to you, when your subconscious mind reveals the idea you've been seeking, for years perhaps, but are not concentrating on consciously at the moment. Inevitably it has been preceded by your considerable and arduous effort of preparation.

Savor the Joy of the New Idea

Enjoy the exhilaration of this step, preceding the actual emergence of the idea. In a sense you can feel the euphoric anticipation of the woman bearing a child, in the interval just before the time of approaching birth.

This is a good period in which to indulge in the pleasure of solving simple, entertaining puzzles such as those at the beginning of this chapter. If you delight in working crossword puzzles, mathematical and mechanical problems, puzzles involving word chains, letters, jigsaw pieces and other such contraptions, relax your mind with them especially during this stage.

But remember the instructions given previously—to stop and let your mind rest if you're completely blocked or frustrated before arriving at the solution. Probably you're headed in a fixed, wrong direction. Go away from the problem, then come back to it later in the day, or tomorrow.

Hasn't it often happened to you that when you return to a puzzle later, the solution seems to fall into place "automatically"? You say to yourself, "Why didn't I see that before? It appears so obvious!"

All this is evidence of how the subconscious mind operates. While you've seemingly dropped the problem, your inner brain has been working on it and arriving at the solution, while you've been simply having fun or applying your conscious thinking in other areas.

Realize that a certain point your mind gets fed up. You must give it time to digest the material you've poured in. Think of it as stuffing actual food into your stomach. You must stop at a certain fed-up stage, or you'll throw your entire digestive system out of balance and prevent smooth, efficient operation. So, it's not only good advice, but essential on your part, to relax and let your inner mind digest quietly all the material you've swallowed in the previous phases of the six-step method.

There's additional substantiation of the merit of this recommendation in the outpouring of ideas that usually follows a creative man's vacation. You've undoubtedly heard secretaries and other employees groan, "Help—here comes a flood of memos about new ideas and new things to do. The boss is just back from his vacation!"

The reason is not that the creative individual has been consciously working at his business affairs while on vacation. It's because the subconscious mind, left alone during the relaxing period, has had the wonderful and too rare opportunity to sort out and rearrange facts and knowledge into exciting, usable new ideas.

That's why so many creative people return after a vacation saying, "Let's go—I'm just bursting with ideas for improvement and advancement."

Decide on Your Best Way to Relax

Select your one best way to relax, or several avenues of escape that suit you most. You've seen a suggested listing earlier in this chapter. Fix your own—resort to your individual choice.

One top creative executive I know releases his mind by working on arduous, complicated but entirely different projects, such as taking apart and then reassembling a delicate watch or another involved mechanism.

A woman who has received enormous payment for years for her creative thinking tackles the toughest double-crostic puzzles she can find. She says that this kind of seemingly difficult effort releases her mind from concentration on her challenging business problem, once she has gone as far as she can go in her preliminary steps, as delineated here.

A brilliant creative advertising writer with whom I've worked will suddenly arise from his desk, grab his hat and tell his secretary, "I'm going up to the zoo for a couple of hours." When he leaves, she sighs, "I'd better relax myself now, because he's going to be pouring out ideas to type in a hurry as soon as he gets back." That detached roaming among the animal cages is his way of lifting the pressure and letting his subconscious mind assess, sort and then spew out the wanted original solutions.

Personal choices of the best way to relax mentally take curious forms. My wife, who is a recognized creative artist, has found that spending an hour on the lawn, squatting and pulling out crabgrass, is a wonderful relaxer for her. "I concentrate so hard on yanking out those vicious weeds," she explains, "that I clear my conscious mind of most everything else. After an hour, I go back to my palette and brushes, and find that I invariably have some fresh new approaches to a subject I've painted that has stymied me."

A vigorous round of golf, or lying down and listening to a stack of string quartets, also provide for her the mental relaxation and refreshment she needs as a hard-working artist. What's your best outlet?

Take a tip from one of the most successful department store heads with whom I've worked. Several times a day he'd walk about the huge store. When he'd come upon a writer, designer or creative person in other departments who seemed baffled by a merchandising problem or need for an advertising headline or idea, he'd order, "Get out of here for a couple of hours, or take the afternoon off. Go for a walk, buy a new hat, drop in at a movie, treat yourself to a double ice-cream sundae or Martini. Your mind is stymied now, going stale. Get away from your problems, forget them now."

He explained to me, "Those people usually come back full of energy and ideas. If they stayed here, pushing at their problems, they'd just keep sinking down further, like a person struggling helplessly in quicksand."

Perhaps you're like me; one of the best practical relaxations I know is to get up, go for my equipment and advise, "I'm goin' fishin'." You too may find that an almost guaranteed way to reel in ideas is to go fishin' for bass, muskies, salmon or whatever is handiest and most challenging.

One last point here: You must really ease up as you approach your relaxation. For instance, "going fishing" won't do. You've got to be "goin' fishin' " and loosen up as thoroughly as bait worms wriggling in a can.

Goin' Fishin' . . . Be Prepared for the Strike

Make this a must in your creative approach. When you're "goin' fishin'," whether it's with a rod and reel, via a walk in the park, reading a fast-moving mystery, daydreaming or whatever is your favorite relaxation, be sure you have pencil and paper handy.

When I first stuffed a pad and pencil in the hip pocket of my fishin' pants, my wife asked why. "I'm goin' fishin' for ideas, too," I explained. "I want to be ready for action when the idea strikes. Just like when a salmon hits the bait, I have to react instantly. My preparation and setting the bait are like preparing to get the idea. When the idea hits, I want to be ready to write it down before it gets away."

Realize that when idea-lightning strikes, it enters a brain teeming with other competitive activities. Before other concerns and needs obscure the bright new idea revelation, write it down. Add all possible details right then and there. You'll have it hooked firmly, enduringly.

You needn't attempt to work out the idea completely at this point, or polish it thoroughly. But set it down in black and white before it gets away. Many a fighting fish has been lost after a long struggle, just before you lift it in the net and land it. And many a struggling idea has escaped because you haven't captured it tangibly in writing or some other method of recording.

Take this advice, and that disheartening, costly escape won't happen to you—that awful moment when you've heard others moan, "I had the idea, but it slipped out of my mind."

Don't allow yourself to say, "It's so clear, I can't possibly forget it." Don't take chances. Write it down, dictate or record it. Then you can't lose. If you should decide later that the idea is faulty, inadequate or impracticable, you can always discard it, without any vital waste of time or effort. Usually, the idea is at least basically sound, and you need only refine it to make it useful and valuable.

The story is told about a leading chemist who was working out a formula that eventually proved of exceptional value. He related that one night he had a turbulent dream. Images formed and re-formed within his dreaming, and suddenly they congealed into the chemistry chain formula he had been seeking for many months. He awakened at three in the morning, the formula so clear in his mind that he knew he "had it" at last, and he went back to sleep contentedly.

But when he arose in the morning, all he remembered was the beginning of the dream, not the conclusion. He tried desperately day after day but couldn't find the answer. Each night, he forced himself to concentrate on the beginning of the dream when he went to bed, but the rest eluded him.

Finally, after many restless, anxious nights, he awakened with the formula clear again. Frantically he wrote down the answer. He told colleagues that never again did he fail to write down a single revelation at the moment it occurred.

It pays to keep alert always to inner responses so you're ready when the idea strikes. It has happened to me often on a train, reading a newspaper. Some items, seemingly unrelated to my problem, triggers a response, and in a flash the wanted idea is exploding and revealing itself in my mind. Hastily I write it down.

The point is that this is a place, unconnected completely with home or office, where I'm relaxed. I'm not expecting a phone call or a visitor or concentrating on anything except my newspaper. In this relaxed state, ideas often pop into being.

Perhaps coming across an item in a newspaper or magazine, or hearing a scrap of conversation, seems like a "lucky break" that triggers the emergence of the idea. Good! Take advantage of every such seeming lucky break. Whip out a pad or scrap of paper and pencil, and write down the idea or inspiration before it vanishes as suddenly as it appeared.

Set Your Automatic Mental Timer

There's a popular joke about an old woman who insisted very firmly that she had a clock in her head. Her relatives sent her to a psychiatrist to correct this. She lay on the couch, swaying her head slowly and saying in rhythm, "Tick-tock . . . tick-tock . . . tick-tock . . ."

After a half-hour of failing to shake her conviction, the psychiatrist suddenly asked her, "What time is it?" She replied instantly, "Ten minutes to three." "Aha," he cried triumphantly, "that proves you have no clock in your head. It's exactly three o'clock."

She answered calmly, "So I'm a little slow—I'll catch up." And she immediately speeded up the swaying of her head and sputtered rapidly, "tick-tock-tick-tock-tick-tock . . ."

No, you haven't an actual mechanical timepiece in your head, but we all have mental timing ability. By concentration, as you embark on step five, you can "set" the clock in your head.

For example, if you must have an idea by the next morning, fix your mind on having a solution the following day, and you'll usually wake up with it, or have it pop up during the next day. That is, of course, granted that you've prepared your mind as instructed in the preceding steps. If you haven't studied and worked on the problem as recommended, you can't expect a solution—any more than you can expect flowers to grow from unseeded soil.

How the Timing System Works

Frequently when I've needed a plot twist for a story or novel, after working to a dead end on it, I've reviewed it in my mind just before sleep, setting my mental timer for the solution to come the next day. Invariably I've awakened with the answer, or had it emerge during shaving, breakfast, or as I sat down at the typewriter.

Some experts refer to this process of preparation as self-hypnosis. I don't care what label is used. The fact it, I assure you, that when the proper preparation and work have been finished, and you set a time limit for the solution, it will usually come through for you, as it does for me and countless others.

As reported earlier, this time limit may be minutes or years, usually depending on the gravity of the problem and the depth of creative thinking required to untangle the facts and possibilities, and to arrive at the big idea.

It may be overnight, as noted. Or, it could be as brief as arising from your desk and sauntering to the drinking fountain and back. The interval could be a long, leisurely lunch, an hour at an exhibit looking at stimulating paintings, a half-hour watching an entertaining television show or listening to a symphony on records.

Or, it may have to be a week, a month, a year or more—while you leave a difficult, weighty problem and work on something else. You must understand, assess and judge the depth of the problem, the practical considerations involved and the timing required for arriving at the big idea.

An outstanding creative commercial artist informs clients that it takes him exactly three weeks and two days to prepare rough designs for a new package or the redesign of a current one. I heard him explain this to a manufacturer this way. He said, "I've set that time limit for myself, and it has never failed me. It takes me a week to research the product, the package and competitive items, as well as general successful packages that might be comparable in some way."

"Then you go ahead and make some designs," the impatient businessman remarked. "That shouldn't take a couple of weeks. All I want to examine first are some rough sketches, then we'll go on from there."

"No," the artist continued. "I find it essential to leave the problem for two weeks after I've loaded up on background and facts. I work on other projects. Meanwhile, my subconscious is dealing with your package-design problem, while I'm purposely not thinking about it."

The tycoon muttered, "You waste two weeks—"

"Not at all," the designer assured him confidently. "When I sit down at the drawing board the fourth week, fresh ideas come pouring out. In two days, I produce a big batch of original, exciting designs. That's how I've won so many prizes. If I try to hurry the process and accomplish the whole job, from start to finish, in a few days, I find that I sketch commonplace stuff."

He concluded, "If you want sparkling and unique designs instead of hackneyed layouts, you must let me work by my own timing system."

Try It. . . . It Will Work for You

Set up and practice your own timing system on each job. On simple matters, you may need only a few minutes interval, such as the common and very sensible coffee break, at home or at work. On complex problems, you'll learn with repetition how much time you need.

Above all, give your mind the essential relaxing period detailed here. Don't try to be a "dead-end kid" who battles on obstinately to try to grasp a solution even when your exhausted mentality tells you it has reached a dead end and can't think further effectively at the moment.

Don't try to be a "whiz kid" who whizzes through a problem to reach what may seem a bright solution. It will probably prove later to be a shallow, obvious and inadequate idea.

Don't hammer at your tired brain, or you'll pound it into unconsciousness so far as thinking activity is concerned. Instead, let it "manufacture" the idea you want.

If your conscious pushes you, realize that you're not forsaking your problems but instead turning them over to your subconscious mind. It will keep working toward the ideas you want and need.

The inner room of your brain has stock shelves loaded with a vast variety of accumulated knowledge from over the years, as well as from your recent investigations. Your conscious mind can't dig and delve into those stacks—it necessarily takes too long. But your subconscious will keep sorting, developing and creating under the surface with astonishing speed, like a marvelous electronic computer.

You can be certain that the thinking in your subconscious mind never stops, except perhaps when smothered by extremely powerful drugs. This has been proved by a multitude of scientific tests.

Accept it—there's a censor in the minds of most of us which may stifle and block original creative thinking when you push on with too severe conscious effort. You must follow step five to relax and remove this self-censorship which often prevents the flow of new, original and possibly unorthodox creative thinking.

Surely you can take the word of Dr. Albert Einstein, who believed in this relaxation step. In substantiation, he said in relation to arriving at usable creative ideas, "There is no logical path . . . only intuition, resting on sympathetic understanding of experience, can reach them."

Take the dosage of relaxation as directed, then on to final, fulfilling step six.

9

STEP SIX: EVALUATE, RECHECK, SETTLE ON THE CREATIVE IDEAS

This is the final, deliberate, hard-working step which combines and brings into practicable usage everything you've done up to this point. Here you decide on the big idea, because the creative person cannot have a mind that's like a bachelor's bed, "never made-up."

Now you evaluate, weigh and judge the ideas you have produced in step four, and the culminating inspirations resulting from step five. Finally, you will have practiced the complete six-step creative method, stage by stage. You'll arrive at the one or more valuable ideas which you'll then put into effect for greatest gain and benefit.

As a preliminary tune-up to this step, here are some "howdunit" practice puzzlers. They're selected exercises in evaluating the elements involved in each problem, and then arriving at the correct solution. Unlike the "whodunits" of popular mystery fiction, the big point in each one is to assess, recheck and discover *how* each answer is unlocked.

Enjoy seeking out the "how" of each entertaining, mind-sharpening little challenge that follows.

"Howdunit" Puzzlers

(Solutions begin on page 253.)

1. What's Her Name? Herbert Grimes met a friend whom he hadn't seen in twenty years. The greeting was warm and enthusiastic. The friend was accompanied by a daughter. Herbert said to his friend, "I never even heard that you were married." His friend answered, "Oh yes, I was married nine years ago."

Herbert then turned to his friend's daughter and asked, "What is your name?"

The little girl replied, "It's the same as my mother's, its—"

Herbert interrupted quickly and said, "It's a great pleasure to meet you, Gwendolyn."

Now you figure it out: How did Herbert know the little girl's name?

2. How the Gray Mustache? Take it on the authority of the M. W. A. (Mustache Wearers of America, sometimes confused with the Mystery Writers of America) that a man's hair will turn gray much sooner than his mustache.

How come the hair on his scalp turns gray sooner than his mustache?

3. Speedier Than Light? George Belfast was a very speedy individual who kept himself in superb physical condition. He boasted truthfully, "In my bedroom, the nearest lamp that I usually keep turned on is twelve feet away from my bed. Yet, alone in the room, without using wires, strings or any other aids or contraptions, I can turn out the light on that lamp and get into bed before the room is dark!"

How can George do it?

4. Penetrate the Proverb. Two brilliant young scholars were talking. One was bewailing the loss of his girl friend and told his companion sadly, "It proves the truth of the famous proverb—'Unseen idiot.'"

The other bright individual nodded sympathetically and agreed, "How true. How true."

How can you evaluate the meaning of their words and translate the "famous proverb"?

5. How to Win the Race? You must imagine, in this "howdunit," that you have a brother and that you both live in New York. You also fortunately have a wealthy uncle who possesses a million dollars but no other heirs. He has given you and your brother each a superb racing car, exact duplicates. Suddenly your uncle dies and leaves a strange will with this proviso, stated in these words:

"The million dollars will go to the one brother whose car comes in *last* in a drive to Chicago starting immediately after the reading of this will. In no case can there be an agreement between the brothers to divide the money."

You realize, of course, that a race to come in last could take practically forever, and neither you nor your brother could get and use the million dollars soon. How can you take action immediately so that you'll get the money? (Evaluate the exact facts and you'll arrive at the winning solution, worth a million dollars in this case.)

Method for Listing Your Ideas

In step four, and at the culmination of step five, you have listed all the ideas created by you to advance or solve your problem. There's a strong possibility that the inspiration emanating from step five is the big idea. You've set this one down separately for special attention.

Now your last step is the vital and essential one of assessment, evaluation and double-checking. You must be as sure as possible. Because having an imaginative idea is not enough.

The aim and accomplishment of this six-step method is to guide and teach you to produce practicable, useful, valuable, productive ideas that will bring you gain, benefit and success.

It suffices for a child to have incredible, imaginative, charming ideas. But your adult ideas are of little or no ultimate value in our society unless they're progressively useful. A nitwit or mixed-up brain may spew out a stream of fantastic thoughts, but they're of no real worth unless they can be applied practically.

In fact, such completely unusable suggestions may likely be a drag and a detriment in organized business or other pursuits, as they probably will waste much costly time of others involved. Even though one idea in a thousand from an erratic individual may be a possible hit, his function is not desirable or affordable.

As a leading industrialist told me regarding a seemingly brilliant but irresponsible man whom he had to release, "He may hit one good idea out of a thousand he suggests, but even a big league manager can't afford to keep a home run hitter with an .0001 batting average."

Shortcut or Thorough Methods

Depending on the amount of time you have available, the scope of the problem and the type of person you are, you may wish to short-cut right to the one idea you immediately consider best. Then you assess and recheck it. However, success is more certain from more analytical, slower progression. It's up to you.

Here's how to seek out the best, potentially resultful idea, by the recommended method. Set down the ideas that you've listed in steps four and five, to assess, recheck and select the one or several you want to submit or apply. Make three headings—Excellent, Worthy, Not Usable—and write your ideas under what you consider the appropriate headings.

It pays to write down your Not Usable ideas, as well as Worthy and Excellent, because the act of relisting them helps you to judge and decide upon their relative and practical value.

How to Judge Your Ideas

As a result of all the work you've put into the solution of the problem in the preceding steps of this method, your mind has automatically improved its powers and abilities to weigh and judge the ultimate idea critically and sensibly.

Thus, in this first phase of listing the ideas in the three categories, you simply reread each possibility you've set down. Give each a minute or more thought, as necessary. Then write it down under the heading you've decided fits it best.

Rechecking Your Judgment

Now you go over your listings again in this manner.

Quickly reread the thoughts you've listed under Not Usable, to see whether any should be retained. You don't have to give this procedure much time. You're simply making sure that you don't overlook or pass by any ideas which might possess greater merit on second sight.

Next, study again the thoughts you've listed under Worthy. Do any of them deserve to be moved up to the Excellent category? If yes, switch them. Don't pass up the gain possible from creating a *number* of bright ideas on a subject or to solve a problem or situation.

Now go to the Excellent rating. If you've added ideas here, study them all in turn. Grade them as to merit—1, 2, 3, and so forth. You then produce a clear evaluation of which idea or ideas to recommend or use.

How to Be Objective

You realize, of course, that these are your personal ideas, your own babies. Therefore you may be prejudiced in their favor. To help maintain subjectivity—seeing the idea from the other fellow's viewpoint—I've developed what I call the "transference system."

This method has proved extremely helpful and effective for me, and for many others whom I've taught or counseled. I've simply taken the position of transferring my viewpoint so that I become the other fellow, the potential customer, for example.

This, if my idea is aimed to sell something tangible to someone else, I try to view it exactly as he would see it and judge it. In other words, what are its merits and benefits for him, not for me. Or, if I'm trying to influence my child with a new idea I've created in respect to his behavior, I try to regard the idea as the child would, not from my own different viewpoint as an adult.

Whatever the idea may be, in whatever category, you'll find that you get a clearer, fairer, more objective view of it when you "transfer" your viewpoint to that of the recipient, not the creator. Seeing through the other person's eyes, in effect, you can reassess your idea with remarkable clarity. You often find flaws or rough edges that you missed or overlooked before. Now you can smooth them out, so that you both gain the greatest benefits that you both want.

Try the "Mirror Test"

Another method of self-analysis of your creative thinking and ideas is a "mirror test." This was suggested and, in fact, made a rule by a noted business leader in his sales department. He instructed his salesmen to try out their sales talks in front of a full-length mirror. By this method, each man addressed the image in the mirror as though the reflected image were the customer he was trying to sell.

Practice this acting game with your creative ideas. Speak them aloud to your reflection in the glass, and try to judge them from the visible "listener's" viewpoint. You'll be impressed greatly by how often you find flaws, large or small, that can often be smoothed and corrected readily. Yet, without exposing those errors or inadequacies to yourself beforehand, you may find that the entire creative idea is rejected by others when you try to put it into practice.

As I state in my earlier volume, "Casebook of Successful Ideas," this rigid, honest phase of self-analysis may well be a pivotal secret of creative accomplishment: "Remember that the 'creative you' must put aside all self-indulgence or self-aggrandizement. Get your kicks through making the sale to the 'customer you.' This concentrated, one-directional effort is a potent aid to creative and business success."

In essence, it's vital that you detect and correct any flaws in your creative ideas before others note and expose them. The methods suggested here, rigorously applied, will accomplish this important function for you. Don't assume. Do expose.

Test Your Thinking and Ideas on Others

As noted elsewhere on these pages, it often helps to try out your ideas on your wife or husband, friends and associates—but with several essential cautions.

Don't be guided by the judgment of someone who is incapable, because of lack of knowledge, experience or other factors, of considering the idea objectively and sensibly. For instance, if your idea applies to a new office system, don't ask the opinion of a poet, regardless of how intelligent he may be. If your brilliant solution is pointed at a problem in raising children, don't expose it to a rigid bachelor uncle for sound judgment.

And don't by-pass this caution as being obvious. It's an unhappy fact that too many brilliant creative ideas have been stifled because some top executive will expose an idea first to his inexperienced wife. She may have no knowledge of the actual problem, yet could be quick to kill it with withering criticism. Ask creative people in advertising how often this has happened. The boss shows a proposed ad aimed at selling inexpensive baby food to low-income families, stressing the economies. His wife, removed by decades from the actual potential user, may say positively, "Nonsense! Any mother would be repelled by that ad."

A story is told about a man whose hobby was raising butterflies. He developed some creative approaches which he revealed to his wife for her judgment. She knew lots about housekeeping but nothing about butterflies. Her first reaction was that it was cruel to let the butterflies struggle so hard in trying to come out of the cocoon. At her suggestion, the hobbyist split several cocoons gently so that the exit would be easy. As a result, the butterflies were incapable of using their wings.

He learned his lesson the hard way: Go to a butterfly expert when you want a confirming assessment or judgment about ideas for raising butterflies.

Don't allow yourself to make that kind of mistake by incorrect methodology. But, pursuing the earlier example, if you were to expose a proposed ad or idea to several young women who were prospective buyers of a baby food, you could gain valuable and objective opinions on the worth and effectiveness of your creative idea. It's out of the normal world of the elderly dowager.

How to Compare and Question

The work you've done previously in fact-finding step three is now very heartening and helpful. You have investigated or researched the subject or the field and produced prime material for practical comparison purposes.

Now go back over that material and compare your ideas with what is available, what is being done, what is being used. What exists at present provides your standards for comparison.

Reassess and re-evaluate the ideas in your Excellent listing, and even under the Worthy heading, if they've boiled down to only a few. Or, confine your rechecking to the Excellent group only.

As one example, for a special kind of cigarette, I created a listing of superiorities which seemed exactly right to me, a valuable creative idea which I could sell. Nevertheless, I rechecked all the elements of my suggestion. Only by this process did I realize that the facts, as I'd set them down, didn't hit the reader quickly or clearly enough. By adding a bar chart device, I perfected the idea. When proposed, it was approved completely. Yet I know that if I hadn't rechecked, discovered and corrected the flaw, my entire creative concept might have failed.

Here's how to conduct your rechecking work thoroughly. Ask yourself the following six questions, and any more that are developed by your own creative inquisitiveness, and write down the answers:

Six Comparative Questions

1. Which idea is most simple and direct?
2. Which is best fitted to solve the problem or put it into effect at this time?

3. Which is most practicable to use most productively and resultfully?

4. Will this idea arouse any new problems too difficult to overcome?

5. Is the selected idea better in every way than the others in the listings?

6. What tests can I make to prove the superiority of my selected idea over the others in my listings, and over the ideas that are the current standards?

From your answers to these questions, you'll settle upon the most effective creative ideas.

Proceed with Testing

The purpose of this testing is to reaffirm your judgment and to reveal any flaws. Carefully recheck all the facts on the field that you've previously amassed. Then test the value and merit of the new ideas against those now in effect or used in the past. This work, sometimes admittedly tedious and trying to your patience, is vital in order to ferret out any objections others might bring up. You'll be able to provide the answers before negative questions arise.

And, if challenges are thrown at you, it's a lifesaver to have the facts and answers right at hand or in your mind. You can quickly strengthen your position and remove opposition, with your points proved by testing against present and past product results and case histories. You're prepared when you've pretested this way—a vital part of producing successful creative ideas.

Make Your Choice . . .
Settle on the Big Creative Idea

Now is the time for courageous and forthright action. You must put aside any inhibitions, timidity or fears, and settle on the big idea, which has really settled itself after you've applied the formulas and questions listed in this chapter.

You must make your choice. You can't temporize like the

pretty girl who had been conditioned by her lawyer father and told a confused young man who was trying to kiss her, "Stop and/or I'll slap your face."

You must make up your mind. You've now earned the right to make your choice, and you can be firm and confident about it. You have eliminated confusion by breaking down the entire problem and challenge into its parts and possibilities.

Thus, you have been able to supply solid, dependable creative thinking, combined it then with reasoned selectivity, and amassed the firm, substantiating support for your creative idea.

Don't Fear Similarity or Difference

Don't turn down your selected idea because "something like it" may have been done before. Have faith in your personal creative selectivity after you've developed the idea carefully and industriously through each phase of the six-step method.

Take a tip from Mark Twain, who demonstrated in one of his writings that man's power of creative selectivity makes the big difference in profiting from past actions and errors. He pointed out that once an animal sits down on a hot stove, he'll never sit there again. Yet that would be a perfect resting place for the beast when the stove is cold.

Don't be like the animal who avoids all stove tops, whether hot or cold, after the one disastrous experience. It isn't the stove top that's wrong; it's the animal's idea about stove tops. The new idea, sitting on a cold stove, would still be an excellent one.

Also, don't turn down an idea because, even though you've assessed and tested it to your satisfaction, you feel that it may fail to be approved because it's so different that it may arouse some disagreement. Learn a lesson from one of the most successful men in the world of commerce, William Wrigley, Jr., who is credited with saying, "When two men in a business always agree, one of them is unnecessary."

Don't be afraid to present an original idea, so long as you're prepared to disprove any conservative disagreement. Your work in step six makes it possible to reveal readily any "hidden possibilities" in your new, different creative idea.

Time to Profit

Now you take advantage of all the time and work you've put in, to arrive at the best, most fruitful ideas, and to profit from them.

As you repeat the six-step creative method in the future, you'll be able to speed the various phases, particularly this final process of evaluation, assessment, judgment, testing and selection. Eventually it may seem almost automatic.

Don't ever pass up this sixth step completely. Don't permit yourself to leap from the illumination of what appears to be the big idea right to the application of it in one jump. Analysis of the lessons and teachings of the greatest creative thinkers throughout the ages affirms this point: This step—evaluating, revising and verifying—may well be the prime factor which differentiates dreaming, or wanting, or trying to be creative from actual productive, successful creative thinking and ideas.

10

PRACTICING THE SIX-STEP METHOD WITH A PARTICULAR PROBLEM

Now let's examine a practical problem and see exactly how the six-step method is used to promote clear, creative thinking, and to produce useful, successful, creative ideas.

To refresh your memory, here's another listing of the six steps.

Six-Step Creative Method

Step 1: Develop the creative attitude.
Step 2: Analyze each problem to focus on the wanted creative solution.
Step 3: Seek out and fill your mind with facts.
Step 4: Write down ideas, sensible and seemingly wild.
Step 5: Let the facts and ideas simmer in your mind.
Step 6: Evaluate, recheck, settle on the creative ideas.

Method Becomes Easier Each Time You Use It

John Stuart Mill once wrote: "One person with a belief is equal to a force of 99 who only have interests." Believe in the certainty of your creative growth through application of the proved six-step method. Don't just dawdle aimlessly and "want" to be creative. Work at it. I assure you again that each creative climb makes the next one easier. Any creative expert will affirm this.

You'll develop your imaginative abilities with your particular personal flair and accomplishment. This six-step method provides a format for your personal, uninhibited thinking and unbounded expansion—no cramping fences to limit the extent of your thinking within each progressive phase.

See now how the method works with an actual creative challenge and solution, taken from real life. This is a specific case history in which I was involved, and it proceeded, step by step, to a successful conclusion.

The example happens to be a business problem primarily, but its lessons are revealing and informative, whatever your problem. The day I wrote this page, I noticed an article in the *New York Times* about a woman who had been a biographer, explorer, newspaper publisher and lecturer before she married in her middle years and became a housewife. She stated emphatically that the same creative principles that had made her a success as a career woman applied to "my full-time job as a wife, mother and hostess."

Problem: Create the Useful, Successful Big Ideas for a New Detergent Product

I've purposely selected a difficult problem for a creative exercise and example. Probably no category is more competitive and therefore provides a tougher problem than to create successful, productive, sales-making ideas for a detergent.

Furthermore, this is an everyday, common item familiar to you and to everyone. You can readily follow and check each phase of the creative process, and understand and participate, as we go along in detail, taking each step carefully. Remember, these same procedures apply to your home, office or other problems.

We've already explored some methods for creating an idea for a detergent product, in Chapter 7. Now we go further, working toward the ultimate big creative ideas that will produce the greatest payoff in a very practicable way, in actual usage.

The problem concerns a moderately successful detergent powder (crystals), already being marketed. It's packed in a box and has been formulated for all-purpose cleaning, useful in almost all cleaning tasks, particularly in the home. The specific challenge is to create new ideas which will improve the product, provide dramatic promotional elements, lift it above the competition and transform it into a zooming success.

Realize this clear point immediately: If you attempt to jump from problem to solution in one huge leap, the challenge seems practically impossible of solution. But, step by step, it all becomes clear, and leads to that fulfilling exultation as possible solutions emerge. And finally you savor, then enjoy deeply the thrilling illumination and accomplishment, the inner reward that comes every time with completing the creative process, in addition to obvious practical gains and benefits.

In solving the detergent problem, and gaining the most useful knowledge from it, I suggest that you read again the chapter on each step as we proceed from one phase to the next. Therefore, before you go further, reread the earlier chapter on step one, then continue. You'll find this procedure very much worthwhile in clarifying each phase of the method for your future use, as well as in solving this problem.

Step One: Develop the Creative Attitude

After you've reread the chapter on step one, not much more need be stated here about approaching the detergent problem with an alert, encompassing creative attitude. You will discover, after rechecking those pages, that your creative attitude has already been aroused and improved greatly, and surprisingly, by progressing this far in the book.

Here, briefly, is a summary of fundamental elements of your creative attitude as we tackle this specific problem:

You are looking at the problem of creating a new detergent-product sales success with an alert, optimistic searching approach that carries with it the assurance of reaching a valuable, useful solution.

You are enthusiastic about making a start on the problem, instead of being balked or confused or blocked by the immensity of the challenge or the obvious difficulties involved.

You're willing to make a beginning toward even a small or partial solution, and then expand to a more complete conclusion and the production of an encompassing idea or ideas.

You have figured out the best time and places for focusing on your creative thinking and working toward idea-construction, best for your personal application and accomplishment.

You're continually aware of the importance of being alert constantly, and you're exercising your mind throughout your waking hours.

You keep developing the "ten basic mental elements of the creative person," as delineated in Chapter 2.

You're ready to apply to each problem all the patience and industriousness that may be necessary.

The searching creative attitude, which you now apply, was summarized in just five words by Sir Isaac Newton. When asked how he made his great discoveries, the scientist answered, "By always thinking into them."

We agree, then, that we approach this sample problem eagerly, alertly, consciously, "thinking into" it.

Step Two: Analyze the Problem to Focus on the Wanted Creative Solution

As stated right at the start, the problem of creating a useful, valuable idea for a new detergent is a very complex and difficult challenge. Hundreds of millions of packages of competitive detergents are sold each year. Countless millions of dollars have been spent, and are being applied to promote such items. Experienced, energetic minds devote their primary thinking to this field.

How then can we expect to come up with fresh, new, practical ideas that will lead to a successful result? We can, and we will. No matter how many dollars have been spent, or how many people have exerted their thoughts and energies to a problem, there's always need for new and better ideas.

You may have read that, back in the early nineteenth century, a government official suggested abolishing the U. S. Patent Office on the grounds that almost everything possible had already been invented. It would be just as ridiculous now to feel, as some reactionaries do, that it's useless to attempt to make advances in detergents or any other field because able and experienced people have already poured in so much thinking and effort.

Let us then approach the problem positively—but, above all, we must be certain that we're focusing on the right productive goal.

Rereading Chapter 5, you studied again the "goal chart," as follows:

GOAL CHART

AIM: ______

	1. WHY?
2. OTHER WAY TO ACCOMPLISH THIS?	
	3. STILL ANOTHER WAY, OR WAYS?
4. WOULD ANY OF THESE WAYS ACCOMPLISH THE PURPOSE BETTER?	

↓

GOAL: ______

Processing the detergent problem through these phases, here's our procedure and result:

AIM: Create a new idea for a detergent. This was our original stated aim. So broad a challenge certainly requires analysis. If this is a matter of product improvement through chemistry, for instance, we're not qualified in this area since we're not chemists. We must therefore pinpoint the need and goal so that we can go toward a solution clearly, intelligently, usefully. We must analyze and simplify by questioning further.

1. Why? Why do we want a new idea for a detergent? There can be many reasons. The challenge here is clear—to produce a detergent product that will be an exceptional commercial success.

2. Other Way to Accomplish This? The obvious way to reach the success wanted is to invent an entirely new type of product that will be completely or radically different from others, and superior to others.

But, as stated before, we're not chemists. Therefore our creative thinking must be applied outside of the area of any brilliant new radical scientific formulation on our part. What other way is open?

We can seek to find a new idea for dramatizing the composition and benefits of the product so that the rewards of using it will become more vivid, and more people will want it and buy it.

3. Still another way or ways? Yes, there are other approaches that can be investigated.

The look of this product itself might be changed to make it visibly different from others.

A notable packaging improvement might be devised, aimed at easier usage, cleaner handling, more compact storage and other such benefits.

4. Would any of these ways accomplish the purpose better? Probably the most desirable and effective would be the creation of a *visible* product improvement which would make the benefits apparent to the prospective user quickly, simply and most impressively.

Goal: Create a dramatically visible and demonstrable idea

for the product which would prove a profitable commercial success.

Note the specific value of going through the analysis provided by step two and focusing on the wanted creative solution. Instead of just generally creating a new idea, we're now concentrating on a special kind of idea.

The result should be to make the product visibly different. The effect should be to project vivid, dramatic proof of benefit quickly, simply and clearly. And the goal is to achieve commercial success.

With this precise, challenging target in mind and now set down accurately, we go on to step three.

Step Three: Seek Out and Fill Your Mind with Facts

Now comes the digging phase, where we collect, pile up and absorb the facts about detergents, past and present. In working on this problem in actual business life, I spent the major part of three weeks seeking out, compiling and studying information on the field.

I won't attempt to list all the material here that I collected in that process. Following through on the suggestions in Chapter 6, I made copious notes as I went along.

In setting a time limit, I had allocated a maximum of three weeks for the fact-finding step. That was essential, since I had a month in which to make a presentation of ideas.

In researching the facts in depth, I checked most of the sources listed in the earlier chapter. I spent many hours in the library; perused books, magazines, newspapers and trade publications; read innumerable pamphlets and other printed literature; interviewed many people in the manufacturing company; talked with wholesalers, retailers and scores of housewives.

Soon I was loaded with pages of notes on detergents. I arranged the material in orderly progression, then rechecked and rearranged for accuracy and clarity.

I referred to the checklist of sixteen fact-finding questions, and set down the answers, point by point. Boiling down the facts about successes and failures in the field, and the chief contributory reasons, here are some of the leading answers I listed:

In using a detergent, women are seeking superior cleaning power.

A product that performs a variety of cleansing tasks has appeal.

Mildness on the hands, and on fabrics and surfaces, is important.

There's sales power in the promise of "extras"—such as bleaching and bluing, in addition to washing. Antiseptic and deodorizing properties would be desirable.

A difference in the actual color of the product has been dramatized effectively.

Proof of better performance has been impressive.

Emphasis on "modern scientific advances" has produced more sales.

Various forms of products—liquid, powder, tablets—are stressed, along with reasons for their superiority.

Proof of faster, easier cleaning is spotlighted.

Comparing superiorities of product with faults of others has produced notable sales results.

Attention-getting product name is helpful.

Economy has proved a vital factor.

Dissolvable packets are an appealing development.

Premiums in packages, or with box tops, show sales strength.

Compact, attractive packaging is a factor.

Lots of price cuts and bargain offers in the field.

Contests are utilized widely for such products.

Demonstration of product in use gets attention.

Sampling is a factor in introducing items.

Under each of the points noted in the preceding listing, I set down details about various existing products as they applied to the economy factor, convenience, "extras" and the other points.

All the data sheets went into a file folder. Then I separated these further into a series of related file folders. I divided the material into categories, including details on manufacture of products, packaging, promotion and advertising statements of competitive superiorities.

Going through each category, I then noted what I considered the most valuable facts in each grouping. Finally I collected this prime information in one summary folder.

By the time I had concluded this fact-finding hunt, at the end of my specified three-week period, I had checked through all the material at least three times. I had absorbed a mass of information by reading and rereading. I had underlined potent items and made special notes of what I felt was of prime interest and usefulness.

I had learned a great deal about detergents, through this twenty-one-day cram course. I had filled my mental "magical jug" with the essential raw material from which would come a flow of information and inspiration for valuable new ideas to solve the problem set before us.

Step Four: Write Down Ideas, Sensible and Seemingly Wild

In poring over the facts, and making notes while digesting and compressing them, I had already jotted down a number of ideas which had been suggested by comparable or different usage in the field.

"You'll find yourself doing the same. When you think of a "new" or adapted idea, write it down immediately. I like to work with a small white pad, jotting down each thought or idea on a separate sheet, then ripping it off and placing it in a folder, or holding the sheets together with a paper clip. How those ideas pile up—what a gold mine of possibilities when you turn back and go through the batch of sheets.

You'll often say to yourself later, "Gosh, did I think up and write down all these ideas? Some of them are excellent."

Yes, you did make that list in just one way—by writing one note and another, and another and another. It's always surprising and gratifying the way one little note at a time, like one drop of water at a time, fills up the pitcher of invaluable inspiration and practical possibilities.

Now let's use the sixteen idea-starter questions listed in the chapter on writing down ideas. Remember, you're to jot down every single idea you get, sensible, or seemingly wild.

Later, you'll assess, evaluate, judge and select.

Checklist of Sixteen Idea-Starter Questions

1. Break down into smaller parts, and list idea for each segment?

Dividing into various parts of the problem, we come up with these ideas when we consider several aspects—product composition, packaging, selling:

A. Product composition.

The new product is in powder (crystals) form. Here are ideas jotted down in this area.

Consider, instead, a liquid which would dissolve more quickly. Color it a rare shade, different from any other detergent, such as "sunlight yellow" or "emerald green." The color difference could be promoted to dramatize product superiority and special benefits.

Make a wafer or tablet which could be packaged to take little space, and used very easily—simply dropped into water. It would dissolve quickly for proper cleaning solution in a washing machine, tub or pail.

Package concentrated liquid in a large, clear capsule, with covering that would dissolve in water fast and make the most effective cleaning solution.

B. Packaging.

Produce a package with a specially long lift-out pouring spout for less spilling, easier handling, no waste, so one can even insert spout directly into a washing machine opening.

C. Selling.

Pack a free item in every box, such as a small kitchen utensil, as a lure in buying this product rather than another brand.

Place a "dividend check" in each package, which provides a price reduction on the next purchase of the product, to keep people buying it instead of switching to another brand.

Add something special to the package—a clear plastic window so people can see the product through it. They'll be more attracted to pick up the package off the supermarket shelf, rather than the less-eye-catching brand in an adjacent display.

2. Adapt and apply ideas from similar problems or products?

(Other product has "free" dish packed in the box.) Have a small children's record included in each box, and call the product "Record" Detergent. The youngsters will urge mother to keep buying the product so they can enjoy a record with another story or group of songs, with each purchase.

(Other products changed color and dramatized the "blue" or "pink" effectively.) Make a product which combine *two* colors of granules, such as blue and pink, with each color of crystals performing a separate function.

3. Adopt and apply ideas from dissimilar problems or products, in related or unrelated categories?

(Attachments are available for tops of liquor bottles which measure out and then pour one ounce of liquid at a time.) Package the crystals in a clear container designed so that the top compartment fills with one measured portion, which is then poured easily into washing machine, tub or other receptacle.

(Other household products have offered linens as premiums, with considerable success.) Print a "certificate" or coupon on the box which enables the woman to send in for a genuine imported Irish linen white handkerchief, free or at nominal cost. Make a big point with this offer in respect to its enticing bargain value. But also challenge the woman to wash the valuable linen with this product, and then see that it comes out whiter and cleaner than with any other brand.

4. List faults; how correct these?

Note how "naturally" ideas spring from this fault-finding and solution-seeking device:

Measuring out a portion of powder or liquid is time-consuming and inaccurate. Make product in one-portion form—a dissolvable tablet, or individual, sealed, one-portion packets. (Note that this idea is a repeat of an earlier one. It's worth jotting such repeats anyhow, as prompted by this particular question and others. They're further substantiation of the merit of possible ideas or directions to pursue.)

Dissolves too slowly. Incorporate in the formula a modern chemical which breaks down particles faster in water, by reducing surface tension or some other means. Give the ingredient a special name, such as "contains Speedol." Promote the improvement through dramatic and convincing photographic or diagrammatic proof-tests.

Doesn't look better than others. Create something visual that shows immediately that the product is different (and better). Instead of having one-color granules, combine two colors, such as yellow and green, with each color promoted as producing a specific benefit, such as cleaning power and purifying effect. (Note that this repeats and reaffirms a previous idea.)

5. List good features: how to expand, increase or improve these further?

Pleasant to use. Granules pour easily, don't make a mess such as a heavy liquid if spilled. Improve the product so that it pours even more readily. Then promote the improvement—"double-sifted for easier pouring, faster dissolving."

Cleans thoroughly. Investigate any new ingredients that could be added to produce even greater cleaning power. Then urge women to try the product with the "imported Irish linen handkerchief test," washing the fabric, as discussed previously, and "see the wonderful difference." Show comparative photographs in the ads—superiority over the previous product, and the contrast with results from using competitive detergents.

Easy handling and storage. Devise a longer pouring spout so that the stream of powder can be directed more accurately when using (a repeat idea). Make the product even more concentrated so that a smaller quantity will be needed for each washing. Thus the same size box will produce more washings, yet it takes up no greater room in the closet. Economy advantages of a more concentrated powder can also be promoted effectively.

6. How simplify it?

In effect, by making the product more "concentrated," it is simplified so that it takes up less space in storage, produces more washings per box, can be purchased less often and therefore cuts down on shopping time. (A repeat variation.)

By making the product in tablet form, it would be simplified, in that it would provide one-portion usage, and a much smaller package for shopping, handling and storage. (A repeat variation.)

7. What can be added or increased to improve?

Offer a combination package of the detergent and a bar of soap made by the same company. These items could be banded together and sold at a saving.

Add to the package a long, transparent window going down the front of the box so the user can see where the powder is almost all used up and should be replaced with a new box. This avoids the inconvenience of running out of the product. This feature automatically tells the user, "Time to buy another package."

8. What can be removed beneficially?

Redesign the package so that it actually takes up less space on the closet shelf. This may be done by making it just a little wider and somewhat shallower. Show by diagram exactly how this takes up much less depth on the average shelf. Band two of the redesigned packages together to prove that they take up only a little more shelf depth than the previous box, and offer a saving over the two packages bought separately. This will help to focus attention on the new benefit and to increase sales accordingly.

9. What extra and new uses and applications?

Revise the formula so that it provides a new "happy medium" between thorough cleaning power and gentleness on fabrics and surfaces. Then actually list its many uses, "from A to Z"—"cleans ashtrays, bandannas, closets," etc.

Demonstrate the extra and varied applications of the improved product with demonstrations in huge supermarkets. Have the demonstrator actually clean a great variety of items—an ashtray, a bandanna, a closet shelf—and point to samples of results right through the alphabet. This proves dramatically, "right before your eyes," that the product will clean everything "from A to Z—from this sparkling bright ashtray to this beautifully immaculate stuffed toy zebra."

10. What complete changes can be made?

Offer the product in its present form, and a similar formula in a completely new tablet form. Promote the choice according to what "you like to use best—you can choose from Exbrand Powder or Exbrand Tablets—getting the superior Exbrand basic combination of effective ingredients in both."

11. Substitute something else entirely?

Instead of the box of loose powder, substitute individually wrapped packets of powder. (A repeat idea.)

Investigate two forms of one-portion packets. One would be in an attractive wrapper such as a brilliant foil which is easily torn open and the contents poured into the tub or pail, to make a solution with water. Another type would be in a light new material which is dissolvable so that you merely drop the entire envelope into the pail of water and soon have the proper cleaning liquid.

12. How about reversing, starting backward, inside-out, reshaping, doing exactly the opposite?

Instead of keeping this as an all-purpose product, repackage it in similar boxes but in three different colors—a red box, yellow box, blue box. Each formula is changed slightly so that the yellow box is best for fabrics; the red box for cleaning hard surfaces such as dishes, sinks, tile floors; the blue box especially adapted for most efficient, safe cleaning of wooden surfaces.

Instead of offering just the one basic product and box, combine the three different boxes in one package, at a considerable saving to the purchaser.

13. How vary the problem and applications?

Instead of concentrating on changing the product, focus on how to improve the presentation of it to the public. Consider more effective selling techniques.

Have a special portable washing machine constructed so that the sides are almost completely transparent (except for essential corner braces) for demonstration purposes. This will be helpful as a dramatic eye-catcher in supermarkets, as a demonstrator points to the fast cleaning action. Prove the speed of washing by use of a timer that ticks off the washing time and rings at the swift conclusion.

Build a special demonstration truck which is then parked near the entrance of a supermarket in the parking lot. Have it completely equipped with interesting washing appliances, photographs, testing machines and other apparatus. An expert explains and demonstrates the best way to save time and effort in the home, including use of the product but not confined to it exclusively.

14. How combine various aspects?

Combine a number of ideas already written down, to improve the product from many viewpoints at once. Thus add strength upon strength for an increasingly successful result.

Take the idea for a two-colored product. Combine the point of having one color aim at extra cleanliness and the other toward the purifying effect. Place the improved product in the specially designed package that takes less depth on the closet shelf. Include in the box a certificate or coupon which is good for a free premium, or one obtainable at nominal cost.

15. Review: how can it be done or handled better?

Change the name of the product entirely, or keep the basic name and add to it in order to help dramatize that it's much improved and different. One possible name—"Exbrand-Plus"—with the "Plus" immediately conveying the promise of something additional, something better. Another variation might be "Super-Exbrand."

16. What more can be done?

Create a special display rack for use in stores. Design a rack which is a miniature of a closet in an average home. Make the shelf depth the same as the average closet (a survey in a number of homes will reveal this; the actual investigation itself can be described to show women that you're thinking of their own practical needs). Print prominently on the display the fact that the new box stores better in the closet, takes up less room, is more desirable than other brands in this and other respects.

Offer a premium of dolls' clothes to accent the fact that even the most delicate fabrics can be washed beautifully and safely with the product. Also, this premium has the advantage that the child will ask mother to get the particular brand so that she can get the dolls' clothes (free or at a big saving). Advertise the offer on some children's television shows so that little girls will learn about it, as well as their mothers (surveys prove that many mothers watch the programs along with their children.)

Run a contest in which users are challenged to coin a word or combination of words that will describe best the superior cleaning action and results with this product—words such as "super-kleen," "cleanerite." Provide a list of tempting prizes, all tying in with cleaning and the household—washing machines, fashion wardrobes, a playroom built in your basement, and such. Perhaps call it the "Exbrand-Plus Cleanstakes."

Send a coupon-bonus offer in the mail to homes. The basic coupon provides ten cents off on purchase of the improved product. Attached to it is a bonus coupon which gives five cents off on a soap made by the same company. In total, the woman gets a fifteen-cent saving, and you get her to try and then keep buying two of your products instead of one. The retailer is pleased also because he sells both detergent and soap, instead of one or the other.

Use a mystery-camera man to travel from one big supermarket to others. Advertise that the photographer, carrying a concealed camera, will be at some supermarket in town for a half-hour each day (not giving the exact hour or store location). He'll snap pictures of people at the shelf buying this product. If he happens to take your photograph, you get ten silver dollars and the photograph. This can be promoted and publicized in the newspapers and on local television to arouse more interest in the product and increase sales considerably all over the area.

Distribute samples of the improved product right in the supermarket, or door-to-door to homes. The sample can be attached to a card which provides ten cents off when the person tries the sample, is delighted with it and goes shopping for a full-size box.

Make a "piggyback" combination package which bands together the regular-size package of the product and also a small "sampler" size. The woman pays the regular price and gets both. She uses the sampler size first. If she's not completely delighted, she returns the regular box and gets her entire purchase price back.

How the Ideas Multiply!

Here's proof for you of the value of the system using the sixteen idea-starter questions. Just by writing down a few creative answers to each question, over forty different ideas have been listed in the preceding pages. Not all are practical and applicable. But here at least are over forty beginnings toward at least one big, usable and ultimately successful creative idea.

When I was actually working on this problem in my daily business life, I wrote down sixty-four different ideas in answering the idea-starter questions. I've left many of them out here for the sake of brevity. But, in my original effort, as you see demonstrated here, I accomplished the long listing by persisting, by going on from question to question, from answer to answer.

When I showed associates my list of sixty-four ideas, just from answering these idea-starter questions, they asked in astonishment, "How can you do it?" I did it, and others do it, and you can do it, too, quite easily, by following this consecutive system.

Learn, as I did, from the great Plutarch, who wrote so many centuries ago, "Perseverance is . . . prevailing . . . and many things which cannot be overcome when they are together, yield themselves up when taken little by little."

You're blocked if you say to yourself, "twenty or thirty or sixty-four ideas on this subject—it's an impossible total." But you're on your way to successful results when you just start putting down one or two or more answers to each question in turn.

As another philosopher, Horace, wrote, "He has half the deed done, who has made a beginning." And it's encouraging to realize, as someone else said, "Creativity is work that is going someplace."

The famed Carnegie project reports flatly, "Discipline is essential to creativity. You put in the work, and the creative ideas will come."

Here's a clear, practical system for making a beginning and then going on to an impressive total. It's hard work, but it succeeds. Each time you try it, you'll prove its worth again. And it will become easier and easier to accomplish.

Try Other Devices

Use, too, the other systems which are described in the chapter on step four. Reread the ideas emanating from the alphabet device, and then go through the alphabet on your own, to add ideas.

Try the very simple like-and-dislike formula, listing first what people may dislike about the product or problem, then what they (and you) would like to have in relation to it.

Apply the split-personality evaluation, becoming the customer who asks to be satisfied, and the salesman who sets forth the points and ideas that help make the sale.

Settle down with a magazine or newspaper and use the turn-the-pages method, checking again the ideas which were developed for the detergent product by this means. Try it on any problem to which you're seeking a creative solution.

As advised previously, use some or all of the methods suggested. When you're finished, you'll have compiled a fruitful and surprisingly long list of ideas. Don't try to settle on any one idea at this point. Go on to step five, for a delightful creative break, sort of a mental coffee break.

Step Five: Let the Facts and Ideas Simmer in Your Mind

In rereading the chapter on step five, you'll note that this is the pleasant time when you let your mind alone. In our specific example, you aim to forget all about detergents. You go on to anything else that interests you, and particularly something that you find entertaining, refreshing and relaxing.

A noted biologist affirmed the value of this step when he wrote that, as far as he could remember, he never found the final creative answer to any stubborn problem by conscious thinking. He said that he realized that subconsciously he went on thinking about the problems all the time—"and my brain must continue to think about them even when I sleep, for I wake up, sometimes in the middle of the night, with answers to questions that have been puzzling me."

Realize that the creative answer is probably just there over the horizon. At this stage you can't "see" it, no matter how much you strain and strive. To repeat that brilliant line of Thoreau's: "I see beyond the range of sight."

The big answer, the big idea, is there, within you, but you can't visualize it wholly and pin it down—not yet. You will. Use the various suggestions given previously on how to relax, suiting the means and methods to your personal likes and pleasures.

And, of course, be ready, when the idea strikes, to write it down and pin it down. In an interview I had with one of the greatest and most prolific writers of popular songs, he made this point emphatically.

After close to thirty years of successful song-writing, the composer emphasized that he still carries with him sheets of paper on which he writes down phrases of music that "come to me." He keeps such scraps of paper alongside his bed at night. The notes of music that he has been struggling to set down melodically all day suddenly come singing through his brain. He knows from decades of experience that he still must be ready to capture the strains in black and white before they escape.

Keep in mind that this creative composer doesn't spend his hours continually dreaming or wandering in a daze, and waiting for inspiration to strike. He puts in long, hard hours of work at the piano composing music. It's the key strains that frequently come to him while he's simply taking a walk for relaxation, or indulging in other pleasant activities, not consciously trying to complete the song he's been working on.

Don't forget to "set your automatic mental timer." If you need the idea "tomorrow," gear yourself as suggested, so that you'll complete your creative efforts the next day. (In this case, with the detergent problem, I had allowed myself a week in which to incubate and produce the big idea.)

Relax and find yourself ready when you achieve that most promising and gratifying moment of revelation, that instant when you feel the surge of tangible inspiration and you can shout to yourself, "I have the idea!"

A *Triple Revelation*

In respect to the timing in this instance, as noted, I had set the following Monday as a limit for my incubation period. As they're supposed to say in the ad world on Madison Avenue, and never actually do, I "put the problem on the back burner and let it simmer." At any rate, I removed the detergent problem from my conscious mind.

On Sunday, I went sailing in a friend's boat. Early in the afternoon, I stretched myself on the forward deck. With the swift motion of the boat, the soft sound of the breeze against the sails, the warm radiance of the sun on my back, I was dozing, half asleep, with nothing seemingly further away from my thoughts than improving the detergent product.

As I lay there, a question filtered into my consciousness, "Why not make it a *triple-action* detergent, with three different colored powders or crystals combined in the one product, performing three different jobs?"

I sat up, stared out at the water rushing by. Tingling with inner excitement, I thought tensely about the idea. Various angles started pouring through my mind. I pulled the stub of a pencil and a little pad from the hip pocket of my shorts.

The actual notes I jotted then are before me now: "Make

the product triple-action, not single or dual. Combine three colors of crystals, one for each action. Three actions might be: cleansing, purifying, deodorizing. Revise name, such as 'Triple-Exbrand,' 'Exbrand-3,' or new name, 'Trio.' "

I savored the special thrill of experiencing the revelation of the big idea, as I always do—as others experience too. You have probably also known it, and you will enjoy it many times in the future by using the six-step creative method. I returned pencil and paper to my pocket, and went back with new exhilaration to full participation in the very pleasant sailing.

I realized that the next day I'd start on the final step of assessing, reviewing and rechecking the dozens of ideas I'd listed in step four, and the culminating idea I'd just noted. Meanwhile, I savored the wonderful creative thrill, as expressed in the words of Marcel Proust, ". . . the joy of a great discovery . . . (which) gives a new and clear form to what we have long been ruminating without suspecting it."

Step Six: Evaluate, Recheck, Settle on the Creative Ideas

You'll find that you're usually eager and even somewhat impatient to start on this phase of the creative process, because this is the payoff. All the work that has gone before is now poured through the funnel into your brain once more. There it's sieved carefully, so that the final creative distillation will emerge at its highest value and perfection.

Let's wrestle now with the detergent problem, according to the procedures recommended in the earlier chapter on step six. (As a comedian put it comparably, "Women are a problem, but they happen to be the kind of problem that men like to wrestle with.")

There's a great temptation at this point to take a short cut and settle at once on the idea which emerged in step five. In this case, it would mean recommending the triple-action detergent. That might be the ultimate answer, but even if it were, it could certainly be refined and improved.

So we follow the thorough system. We go back over all the ideas previously set down. Now we re-evaluate and list them separately under the headings, Excellent, Worthy, Not Usable, as recommended earlier:

EXCELLENT

Enclose the powder in individual packets, just enough to dump into a washing machine or other vessel for proper solution.

Pack a free item in every box, such as a small kitchen utensil, to keep people buying the same brand. (Rechecking shows that this has proved very effective for some other products.)

Print a coupon on the box, offering an "imported Irish linen handkerchief" at very low cost. Tie this in with washing the fine handkerchief, to prove how much whiter and cleaner it comes out when this detergent is used in a test.

Incorporate in the formula a modern chemical which breaks down particles faster for speedier washing, and can be demonstrated by visual proof-tests.

Have a window near the bottom of the box, to show when product is almost used up. (Note how this idea, as improved, is transferred from Not Usable category.)

Combine varicolored product with improved packaging and a coupon offer on the box, for multiple sales power.

Improve or change the name to dramatize the improvements.

Distribute samples of the improved product, along with coupon for ten cents off on purchase of a large box.

Triple-action idea produced by step five.

WORTHY

Make a wafer or tablet which would take up little space and be used very easily by being dropped into water and dissolved. (An excellent idea, but it must be assessed only as "worthy" at this time because manufacturing machinery and procedures would have to be changed completely.)

Package concentrated liquid in a large, clear capsule which would dissolve in water. (This is a dramatic and appealing concept. But rechecking reveals negative aspects. Long research and development would be needed before the product could be marketed. The manufacturer would welcome more readily an idea that could be put into effect more quickly and easily.)

Produce a product with a specially long lift-out spout, for greater accuracy, economy and speed in use. (This is a good "secondary" idea, not an important enough improvement by itself.)

Place a "dividend check" in each product, good for savings on the next purchase. (Evaluating this reveals a weakness in that the idea isn't particularly new or dramatic.)

Insert a children's record in each box so that the youngsters will ask mother to keep buying the product. (Rechecking shows that this idea would have high appeal. A negative aspect is that the price of the product would probably have to be boosted because of the comparatively high cost of records.)

Improve the product by making the crystals smaller, for easier pouring and faster dissolving, promoting this "double-sifted" feature. (This is a worthy but not especially dramatic improvement.)

Make the product more concentrated, for economy and to provide a smaller, more easily stored package. (Competitive checking reveals that a smaller box would look like a poorer value at quick glance, a conclusive negative aspect.)

Offer a combination package of detergent and a bar of soap. (An effective but not a novel idea.)

Redesign the box so it takes up less shelf depth. Band two boxes together and offer at a bargain price. (Assessing this idea shows that it has considerable merit but not very striking originality.)

Revise the formula to combine gentleness and high cleaning power so that the product is safe for cleaning everything from A to Z. (Reconsideration indicates that this is a sound idea, but not as dramatically impressive as others.)

Offer the product in both powder and tablet form. (Assessing this idea reveals a weakness—that buyers might become confused, even though the thought has merit in appealing to users of both types of products.)

Use a portable, transparent washing machine for store demonstration purposes. (Checking shows that such demonstration is effective but very costly on a nationwide basis, even when confined to the largest stores in each area.)

Build a special demonstration truck to educate women about best washing procedures. (Investigation reveals that this is very costly on a national basis but is worth considering in the future for selected "problem" areas to combat particularly severe competition.)

Design a special display rack for stores. Build it to look like a home storage closet. Focus attention on the easy-storing and other features of the product. (Research measures this as a worthy idea, but the costly display would probably have to be linked to an exceptionally large product order from the store getting it.)

Offer a premium of dolls' clothes. (This was reassessed as having considerable appeal but not as much as some of the other premium ideas created at this time.)

Run a contest linked to the improved function of the product. (This was considered a good idea but one to be reserved for the future. Promotional money should be concentrated directly on the improved product itself at this point, rather than diverting some of the attention to the contest details.)

Send a coupon-bonus offer to homes. (Same consideration as in previous paragraph.)

NOT USABLE

Instead of a powder, make a liquid product, as the latter would dissolve more quickly. (This idea was discarded because rechecking shows huge obstacles apparent. There's as much tough competition among liquids as powders. Entirely new manufacturing and packaging procedures would have to be set up. Also, there's nothing dramatic or novel about offering a liquid form of the product.)

Make a two-color product. (This idea is superseded by the tricolor inspiration.)

Provide a top compartment on the package which would measure out one portion at a time. (Investigation reveals that the package itself, without the product, would become far too costly, unless an entirely new measuring invention, not available now, could be developed.)

Insert a window that extends to the bottom of the box, to show when package is almost empty. (Research reveals that the box would be weakened considerably by such a window. However, a fine offshoot idea emerged from this investigation—to have a smaller transparent window near the bottom of the front panel only, thus keeping the box strong yet showing when the product is almost used up. You recall that this idea was placed in the Excellent category.)

Package the powder in individual packets of material that dissolves completely in water. (Investigation shows that this idea requires technical development but is worth prime consideration for research and future possibilities.)

Repackage the product with three variations of formula, in three different colored boxes combined in one package. (Assessing this shows that the final package would be too costly, also that there's often some resistance among shoppers against buying three different products for different uses, all at one time.)

Send a mystery-camera man to stores. (Research reveals that this would be too costly on a national basis, but it might be tried eventually in special "problem areas.")

Make a "piggyback" combination package of sample size and regular box, with full money-back offer if sample isn't satisfactory. (Assessing this idea led to decision that it was worthy but that the extra packaging cost involved would not provide sufficient extra sales power at this time.)

Note that in addition to the listings you have by categories, you also have produced some creative ideas that you now put aside for possible future usage, such as the wafers and individual packets. These may eventually prove of considerable value to you. Such future ideas provide a bonus that you'll find occurring frequently from your efforts evolving from the six-step method.

Rechecking One's Judgment

In rechecking my own ideas, and my assessment of them, I proceeded to employ all the devices suggested in Chapter 6:

Reread the listings under the three categories, and settle on those previously placed under Excellent. In this process, I shifted the idea about enclosing the powder in individual packets from Excellent to Worthy, making the note that it would involve considerable experimentation and manufacturing change. Therefore I decided that it would be better to postpone its development for the future, rather than to recommend applying it right now.

Graded the ideas under Excellent according to merit, as follows:

1. Triple-action product.
2. Combination of ideas listed.
3. Transparent window near bottom of box.
4. Add modern chemical for speedier action.
5. Print coupon on box, offering handkerchief.
6. Change name to dramatize improvement.
7. Pack free item in box.
8. Distribute samples, with ten-cents-off coupon attached.

Requestioned my judgment in respect to the ideas and the evaluation of them by considering the points as though I were the person buying the product, rather than the one concerned with improving and selling it.

Discussed the innovations with my wife and with other women who were detergent users. Also questioned experts in the field whom I could trust in respect to fair judgment and discretion.

Asked the seven comparative questions listed in the earlier chapter on step six and then used the answers to affirm or revise previous judgments.

Went back over the factual material in detail, specifically testing and comparing the merits of the new ideas with facts and histories about comparable and competitive products and results.

Settling On the Big Idea

After assessing, checking, rechecking, reviewing the various forms of testing provided by the six-step method, we come to the following conclusive "big idea." In this case it's a combination of several phases from the Excellent category:

★ Change the product into a triple-action detergent.

★ Dramatize the triple-action visually by having three colors of granules or crystals combined in the one powder.

★ Emphasize three actions instead of one—yellow crystals for deep cleansing, blue for purifying (antiseptic, antibacterial) action, pink for deodorizing (clean, sweet-smelling) effect.

★ Call the improved product by a new name, "Trio," to parallel the triple-action benefits. Or, alter the present name, such as "Exbrand-3," for the same purpose, to spotlight the three-way action.

★ Revise box with a transparent window near the bottom of the front panel to reveal the three-color difference to the eye instantly, and to warn the user to get a new box by showing when package is almost empty. (A dotted line printed at a low point, and suggesting the need for getting another package, would be helpful to the user.)

★ Incorporate a modern chemical in the formula, to speed dissolving and cleaning action.

★ Print coupon on box, offering imported Irish linen handkerchief at low cost. Show photographs dramatizing the handkerchief proof-test.

★ Distribute small samples of the new triple-action product, in transparent packets that reveal the tricolored granules. Attach sample to a coupon worth ten cents off when product is purchased at store.

Now You Profit

Now that all your efforts have culminated in a big creative idea, or a series of ideas as in this detergent example, you reap the fruits of your labors.

If it's an idea, as in this case, involving big business, you present it in detailed, impressive form accordingly. If it's an idea involving your home or personal activities, you put it right into effect with confidence and knowledge that you'll get the result you want.

As proved by this detailed example, the six-step creative method works. And you may feel assured that, as you use it again and again, the procedure will become increasingly easy.

Take heart from the story about a child from the city pavements who was spending his first summer in the country and learning to run around barefoot like his country cousins. Asked how he like going barefoot, he thought about it carefully. "Well, at first I could hardly walk," he finally said slowly, "but now the rocks seems to get softer every day."

So it is with creative thinking. The rocks get softer every day.

11

HOW TO FOLLOW THROUGH AND APPLY YOUR IDEAS

To put over your ideas successfully, it's necessary to follow through properly, logically and energetically. That's true whether it's a creative plan for decorating your home, a proposal for new office procedures, a way for you to earn more money as a teen-ager, or whatever it is.

Here's what happened with the actual case history of creative thinking on the detergent product.

I presented the ideas in the form which will be given to you in detail on the following pages. You can adapt this basic format for the small or large creative project. The presentation in this case was placed before a large manufacturer.

As a result, a contract for advertising was secured, with a potential involving profits on the expenditure of many thousands of dollars, possibly millions of dollars, on advertising and promotion.

Here's just one proof that the six-step creative method is practicable and productive. It has been proved by myself and others in preparing and presenting ideas of varying types. It can be immensely valuable to you in all the years ahead, wherever you apply your creative efforts.

If your problem is a simple one, such as feeding a child correctly (as mentioned earlier), simply go right ahead and put your ideas into practice. You usually don't have to present ideas to a group, or consult with a board of directors or anyone else.

Go to it. You may modify your conclusions and course of action as you go along. But you'll retain the pure, simple basic of your idea as you head toward and achieve the results you want.

If your ideas are of such scope that they are to be presented to others, you simply compress the work and conclusions you've achieved by the six-step method and make your presentation in the following form. Keep in mind this useful guide: "Never underestimate the intelligence of your audience, nor overestimate their knowledge."

But don't inflate the facts. As a wit put it, "People, like boats, toot loudest when they're in a fog." Another commented, "A gentleman doesn't blow his knows."

Your proposals may be written out formally (usually the case), or delivered verbally, or use a combination of both. Give your presentation careful thought; remember Mark Twain's pithy comment, "It usually takes me three weeks to prepare a good impromptu speech."

Important Considerations

Before presenting the idea, consider the following factors, and be guided accordingly:

1. Be sure that you're reaching the right person or group of persons. These people are sometimes referred to as the decision makers. If you don't place your ideas immediately or eventually before the one who can say, "Yes, go ahead!"—there's very little chance that you'll get an affirmative decision.

This is a factor you must work out sensibly and conclusively. Don't blame the merit of your creative idea if it doesn't get a proper hearing. The best idea can't be productive if left to wander in a vacuum.

Remember this rhyme? "I shot an arrow into the air, it fell to earth I knew not where." You must aim the presentation of your idea at the right target, or you can't score the bull's-eye you want.

2. Study your audience, and approach them accordingly. A

coach of one of the most successful basketball teams in the record books told me, "One of the prime secrets we use in beating our opponents consistently is that we study them ahead of time. Then we know our best approach."

Whenever possible, study or investigate beforehand the man or group or committee about to judge your ideas. Obviously, you shouldn't make a long presentation to an impatient person who insists on brevity. Conversely, you shouldn't plunge ahead in quick 1-2-3 fashion if you must impress an executive whose habit is to digest material slowly.

I've heard it said that "a sales talk is like a wheel—the longer the space, the greater the tire." Aim for brevity, but never sacrifice clarity. People are seldom in love with a "wordy cause."

Also, beware of promising too much. Let your proposals prove their promise by their worthy content. I recall with amusement the statement of one bright speaker who was introduced so enthusiastically that when he arose, he said, "After such a glowing introduction, I can hardly wait to hear what I'm going to say."

3. Seek out the best time and timing. It may seem silly but it's true that even the hour of the day can make a vital difference in the success or failure of your presentation. I know of one man in a high position in the advertising division of one of the largest financial organizations, of whom it is said, "You'd better see George in the morning if you want an okay on your proposition. He's murder after lunch!"

This is admittedly an extreme example. You can't always pick the right hour of the day or the best week or season to make your presentation. But try to, as much as is humanly possible.

As an example of another kind of important timing, the great mystery writer Dashiell Hammett told me that an editor had rejected a story early in his career. Hammett considered the tale an excellent one and took the rejection painfully, upset that so fine a creative effort had failed.

A year later he again shoved the story into an envelope, without a note, and sent it back to the same editor. This time the story was accepted enthusiastically. When Hammett asked the editor for an explanation, he was told, "The first time I had just bought a story on the same subject, so I wasn't interested at all in yours, regardless of its merit."

Even with a great creative story, in this instance, timing made the difference in success or failure. This can happen to some of your creative ideas, a vital point to realize.

In respect to timing, it pays to investigate and proceed accordingly, whenever possible. If your idea would involve someone in a considerable expenditure, as another example, and you find that he's overspent at the moment, hold back your presentation if you can until a more propitious time.

But when the timing seems just right, don't hesitate, make your move. Publius advised back about 42 B.C., "You should hammer your iron when it is glowing hot." Rabelais wrote in the early 1500's, "Strike whilst the iron is hot." John Heywood stated it in the mid-1500's: "When the iron is hot, strike." Take this tip which has been passed down through all time.

4. Keep your language, oral or written, clear and simple. You must have heard something like this, surprisingly often, about some very capable person: "When Henry is just chatting with you, his words and phrases are simple, understandable, crystal clear. But when he's making a presentation, on his feet or in writing, his language becomes so involved and pretentious, you can't tell what he's driving at. He makes you feel like you're wrestling with an octopus."

Too many people go hifalutin when they're trying to present an idea; they think that many-syllabled words are most impressive. They're not. It pays to check carefully over what you're going to say, or what you've written, before you make your presentation.

I can't tell it to myself too often; neither can you: "Simplify, simplify."

Let's run over these basic points once more: reach the right person; study your audience beforehand; seek the best timing; say it simply. And present it confidently. It has been said that "every time a person puts a new idea across, he finds ten people who claim they thought of it before he did—but they only *thought* of it." You *do* it!

Basic Presentation

Referring back again to the six-step method, the first step—developing your creative attitude—has no specific place in the presentation. Nor should you be directly concerned about steps four and five. On the other hand, step six provides two phases.

Actually, boiling down all your work to the presentation is usually as simple and direct as A, B, C, D:

A. Analysis (from step two).

B. Facts (from step three).

C. Review of ideas (from step six).

D. Idea recommendation (from step six).

This is your basic presentation structural guide. You may vary it as you wish, according to the size of the problem. Present it in as much or as little detail as you think fits the situation best.

As pointed out previously, this is not a method for machines or robots, but for you as a thinking, wanting, mentally active individual. This is a guide, a specific method that works, that will prove its value for you. But using it and applying it is entirely up to you.

One might liken it to playing the piano. You are provided with the instrument and the method by which you can positively learn to play the piano. But *you* must practice in order to learn. No one else can do your practicing for you.

There's one vital difference in the comparison. Special personal talents are necessary to play a musical instrument brilliantly. It's not so in producing ideas. You can formulate excellent, usable, profitable ideas consistently by learning, practicing and applying the six-step creative method. You don't have to be a genius. That's proved by the fact that there are very few geniuses in the world, but many successful creative men and women.

Delineating the Presentation

Here's how you go about co-ordinating your presentation:

A. Analysis

Usually you'll cover briefly, or in detail, the phases of your analysis of the problem in step two, leading to the goal. Or, you may set down your analysis conclusion directly.

In the case of the detergent problem, in my presentation I noted the "why" and the "ways to accomplish this," leading to the "goal—create a dramatically visible and demonstrable idea for the product which would prove a profitable commercial success."

B. Facts

In this section, you set down the most important basic facts which emerged from your fact-finding studies and procedures. Touch on these lightly, or in depth, depending on the scope of the problem and the interest and patience of your audience.

In the case of the detergent presentation, I spotlighted the principal basic facts noted previously, thus building a solid foundation of understanding for the new ideas which would emerge.

C. Review of ideas

Now you come to the creative ideas which you listed in step six. In some cases, you'll cover only those which you had noted as Excellent. Sometimes you'll find it effective to run over all the ideas, even Not Usable. This often serves to establish, and to impress on others, the scope and depth of your thinking.

When you show ideas you've discarded, and explain why, you will have answered many questions, in effect, before they're asked. This is always an impressive gain.

In the case of the detergent, I included all the Excellent ideas in the presentation, a half-dozen of the Worthy ideas, and also touched very briefly on three in the Not Usable category. This provided specific evidence that the problem had been covered from a great many aspects. The scope and depth of the investigation and the probing and conclusions were complimented and appreciated by the people who had to be sold.

D. Idea recommendation

Finally you present your idea recommendations, with the confidence and enthusiasm that come from all the knowledge you've gained before producing them. Don't be apologetic. The exhaustive groundwork you've put into the construction of the idea eliminates any need or reason for apologies, since your sound proposals are anything but inadequate.

The analysis, facts and assessment of other ideas, which you have covered in the course of the presentation, produce the assurance that the ideas can prove usable, productive and profitable. You say so specifically, linking back to the facts point by point in most cases.

In the detergent presentation, I referred again to what comparable products, and examples in other fields, had done successfully. This provided sound and specific evidence that the new ideas recommended should prove even more successful. As I noted before, the ideas and the presentation made the sale. This will happen for you also.

You can't always score perfectly in selling the presentation, or bringing your creative ideas to a successful conclusion. There are too many imponderables involved, such as timing factors that you can't foresee or control, immediately availability of funds if needed to carry the idea to conclusion, and other points.

But the six-step method, and resultant A-B-C-D presentation, will score for you with a high batting average. It's a solace that not even the greatest hitter in the entire history of baseball batted .1000. Practically phenomenal averages were over .400; and anyone consistently hitting one out of three in the game (and in most fields of endeavor) is considered an extraordinarily successful individual.

The Success-Making Consideration

The big point in which you can have confidence that you'll be successful in putting across your creative ideas is this: the six-step method prepares you thoroughly.

You know the answers to the probable questions of others before they're asked. Why? Because you've already put the questions to yourself in the course of pursuing the method.

You have considered the negatives beforehand, along with double-checking and triple-checking the positives. All this took place before you put together the presentation either on paper or in your head.

You have answered and overcome the negatives in the course of your orderly, careful, progressive creative thinking.

Because you know the facts, pro and con, you're sure that your ideas are sound and can be successful. Don't let people tell you that your ideas won't work if the *facts* proved during the six-step creative method tell you that they will function successfully.

Keep Following Through

If your ideas are not accepted at first presentation and you're sure they're right, keep following through. Like Hammett, with any of his excellent stories which at first were rejected, he'd send them to another editor, then another and still another.

This masterful creative author told me that, in his early writing days, he had a list of over twenty editors of magazines where he thought his work might be used. He said that after a story was rejected by the entire list, he'd start it on its rounds all over again.

That's how he sold the story mentioned before, and many others. His advice, repeated often to writers, and a good point for every creative person to remember in any kind of endeavor, was, "A story can never make a sale while it sits in a desk drawer. Get that manuscript (and idea) out making the rounds. You'll be surprised at how often you make a sale the second time around, even the third."

It is reported that Westinghouse invented and completed his air brake while still in his twenties. But it didn't become a success and achieve recognition as a great and needed invention until more than a decade later. Lest you become discouraged, realize that even with so extraordinary and so valuable an idea, this creative genius had to fight over ten years to win the approval and usage for his idea that it deserved so richly, and even so obviously.

After you devise a worthy idea, produced on a sound foundation, checked and rechecked through the six-step method, and presented as suggested here, fight for its usage and acceptance as much as necessary to achieve recognition and approval for it.

Present Your Ideas Creatively

One of the most important points in putting over a creative idea is to emphasize the "you factor" throughout. That is, concentrate on the benefits for the "you"—the person you're addressing. Remember that "an egotist is a person who is always me-deep in conversation."

If you're proposing a new creative idea to your club or organization, show exactly how it will help "you, the members of the club." If it's a recommendation to the P.T.A. or school authorities, accent the gains for "you, the parents and teachers of the children." If it's a business idea, spotlight the "profits for you, for your business."

Use creative devices to dramatize the benefits for "you." Even if the idea is small in scope, it usually pays to write it out, in a few words and pages, and show it in a loose-leaf binder.

In the case of the detergent ideas, I used a large easel binder, with just a few words lettered in large print on each page. As I talked, the group before me concentrated on the large words or pictures, about which I built the particular point involved at that stage.

Sometimes you can capture the essence of your idea by making a single chart or diagram on a large card. By holding up and referring repeatedly to the card, you communicate better to others the specific merits of your idea, and thus help them to understand, to recognize its benefits and approve it.

The advantage of a little extra creative "showmanship" were demonstrated very specifically for me by participation year after year as one of the teachers of a creative writing course conducted at New York University by the Mystery Writers of America. The professional members, including some of the leading writers of mysteries, were (and are) the instructors.

Some of the outstanding authors could not get their ideas over to the bright students, who ranged in age from the teens into the seventies. The reason was that they hadn't prepared their material properly. Instead, they presented their points in rambling, disorganized fashion. Thus, they couldn't put across their valuable suggestions with the impact and clarity they deserved.

The most successful author-teachers, most able in "selling" their ideas to the students, and thus providing the most specific help, were those who had prepared well. They illustrated their lessons with anecdotes, examples, actual case histories and exhibits.

In teaching the subject assigned to me, "How to Plot a Story," I outlined my ideas on paper. Then I illustrated each point with simple sketches that I drew myself. I bound the sheets in a large loose-leaf book with an easel back. As I talked, I turned page after page, each picture focusing attention and aiding understanding of one step after another in plotting a story.

Because this presentation went over so well, I was asked to tackle another subject later in the course, "Building Suspense." Here again, once I had outlined my ideas, I decided to dramatize them for greatest value for the students.

Using one of my mystery novels as a case history, I charted the progress of the plot with a row of sketches connected by a rising and falling red line. This showed exactly how and where suspense was built to peaks in the book at specific intervals.

When I arrived at the class that night, in a large room at the university, I enlisted the aid of two students after I had introduced my subject. I had drawn my hieroglyphics on a hundred-foot roll of plain white shelving paper. As my helpers unrolled the paper, I attached the serpentlike sheet to the wall with short strips of cellophane tape.

The class was in an amused uproar as they saw the cartoon-like mural stretch along almost three sides of the classroom. Then, as I proceeded to delineate the building of suspense throughout a devious plot, I had my onlookers' attention every step of the way.

Keep it in mind—the fact that bright creative slants used in your presentations can help greatly to "sell" your creative ideas.

Modification Sometimes Makes the Sale

This is an important caution to every creative person: Don't be stubborn about having your ideas accepted without change, for "stubbornness is a symptom of hardening of the mind." If the slightest change would ruin your idea, then resist alteration and fight it, of course. But keep in mind that the whole concept of changing things is one of the basics of creative thinking.

If others suggest changes or modifications in your pet ideas, at least listen calmly, sensibly and judiciously. "Why not?" are two words that have proved to be great spurs to make a good idea even better. "Why not shorten this or lengthen that?" "Why not add another color or take one element away?" As Alexander Pope wrote, "An obstinate man does not hold opinions; but they hold him."

Knowing your idea thoroughly and confidently, by producing it through the progressive six-step method, you should be able to recognize readily any faults in modifications suggested by others. Thus, you can reject them politely but convincingly.

And, by the same token, you can realize the merits of valuable suggestions if you keep your mind open—the essence of the creative viewpoint. It pays to accept worthy modifications generously, and utilize your abilities to carry them even further. Such changes can make your good ideas even better.

In the specific case of the detergent idea, my recommendations had to be modified to set aside the change to a window on the front panel of the box. It was pointed out to me that this would be costly and impracticable at this time. I agreed, as this modification eliminated an element that would have delayed speedy introduction of the tricolor product.

Ask any successful creative person whether suggestions and changes from others have ever improved their ideas. You'll hear a uniform "yes." It's worth remembering that to modify often means to succeed in the follow-through and application of even the most perfect-seeming creative ideas.

We can profit from these words of Mark Twain, "The difference between perseverance and obstinacy is that one comes from a strong will and the other from a strong won't."

12

CREATING IDEAS BY TEAMWORK

Is effective creative thinking to produce successful ideas entirely a function of you, the individual? Or, in this modern day of the large business and the huge organization, is "group thinking" the best way to create valuable productive ideas?

The answer is not, and need not be, either one or the other exclusively.

What we're concerned about in this book is to help you achieve the most gainful results for you, the individual, whether you're a businessman, housewife, student, professional person, whatever your vocation or avocation. And every word in this volume is written toward that end, to improve your creative powers, for your practicable benefit.

Therefore, be assured of this fact: The six-step creative method will help you produce more and better creative ideas both alone and with the assistance of or in co-operation with others.

Strike Sparks Off Other People

Examples of how you can improve your creative thinking and results with the help of others were shown in Chapter 7, through the question-and-answer approach explained in that section. By throwing questions about your problem at your wife or husband, friends, associates and others, you noted how you struck creative sparks that produced some helpful answers. (I recommend that you turn back and reread the paragraphs on the "Question-and-Answer Approach.")

In planning and writing this book, a considerable creative undertaking, the outline, principles, methods and words are my own. But I gained greatly at the beginning of the project, and at intervals throughout, by sessions with one, two or three of the bright people at the publishing house.

For instance, in discussing ideas for the volume, I stated at lunch with two editors that I was not aiming to aid the natural-born "creative genius" (count them on the fingers of very few hands). My targets, I emphasized, were average and above-average men, women and young people in every walk of life.

One of the editors responded immediately, "Sure, you're telling a man, in effect, 'If you're a plumber, you can go further and get more out of your work and out of life by being a *creative* plumber!' "

That spark struck and built a fire in my mind that burned throughout the writing of this book. I was able better to concentrate on detailing the method most clearly and simply, so it would be of the quickest, surest and greatest aid in helping each reader to make the most of his creative powers in his personal area, just as it could help the plumber to be a creative plumber.

In other ways, too, my creative thinking about the book was deepened and broadened by chats and conferences with the alert publishing experts. Ideas about provocative puzzlers, for example, were inspired and improved by their comments. And, in explaining facets of the creative method for them, I was then able to delineate the basic format most understandably for you. Also, by seeking out leading creative men and women, and discussing the subject with them, I added to my mass of notes and research material for this volume.

Keep in mind that discussion with others can expand your creative efforts and ideas, rather than limit or thwart them. Your good sense will help you to discard the unfounded negatives and the negators whose first reaction invariably is, "It can't be done." You'll find that even the pessimists can be helpful if regarded thoughtfully. For, when you answer their "can't be done" with your explanation of how it *can* be done, you often clarify and improve your ideas for yourself.

So, beware of the automatic "no men" and those who profess knowledge without knowing anything about the subject (like the earlier example of the wealthy dowager who shouldn't have been consulted about packaged baby food). But do try to strike sparks off sharp, flinty minds whose reactions can help ignite your own thinking and ideas.

A leading research man, advising a group of eager young college men and women, told them, "Always expose yourself, as much as possible, to provocative and stimulating situations and people. It will stimulate your own thinking." That's good advice for creative improvement, whatever your age or pursuit, as I've advised repeatedly on these pages.

A successful writer pointed out that, like a machine, the creative part of the mind suffers from disuse and complete inertia. I've never heard of a hermit who became famous for his creative ideas. You needn't be gregarious, but you can gain from searching contact with others. Speak up; keep in mind the admonition: "It's natural for some people to be quiet—they have more to be quiet about."

The key point in benefiting the most from talks and meetings with others is to ask specific and provocative questions. And, as recommended so urgently heretofore, jot down notes of helpful and inspiring answers.

You needn't be like the man pictured in a cartoon, who at a lecture hammered at a portable typewriter on his lap, angered the people near him and explained apologetically, "I'm only taking notes."

If you'd seen me at lunch with my publishing associates, while this volume was being written, you'd have observed a small white card and pencil on the table, alongside my plate. On one side of the card, I'd written previously a list of key points and questions for discussion. On the other side, I jotted vital answers and comments as the luncheon and conversation progressed.

As a creative individual, make it a point to be many people in one. You're not just a thinker, but also an investigator, an evaluator, a creator, a doer. Just as you use the services of others—the grocer, the retailer, the carpenter—in your daily living, welcome the help of others in expanding and improving your creative thinking and ideas. Realize that you inevitably need the aid of others in carrying through even the greatest ideas, with or without modifications.

Do You Gain from Organized Group Thinking?

There's been a lot of talk, writing and controversy about the value of group thinking such as organized meetings sometimes referred to as "group brainstorming." If you should be involved in such sessions, you'll usually gain most by applying everything you've learned, in this book and elswhere, as a creative-thinking individual.

Group brainstorming is described by one of its proponents as "creative collaboration by groups . . . organized ideation by a number of people gathered together for that purpose . . . using the *brain* to *storm* a problem."

The usual procedure is to get a group together and have the members react to a problem by throwing in their "instant ideas," no matter how wild or woolly. The aim is toward quantity, not quality.

Part of the procedure is, to a degree, akin to your personal activities during step four, at the stage when you write down ideas, "sensible and seemingly wild." A vital, tremendous difference is that members of the brainstorming group have not preceded this phase by the all-important preparation of going through steps one, two and three thoroughly and carefully.

One of the nation's leading psychologists and experts in this field has stated flatly, after considerable study and testing, that worthy solutions to problems of some depth are "more likely to come from one person staring at the wall than from any group-think session."

Another noted educator and researcher studied many series of tests and experiments at one of the most highly regarded universities. He then reported that ideas produced at group sessions were far less valuable than those emanating from a similar number of persons of comparable intelligence when they worked separately. He referred both to quantity as well as quality of ideas.

An article concluded that, in repeated tests and comparisons, lone thinkers produced double the number of ideas per person, and more original and useful ideas, than the same number of people participating in group-think sessions. Other researchers report that "careful experimentation has tended to leave the results at about a draw." The proponents of brainstorming produce figures that show remarkable and superior results.

From a practical viewpoint, I'm concerned here about the increased creativity of you, the individual. Your very limited ability to gather a group when wanted makes the pros and cons of brainstorming relatively unimportant here.

It would be unfair for me to try to convey to you all the facets and evaluations here about group thinking, brainstorming, or whatever other label. Entire books have been written on the subject, and I recommend that you read them also. As a thinking creative individual, judge and decide for yourself.

I have participated personally in a number of so-called brainstorming sessions, not always through choice. In some cases, I've found it a waste of valuable time and mental energy. I've also noted that some sensitive, productive creative individuals become so upset by the brainstorming "group-processing" effect that their production of ideas has suffered for days and even weeks because they became so confused, angry and upset.

But I personally have gained at times from such meetings in this specific way that I recommend to you:

After leaving a brainstorming session, I then try to forget everything I've heard there. I approach the problem right from the beginning with the six-step creative method. At step four, I refer to any notes I made at the group meeting, and use those points to stimulate my own quantity flow of ideas. In this way

I have benefited specifically. I suggest that you utilize the same procedure to increase your production of valuable, usable ideas.

In short, if and when you're involved, consider group thinking or brainstorming as a tool to aid your individual creative thinking and production of ideas. To my knowledge, even the most enthusiastic backers of brainstorming do not advocate it as a substitute for individual, original creative effort.

No matter what is produced by a group, it finally is up to some individual to bring the findings to a culmination point, for "the great works of the world always begin with one person." There's little question that even this can be done best by the alert and trained creative person. Be yourself, don't succumb to doing it the "herd" way.

Thus, in respect to group thinking, the ability to think creatively can be of great value to you, and of benefit in your work with others, whatever the session's concern, whether a women's committee's problems, or big business or any other activities.

At this point, I recommend that you "brain-prod" yourself by exercising your brain muscles, either in solitary or in the company of others, with the following activating puzzlers:

Five Brain-Prod Puzzlers

(Solutions begin on page 254.)

1. How Start a Fire? How could you start a fire just by using one or more of the pictured objects? No, you can't add matches or kerosene or other combustible materials.

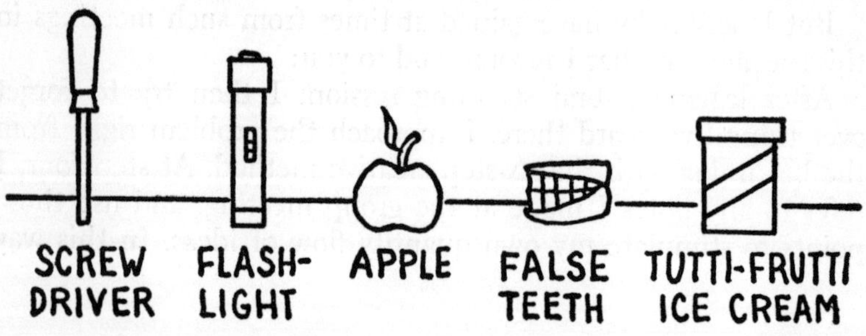

2. How Cut the Pie? How can you cut this pie into eight pieces by making only three cuts? You're not permitted to cut the pie in half and then put the pieces atop one another before making the next cut.

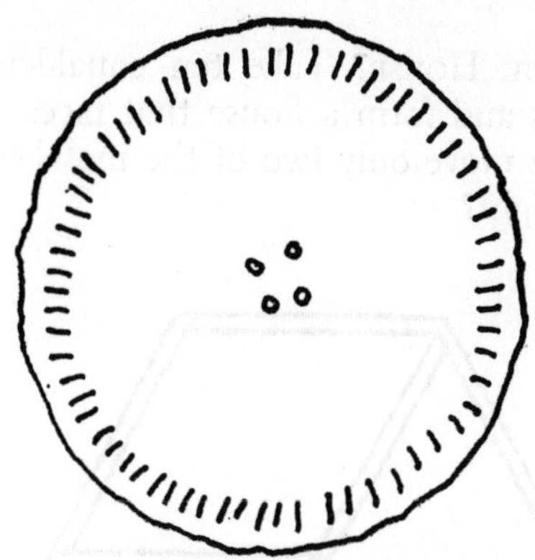

3. How Arrange the Diamonds? A wealthy lady brought seventeen large, loose diamonds to a jeweler

and instructed him to arrange them in a pendant so you could count nine diamonds in six different ways, either in straight lines or in lines at right angles to each other. How did he arrange the diamonds?

4. How Win the Coins? You're shown six coins arranged this way:

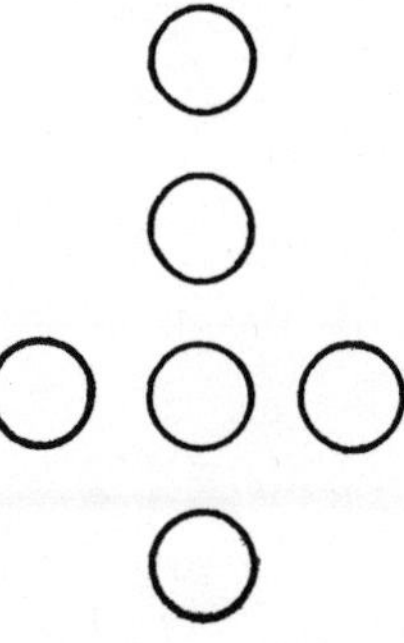

You're told that you can keep the coins if you move just one somewhere else to form two rows containing four coins each when added up either horizontally or vertically. What move would you make?

5. How Alter the House? Take ten equal-length matches, toothpicks or sticks and form a house that faces left, as shown here. Now, can you move only two of the matches to make the house face to the right?

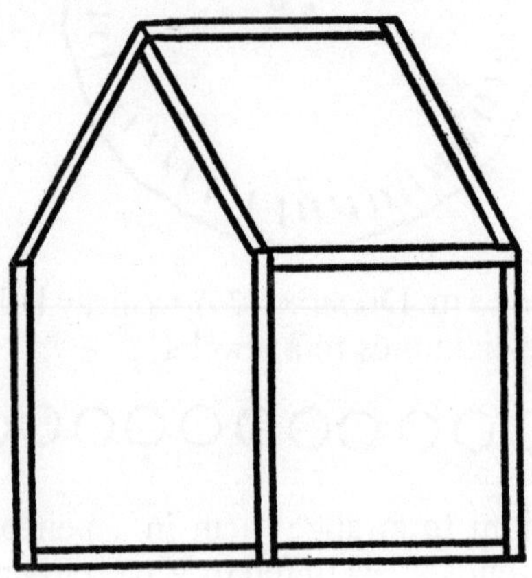

13

HOW TO USE WORDS CREATIVELY TO CONVEY CREATIVE IDEAS BEST

Here are the twenty-six basic tools available to you to convey your creative ideas:

a b c d e f g h i j k l m n o p q r s t u v w x y z

How you use the words formed from those twenty-six symbols can increase or decrease your chances of success conclusively when you try to sell your creative ideas to others. How can you use the words best?

An illustrative story is told about the exciting painter, Picasso. He was asked to write some words to explain his philosophy of art and his creative aims in painting. His comments were to accompany the reproductions of some of his paintings in a book.

Month after month, the editor kept after the artist to write his comments. Picasso refused. Finally, with the printing deadline near, the editor begged for a few paragraphs, even for several sentences.

Exasperated, Picasso drew the alphabet large on sheets of paper and told the editor, in effect, "Here's the alphabet. Make up your own words about my paintings, using these letters."

In desperation, the publisher finally printed the book without any words by Picasso. But the volume reproduced the beautifully artistic alphabet letters which the genius had drawn, along with the story retold here. Obviously, the painter felt that his pictures spoke for themselves; he didn't need words to explain them to anyone.

However, with your creative ideas, the words you use can help make the big difference in whether people understand them and "buy" them, or not. That doesn't mean the words you use should be grandiose or of high literary quality. But they should be specific, simple, clear, precise.

This point is highly significant as it may apply to you. When I taught advanced retail advertising writing at New York University in the evenings, I found one dominant fault among students ranging in age from the teens into the sixties. In practically all cases, the sentence structure and word usage were complicated and involved. It took week after week of rewriting, and rewriting again, to produce simple, effective creative writing.

Ernest Hemingway was one of the most highly respected of American novelists, yet the words he liked best and used most were short, pithy words such as "true," "good," "straight." The fact that he used them explicitly made them strikingly effective.

Using words to convey your meaning most precisely and vividly is actually using them creatively. Researchers at a California university stated specifically that the able use of words, and a wide vocabulary, are closely related to much successful creative work.

A leading essayist wrote, "Versatility in the use of words is not a social grace, it is creative." Hunt for, refine, decide on just the right word. Careful use of words conveys and clarifies creative ideas best.

Take Time with Your Choice of Words

A man or woman rises to present an idea to a group—in a home, a club meeting, a business group, wherever. He'll start by saying perhaps that he has a "fantastic" idea, that every phase of the plan is "fantastic," that results will be "fantastic."

You've heard people talk like that. And you know that they're most unbelievable and unconvincing. For, if even the smallest detail is "fantastic" or "fabulous" or "stupendous" or "terrific," then nothing about the whole is truly and believably fantastic in the full dramatic meaning of the word.

Consider, as an example, a headline for a poster for National Library Week which would reproduce the twenty-six letters of the alphabet and then state: "Your public library has these [letters] arranged in ways that are fantastic, fabulous, stupendous, terrific."

Reading that line, you'd probably shrug and remain totally unimpressed. You've read words, but without any penetrating meaning. Note the difference in this line actually used for National Library Week, under a reproduction of the letters of the alphabet: "Your public library has these [letters] arranged in ways that make you cry, giggle, love, wonder, ponder and understand."

These words arouse you; they're explicit action words, picture words, "words with muscles" that hit you with forceful, driving impact.

As further substantiation of the power of words used most effectively, the message went on to say, "It's astonishing what those twenty-six little marks [letters of the alphabet] can do. In Shakespeare's hands they became *Hamlet*. Mark Twain wound them into *Huckleberry Finn*. James Joyce twisted them into *Ulysses*. Gibbon pounded them into *The Decline and Fall of the Roman Empire*. Milton shaped them into *Paradise Lost*. Einstein added some numbers and signs and they formed "*The General Theory of Relativity* . . ."

You may be saying, "Great, but I'm not an author . . ." You don't have to be to harness the power of words most effectively to convey the clearest meanings of your creative thinking and ideas.

Your primary rule should be to use words best by choosing them carefully. Take a little extra time to check back after you've written out each creative idea and its explanation. Ask yourself, "Can I use a word that carries forward my meaning more precisely and forcefully here, there, there?"

For example, a "wonderful invention" is vague and general, not very meaningful to you as an individual. But a "money-saving invention" does excite your interest because it offers you a precise and desirable benefit. You want to know immediately, "How will it save money for me?"

The point was proved again in a test of packages of a product for the home. Different groups of women were offered identical packages, all at the same price, but one was labeled "Economy Size," another marked "Giant Size" and a third identified as "Money-Saver Size." The overwhelming majority of shoppers went for the "Money-Saver Size" because it conveyed the promise of the most specific benefit for them.

Precise Words Multiply Gains Enormously

How would you describe very large strawberries most effectively to gain the greatest number of sales, if you were trying to sell them, just as you try to sell your creative ideas?

A leading nursery offered exceptional strawberry plants by mail, describing the fruit as "Giant Size." Sales seemed satisfactory. I was involved in this case and wasn't at all satisfied with the description. I wanted to be specific, to create an irresistible picture of the strawberries in the minds of prospective purchasers, through explicit words.

I asked, "How big are the strawberries actually? Are they as big as cherries? As peaches? As plums?" As a result of actual comparisons, the choice species was offered as "Plum-Size Strawberries." Just the change of two words multiplied sales many times over—immediately.

Similarly, I changed "Large-Size Gladiolus"—which grew five to six feet tall—into "Man-High Gladiolus." I suggested changing the description of a variety sold simply as "Everbearing Raspberries," which produced crops spring, summer and fall, to "Three-Season Raspberries." In each case, sales were doubled and tripled and more, by changing just two little words. (How potent, for example, can be just three little words, "I love you".)

A big point to realize is that, before the words were changed in these cases, many sales had been lost in effect because of unimaginative, unrevealing, inadequate descriptions. Similarly, your creative ideas may be badly weakened, and their effectiveness even overlooked almost entirely, if you don't use the most specific and meaningful words to describe them.

Know More Words . . . to Choose the Best

You needn't wonder or doubt whether a better vocabulary will help you to greater success with your creative ideas. Reports of research and testing involving well over a quarter-million persons prove the benefits of increasing your vocabulary. That's true in spite of the claim by a comedian that "a synonym is a word you use when you can't spell the other word."

The records show conclusively that in tests including many different types of workers, along with college and high-school students, knowing the precise meanings of a greater number of words has proved to be a leading factor in helping persons to produce outstanding successes in the business world. The same was revealed in helping individuals to advance in other daily pursuits, as well as in schools and higher institutions of learning.

Close to the top in the list of factors contributing to success is "the ability to understand and use more words," as reported by other studies. In rating various groups of workers in respect to vocabulary, those who were highest in position and earnings also scored highest in being able to identify, explain and use more words more precisely.

In fact, the highest earners and highest scorers achieved ratings up to three times as great as those in the lower positions. Yet the scoring was not related to educational background as much as to acquired knowledge. In a special analysis of a group of executives, it turned out that those who had a formal high-school education or less averaged as high as a comparable number of leaders who were college graduates.

The excellent, intensive studies proved these three points of vital importance to every creative-minded person:

1. Those persons with the largest vocabularies were almost invariably the most successful, regardless of formal education.

2. It's quite possible, without great difficulty, to improve your vocabulary in not too long a time, by study, application—and by caring.

3. With an improved vocabulary, chances to achieve greater success are considerably multiplied.

Similarly, there's no question that a better vocabulary, and precise use of exactly the right word to convey the thought most explicity, can improve your chances for greater success with your creative ideas.

How to Improve Your Vocabulary

Here are some specific tips to study and follow, in order to improve your vocabulary:

1. Don't pass by a word that you don't understand, in whatever you're reading—book, magazine, newspapers, pamphlets or other literature. Jot down the word before you continue, for investigation later.

2. Look up in the dictionary any word whose precise meaning you're not exactly sure about. You'll usually gain not only a clearer understanding of the word but also extra definitions of it. They, in turn, often lead to ideas about new ways to use the word.

3. Concentrate on the meaning of the word, as delineated by the dictionary definition, so that you fasten its exact import in your mind for future use. Just a glance in the reference book isn't enough to assure remembering.

4. Study other words used in the dictionary description of the one you've looked up. This will help to add anywhere from a few to ten or more words to your vocabulary, though you've only looked up one originally.

5. Look up the word in a thesaurus to familiarize yourself with other words related to it. Thus you add more words, meanings and shades of differences to your vocabulary.

By this simple, painless and absorbing method, you'll expand your vocabulary gradually but surely. You can be certain that you'll increase your knowledge and range of words by this system. Repeated testing has proved that similar procedures have boosted individuals from low grades to high scores in vocabulary knowledge.

How to Use Words Best

Here are basic guides for using words most effectively to convey your creative ideas most clearly and convincingly:

1. Consciously choose the precise word that will reveal your meaning most swiftly and clearly. Don't use a key word just because it comes to mind first. It's worth a bit of extra thought and concentration to find a better word, a more specific "word with muscles."

2. Choose the simplest word if there are several possibilities to express your meaning. Long words usually take longer for the reader or listener to untangle. But don't discard a word just because it's long if it expresses the exact shade of meaning you wish to convey.

3. Seek out words that make pictures, whenever possible. "Plum-Size strawberry," for example, instantly makes a picture in the mind of a big, plump, delicious strawberry—you can almost taste its sweet, tangy juices.

4. Don't hesitate to employ slang words and expressions where they fit precisely and picturesquely. In describing a food, for instance, you might tell more about its hearty nourishment when you say, "it puts meat on your bones," than with a paragraph of analytical details. Similarly, while you're usually clearer when you're being grammatical, allow yourself to use an ungrammatical phrase or construction if you feel that it will help your audience to understand and absorb the point more readily.

5. Use rare and complicated words with discretion. If a long, unusual or little-used word is the only one that expresses your meaning exactly, by all means use it. But if it will cause your audience to concentrate on the word, rather than on your thought, it's usually wiser to replace it with a simpler, more quickly understood word.

6. Use repetition when it hammers in your point more quickly and firmly. For instance, the amateur author usually takes great pains to seek out substitutes for "said," rather than to repeat it, even when that swift small word serves best. But professionals, like the great O. Henry, have used "said" repetitively, unless

shades of meaning were expressed more precisely by more dramatic and picturesque verbs, such as "cried," "wailed," "groaned," "snarled."

Also, don't hesitate to use the same word twice in a sentence or paragraph if it then becomes twice as expressive (there—I used "twice" twice in the same sentence, and I'm glad).

7. Use as few words as possible to express your thoughts and meanings. "You can't see the forest for the trees" might well be amended to, "You can't see the meaning for the words." Cut out excess words, as much as possible, to make a clearing for your creative thoughts and ideas. You'll be helping others to "see through" to the meat of your ideas most quickly and easily.

Consider the following business letter, which is a too common example of overwriting:

> Regarding your letter of August 19th, please be advised that we have looked into the matter and have taken steps to rectify the situation. You wrote in your letter that the three cases of materials which you had ordered had not yet been received. We checked carefully and found that the order had been inadvertently delayed but was shipped yesterday. We trust that this will be satisfactory to you, and we thank you again for your order and look forward to serving you further in the future.

By chopping out wasted words, the same facts could have been conveyed this simply:

> Referring to your Aug. 19th letter, your order was shipped yesterday. Thank you for past and future orders.

Note how the reader has to wade through a swamp of words in the first letter to get to the meaning. The same message is conveyed quickly and clearly in the second letter, via just two short sentences.

Comparing this example to the exposition of one of your creative ideas, realize how much more quickly and clearly the other person would "get the idea" when expressed with simple brevity, as in the second, short, but far more meaningful, letter. So often it's true that the fewer the words, the greater the understanding.

Always Reread for a Clearer Second Look

Not only creative people in general, but even experienced writers, produce peculiar inverted sentences with laughable results. A rereading, a second look, is essential to make certain that each sentence is clear and true, exactly as you mean it. You don't want to be caught in any amusing mixed-up meanings like these, culled from actual lines that have appeared in print:

"Wanted: a woman to wash, iron and milk two cows."

"I saw a man digging a well with a large nose."

"Wanted: a room by two gentlemen 30 feet long and 30 feet wide."

These twisted sentences are exaggerations, of course, but they illustrate a significant point to keep in mind.

Break Rules, if Need Be

As I've warned repeatedly throughout these pages, beware of obviously "classy" language when talking or writing about your creative ideas, in conveying them to others. Your words should be used to express your meaning, not to bedazzle and impress others with your knowledge.

And don't worry or let hidebound rules get in the way of your clear expression.

The story is told about a high military official in the Pentagon who sent around a memo including a sentence such as, "Remember the exit you must go to." Some anonymous subordinate returned the memo with that sentence circled, and a line added, "Never end a sentence with a preposition." The irate official immediately dispatched another memo which described the incident and ended, "This is the kind of impudence up with which I will not put."

I keep recalling this story to myself as a reminder to break the rules if necessary, and to concentrate on choosing and using the precise words, phrases and sentences that will be most understandable and convincing to my audience. I urge you to remember this also, and to make a pact with yourself that fuzzy or pretentious words and phrases are the important things "up with which you will not put."

Warning: Don't Waste Words!

At one stage early in my writing career, I received a small printed sign from the local authorities, during a drought period. The card read, "Don't Waste Water!" We were requested to attach the sign over the kitchen sink. Later, I tacked the little card on the wall next to my desk, after changing a word so that it read, "Don't Waste Words!"

This sign served as a constant warning and aid to me in my writing. It continually reminded me to leave out and then go back and cross out any unnecessary and therefore "waste" words.

Words are the precious stones you use to formulate the jewels that are your creative ideas. Don't squander a single valuable word, lest your meanings become obscured and your worthy creative ideas lost in a confused welter of phrases and constructions.

Strive to say it simply, precisely, accurately—and you'll usually say it well. When you've finished writing up each creative idea, go back and check each line against the seven basic guides to "how to use words best."

Then revise and rewrite accordingly, if necessary. This action may make the difference between success and failure in "selling" your bright creative ideas.

Napoleon is reputed to have said that you can "rule men with words." It is certainly true that you can influence others to approve and accept your worthy creative ideas more readily when conveyed through the clearest, most expressive words.

Five Fun-With-Words Puzzlers

(Solutions begin on page 257.)

Playing with words, games with words, can help increase your vocabulary and your facility in using words most effectively. Here are some entertaining puzzlers that will also help stimulate your creative thinking and skill with words.

1. The Hidden Word. What three-syllable word is hidden in these letters?

2. Climb the Word Ladder. Here's how you climb the word ladder in five rungs, at left, from Love to Hate, changing only one letter per rung, forming a complete word at each rung.

Now, step up your creativity by climbing the ladder from Seed to Crop. Here are hints to help speed the verbal ascent:

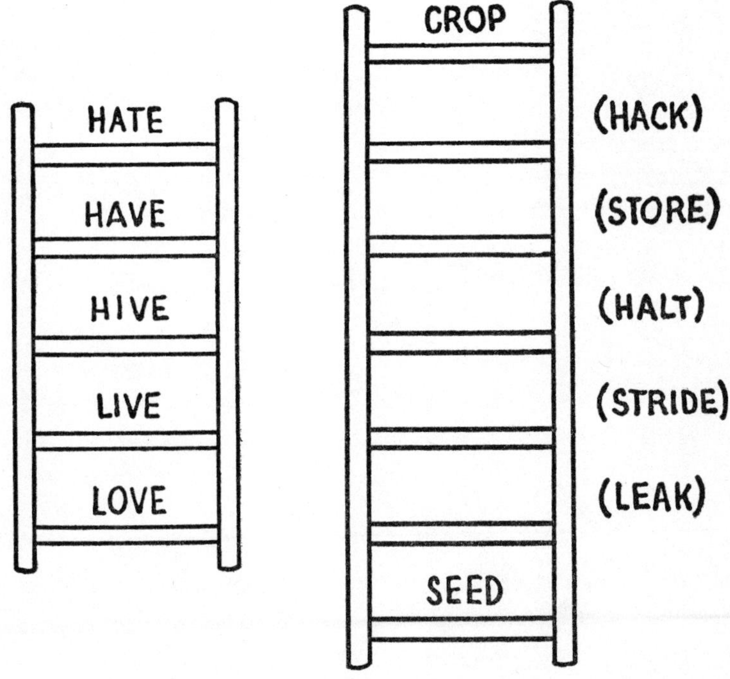

3. FIND THE PHRASE. This is tricky. What common five-word phrase is revealed by a study of this peculiar word: *Wether*.

4. PLACE THE PUNCTUATION. The following string of words doesn't make much sense without the proper punctuation. The challenge to you is to form these words into a clear sentence by adding commas and quotation marks, but not changing the position of a single word.

It was and I said not are and and and are are different.

5. MAKE A WORD GROW. "Ergro" is not a word. But you can make it grow into a word by adding three letters in front, and also the same three letters—in the same order—in back. Dig into this one to find the surprising solution.

14

HOW TO FIND UNLIMITED CREATIVE OPPORTUNITIES

You've probably noted an interesting series of advertisements in leading magazines which has as its theme the phrase: "Another creative solution to a problem."

One of the pages tells about a serious problem that was plaguing many manufacturers. The inside walls of the ordinary corrugated box were found to be abrasive, causing tiny scratches and scars to appear on merchandise such as refrigerators and furniture, while in transit. The advertisement states that a new container inside was developed that doesn't scratch, regardless of rough handling, even when shipped thousands of miles.

Credit for the solution is given by the huge industrial firm to creative thinking and action. Here's further evidence that the great value of creative thinking is recognized today more than ever before. Creative ideas are wanted, sought and paid for generously.

Such an attitude indicates an unlimited opportunity for you. The six-step creative method will help you to take advantage of the opportunities. In the case of the scratchproof cartons, for example, the progression was undoubtedly worked out according to stages such as specified by the method:

1. Problem approached with an alert, seeking, creative attitude.

2. Analysis revealed the wanted solution—a new, nonabrasive surface.

3. All available facts researched and examined thoroughly.
4. Many ideas set down toward the solution.
5. Facts and ideas simmering.
6. Best ideas evaluated, rechecked, final solution reached.

In this case, technical knowledge was an important factor, of course. But strictly technical skill and knowledge often lack the spark which ignites those basic assets into great ideas. The creative approach usually provides the essential spark.

You must exert sound creative thinking and produce the ideas which make the successful solution a reality. It's up to you to take the creative steps that will provide a continual series of small and large successes for you, as revealed by the examples that follow.

Making a Hobby Into a Career

An intelligent man felt restless and unfulfilled by the profession which occupied his days. What he did about it (this is a meaningful case history for you, regardless of the nature of your creative problem) is charted by the six-step method:

1. He decided to do something about his situation. Instead of complaining about his lot, he adopted the progressive, searching creative attitude.

2. Analysis revealed that he'd like to spend his time working with books, as he had found that collecting rare books was a most satisfying hobby.

3. He studied all the phases of book publishing and selling, collected the facts.

4. He wrote down many ideas, even those that seemed wild.

5. The facts and ideas simmered in his mind, as he continued with his daily occupation.

6. He arrived at a unique creative idea, to publish small limited editions of books long out of print, some of them even centuries old. He tracked down books available only in one or two copies anywhere in the world, worth thousands of dollars each, but whose contents were wanted by hundreds of libraries and individuals. He'd get permission to reprint such a book, then pro-

duce whatever number would fill the demand, only a few dozen or hundreds of copies, varying in each instance.

Then he charged as much as necessary per volume to provide a profit, ten dollars to a hundred or more per book. He gave up his profession entirely as his unique publishing venture became a successful business. The change amply satisfied his desire for a new, more rewarding way of life.

This case history is significant beyond its interest as a creative success story. It's only one example of how others have advanced and improved their lives through creative thinking.

How Others Achieved Success

Similarly, an active-minded woman whose children had grown up and left her with little to do started collecting antiques and eventually established a rewarding antique shop. (She did *not* put up the sign: "We buy old furniture—we sell antiques.")

A man who was dissatisfied with his sales job in a sizable firm approached his problem creatively. Self-analysis revealed his special interest in finance. He enrolled in selected courses, gained specific knowledge. Then he advanced some creative ideas about accounting systems which won him a job in the financial division of the firm. Later he became the assistant treasurer and ultimately the treasurer of the company. He told me, "I credit my entire success to my first switch from hopeless bellyaching to energetic creative thinking."

A man with a small bakery shop developed an ingenious creative idea with an amusing reverse twist. He had noticed the sign in doughnut shops (you've probably seen it) which read:

> As you journey through life,
> Let this be your goal—
> Keep your eye on the doughnut,
> And not on the hole.

However, thinking creatively, the baker fixed his eye on the hole rather than on the doughnut. He cooked the doughnut centers and offered his customers "Delicious Doughnut Holes."

People were interested, tried them, came back for more. Aided by other similar bright ideas, the little bakery shop grew into a big business.

An enterprising woman who enjoyed gardening was seeking more activities. She belonged to a small, disorganized garden club. I advised her how to think creatively. Using the six-step method, she and her friends came up with so many bright ideas that the club became a beehive of interest and activity. As the new president of the club, this woman now says enthusiastically that she never enjoyed her days so much, and she gives the credit to creative thinking.

Whether your interest is in changing or advancing your career, business, daily activities, or just in making your hours more interesting and productive, creative thinking as recommended and illustrated in this book can help you.

The World Wants Creative Ideas

Here are just a few of the creative ideas, and activities growing from alert creative thinking, which have won success and many benefits for people in many walks of life. Demosthenes said that "small opportunities may be the beginnings of great enterprises." These examples may prove of inspiration and aid to you:

A woman converted her station wagon into a "Bookmobile," establishing a book rental library on wheels. She added considerably to the family income, along with new interest for herself.

A creative-minded operator of a drive-in movie theater installed a laundromat so that women could have their laundry done while they watched the film. Income went up both at the box office and at the washing machines.

A camera hobbyist started shooting portraits and action photographs of children in their homes, added photographs at weddings and movie camera action shots of golfers, which he sold to them so they could study and improve their swings. Soon he had a thriving business which was more fun and more profitable than his job.

An ex-secretary with a few hours to spare each day recruited other housewives like herself. She established a "part-time office help" service which was profitable for all concerned.

The owner of a huge indoor auto parking building pulled more customers by inviting patrons to set a three-minute timer alarm clock when they called for their cars. If the bell rang before the car was delivered, the parking would be free.

A pair of creative-minded teen-agers popped up with a unique summertime money-making idea which was a big hit. They offered a pre-party pest-control service. They were in great demand for spraying premises right before a big outdoor lawn, barbecue or cocktail party, so that pesky insects (not of the human variety) would stay away.

A talented young couple increased their income with a gift-wrapping service, using their creative ideas for decorations that were the talk of every party.

A florist attracted more customers in other cities by sending them a color snapshot of the bouquets they'd ordered by wire, as proof of his artistry. Their word-of-mouth advertising boosted his business.

These are just a few examples of how others profited in daily activities through creative thinking, as you can do also if you're so minded.

The Brightest Ideas Are Still to Come

If you should have the impression that all the bright ideas have been used up, note just a few here, most of them familiar to you. These are innovations in fields which some people thought provided little opportunity for new twists and developments.

Gift decanters and special factory wrappings to boost liquor business at Christmas.

Parking meters to provide more parking spaces and increase community income.

Belts made more comfortable by combining leather with elastic materials.

Nail polish that doesn't just cover, but also glitters, glows, "frosts" the nail surface.

Deodorants not only in jars and bottles, but in sticks, roll-ons, sprays and mists. (What's next?)

Shoes with elasticized inserts for easier fit; laceless, backless, toeless.

Huge, colorful playing cards for just admiring, or for use in constructing paper buildings—as a new kind of toy.

Serving made easier by revolving trays, tiny to table size, even built into the table.

A "heartbeat comforter" for the young baby's room, that makes a low heartbeat sound like mother's, and helps keep infants from crying.

Garden plants in peat pots which combine with the earth when planted.

Electrified wire mesh under a driveway surface which can be heated to melt snow as soon as it falls.

Sunglasses made glamorous by jewel-like stones, painted decorations and flaring designs.

Complete concentrated liquid meal in a can, for reducing or quick eating.

Pressed-powder compacts providing face powder and cream combined in one product.

A towel-pole that stretches from floor to ceiling, for space-saving in the bathroom.

Sandals with a built-in arch lift for flat-footed pedestrians.

Insulated plastic tumblers to keep icy drinks cold longer, and no freezing the fingers.

Mood-lighting switches that control light gradually from dark to bright, instead of just on and off.

Nonfat frying pans with slick surfaces that eliminate the need for butter or any grease.

A two-compartment cake decorator bag, so you can put two different icings or other toppings on cakes and cookies.

Impregnated shelving paper and specially treated floor waxes that also kill bugs.

A wrist watch with six changeable cases in color to match the clothes you're wearing.

The list of ingenious inventions that represent bright new creative ideas could go on almost endlessly. And, what about the opportunities ahead?

A research project turned up hundreds of "I wants" from people who were asked what product improvements they'd welcome. Among these were: no-burp baby nipples, electric vegetable peelers, spray-on product to make garbage odorless, no-spill coffee cans, eyeglasses with changeable color frames to match clothes, and even an "automatic bed-maker" (substitute for a wife?).

Where there's a need to be filled, there's an opportunity for a bright creative idea that will prove profitable for the creative thinker. A simple start is to list some needs now, and then create the ideas to fill them.

You now know the six-step creative method. What are you waiting for? Keep in mind that creativity is like a rifle, in that it can't shoot higher than it is aimed.

15

HOW CREATIVE POWER CAN HELP YOU TO GREATER SUCCESS AND A HAPPIER LIFE

One immediate gain is certain for you. If you've studied and practiced the six-step creative method as you've gone through this book, then you'll be a different person at the last page than you were at the first page. Because one big change derived from creative thinking is an immediate difference and improvement in one's mental attitude and outlook. You'll have a more alert, eager, searching viewpoint.

It has been affirmed again and again that, as a prominent educator has said, "Knowing the principles of creative thinking is a big step toward developing creativity." And, as you apply the progressive steps, you cannot help but improve and profit from your awakened and activated creative abilities.

A modern philosopher put it this way: "Education for creativity is nothing short of education for living." Another commented, "A person needs more than an aim in life: he has to have some ammunition to go with it."

A New Adventure in Living

Another noted educator writes that the creative person is one participating deeply "in the full, vigorous adventure of living." More leaders, discussing creativity in a symposium, list as its benefits for you "absorption," "intensity of consciousness," "peak experience," "fulfilling participation," "delight," "ecstasy."

And, above all, the "joy of creating ideas" was hailed repeatedly in the discussions of psychologists and professors and heads of great educational institutions, all meeting at a leading university. Creativity adds and multiplies when we share it with others.

A noted writer says, "There is nothing so exhilarating as the feeling that comes from discovering and creating something all your own, whether it is a song, a recipe, or a new twist to an old idea. Creativity is an inner resource that can be called on endlessly to enrich work and play. Imagination makes life continuously exciting and keeps us forever young."

Note well, in the days and years ahead, the value of your new creative spirit, knowledge and ability as an "inner resource" to make all your life more productive, joyous and fulfilling, helping to keep you "forever young." Arnold Bennett advised the use of "the creative effort as an antidote for worry . . . healthful exercise of imagination that drives out worry, promotes mental health."

And, from the viewpoint of monetary gain, a financial wizard said dryly, "The best way to raise your standard of living is to raise your standard of thinking."

Creativity Is an Ability, Not an Age

There are no age limitations on creativity. Note some of the great creative advances made by people in their youth:

Samuel Colt constructed his first models of new pistols at the age of seventeen.

Marconi first created a new system and transmitted signals without wires at twenty-one.

Louis Braille invented a method of printing for the blind at twenty (he had lost his sight due to an accident when he was three, and overcame this to become a benefactor to millions all over the world).

Jane Austen wrote *Pride and Prejudice* at twenty (and it took publishers sixteen years to "discover" its enduring merit—something to encourage you if your creative ideas are not always accepted at first presentation).

Jumping to creativity in later years:

Benjamin Franklin invented bifocals at seventy-eight, and other creative advances up to the age of eighty.

Robert Bunsen, who developed the Bunsen burner, scored his greatest creative achievements at twenty-six.

Alfred Tennyson wrote *Becket* at seventy-five.

Christian Pfaff, the great chemist, synthesized fumaric acid at seventy-two.

And, as an example of the lasting ability to be creative, Galileo started his discoveries of monumental advances at the age of seventeen, scored additional successes all through life, and produced the telescope at seventy-three.

One of my favorite stories, illustrating the value of creativity in helping to promote the spirit of youthfulness, concerns an incident with a progressive, creative businessman who was well into his sixties. I presented a new expansion plan to him. He examined it eagerly, was about to approve it. Then his face fell pessimistically into worn lines.

"I don't know," he sighed. "The proposition is very appealing, but I'm not as young as I used to be."

I said quietly, "You never were."

He frowned and asked, "What do you mean?"

"Even at eighteen," I explained, "you were never as young as you used to be at seventeen. At fifty, you were never as young as you used to be at forty-nine. Today, you're not as young as you used to be yesterday. But if you feel a moving creative spirit within you, then you're always young, at any age."

He straightened up, grinned, tapped the plan on his desk and said vigorously, "What are we waiting for? Let's go!"

As Charles Kettering said, "My interest is in the future, because that's where I'm going to spend the rest of my life."

Hard Work Produces Creative "Miracles"

A college president, an enthusiastic and energetic creative leader, said in an interview, "Work is fun, especially when you're part of something that is going somewhere." The essence of being creative is that you're advancing, going somewhere.

Another alert observer wrote that creativity is not just "an aptitude but an attitude, applicable to making a lemon pie or building a rocket." Combine the aptitude and the attitude with the correct creative procedures, hard work, discipline and persistence, and you can't help but produce creative successes.

Do you feel perhaps that you're overburdened already, saying, "I haven't the time?" An article about a woman who is a best-selling author and successful playwright states that she "holds down at least half a dozen full-time jobs, five of them boys."

Asked how she manages, she said, "I simply take first things first." That's exactly how you learn and succeed with the six-step creative method. As you approach each problem, you advance step by step to the ultimate, wanted solution and forward-moving result.

But you must work at it. You learn best by *doing*. As I said earlier, use this book as a "workshop course" where you produce ideas, not just read about them. That's how I started writing mystery stories; I took a workshop course with a successful author; I wrote a story for the course, then sold it to a magazine. I went on from there, writing and selling more stories, and then books on various subjects.

On the other hand, a young woman who took the same course at the same time never became a published author. She had talent and ability. But she lacked the industriousness to fill one page, and then another and another—actually putting words on paper. She was always "going to do it," but neither a publisher nor anyone else pays off on "going to."

As the vice-president of a large and demanding business organization, I am frequently asked how I also manage to write books, articles, stories, a weekly column in a publication. I usually reply with three simple words: "By doing it."

That's just part of creativity, of course, but a prime essential. I know (and you do, too) so many people who are "going to write a book," "going to redecorate the house," "going to streamline a routine." But the only way they can even begin to produce the creative success is "by doing it." Heed the advice of a leading statesman: "Now is the time for all good men to come to."

It's worth recalling frequently the pithy admonition, "He who rests on his laurels wears them on the wrong place." An editor said, "Putting off an easy thing makes it hard; putting off a hard thing makes it impossible."

You're never too young to win creative success by hard work and proper methodology. A young man in his teens learned the six-step method from me. While attending high school, he worked at the local supermarket. There he suggested creative ideas and put them into action, such as a huge combination display of cider and doughnuts which sold out both items in record time. When he graduated from high school, an executive of the huge chain approached him and asked him to take their managerial course, with the promise that he'd be made a store manager at a substantial salary before he was twenty. The executive said, "We want you because we can't find many men, young as you or much older, who combine a bright creative attitude and ability with the eagerness to work hard putting across their ideas."

The young man declined because he had determined to go on through college and become a doctor. I know that he'll apply his creative thinking just as industriously and effectively in medicine as in the supermarket.

Make a beginning, then follow through, and you'll agree with Genghis Khan that "it is the completion that gives the greatest value to an action." Use your spare time to perfect and put across your ideas, if necessary.

The Wright brothers earned their living by repairing bicycles and devoted their spare time to building the airplane which was their miraculous achievement. A woman who was raising a sizable family applied her spare hours in the greenhouse her husband built in his "spare time"; she started raising and selling exotic plants, and soon developed an enterprise so successful that it became a full-time thriving business for the couple.

One expert warns that creativity should not be considered "something you use only on Sundays." Work consistently at the exciting pursuit of creativity, and you cannot help but gain. A national business magazine states succinctly, "An effective creative thinker can often equal and surpass the achievement of a more brilliant person who lacks the technique."

The six-step method is a technique, a tool for you. But you must use it. Wanting to is the spark of all creativity. Socrates made the point truly: "Go your way and remember that when you want knowledge as much as you want air when you are under water, you will get it."

The Sky Is Not the Limit

With the advent of the space age, a humorist commented, "Anybody who still thinks the sky is the limit has no imagination."

There's no question that creativity is more highly regarded, wanted and honored than ever before. The president of an advertising agency stated in a magazine article, "Today, the creative man is king." The head of a television station, addressing a convention of broadcasters, said, "The key to our future success lies in ideas, creativity and courage. The great accomplishments of this country have started in the minds of individuals who dared to put their ideas into practice."

A national magazine, listing the abilities needed by a person to go to the top, features among the foremost needs "the ability to produce new ideas." A scientist affirmed, "Creativity can shape the milestones of history." A historian notes, "Creativity may be the outstanding characteristic of our age." A university head proclaimed, "The future of civilization depends on the quality of the creative thinking in the world during the years to come."

The great journalist Lincoln Steffens inspired thousands by stating repeatedly in his writings that nothing has been done quite so perfectly as it should be, and so, practically everything needs to be done over, and *better*. And the opportunities are greater than ever before, if you'll see them and seize them creatively.

The sales head of a large organization said that the primary aptitude he seeks in hiring and advancing a man is "creative salesmanship." Another affirms that the man who moves ahead is "not just an order-taker. He doesn't sell just merchandise; he sells ideas. He offers specialized treatment of the customers' problems—market research, promotion, merchandising and development services, all tailored creatively to the individual account."

The value of creative efforts continues to increase. A company head cites the results from various exhibits at trade shows. Comparing use of an ordinary, attractive booth, with a creative exhibit utilizing charts and motion—both costing about the same to construct—he reports over three times as many inquiries leading to sizable orders when the creative exhibit is used.

Another executive summed it up this way: "We have proved that creativity is a down-to-earth working tool, and there's nothing mysterious about it. But it's up to us to take advantage of it." He added, referring to the joys of being creative, and the individual inner gains, that "they say 'creativity is its own reward,' but it can be highly profitable as well."

Rechecking the Six-Step Method

When I finished the manuscript for this book, I asked a dozen top executives and leaders in business, organizational and community activities—women as well as men—to read it.

The reaction of one was typical of all: "That's exactly the way I think and work; I didn't realize that I went through these steps and progressions, yet that's just the way I do it."

All of these successful people said they were eager to buy copies of the book, for themselves and associates and friends so that they could read and reread. They realized the need to be refreshed constantly and helped by the method, as set down simply and clearly.

Many others could have written down these points. I've delineated them here for you, as well as for myself. I know surely that repeated restudy of the method as laid out here will help me in all my future creative thinking and development of productive ideas.

Creativity Is Always a Beginning

This six-step process is not the all or the end-all. It is a springboard, a beginning for your advancement and greater accomplishments, for your personal gain and for the benefits you can bring to others.

It is an enormous loss to the world and to the individual, I believe, as a company president said in an address, that innumerable men, women and youngsters "have never exercised what creative talents they may have unknowingly possessed." A leading novelist affirms that "what man can imagine, he may one day achieve," just as surely as that the space age is "the end result of man's first mad, unreasonable image of himself flying," going back to centuries ago.

I must emphasize once more the all-important point that the six-step creative method is a structure, a format to help you assert your own individuality and talents best. Rather than finding it restrictive, you will apply it to seek new truth and directions, avoiding any limitations of holding to the familiar or being confined to the commonplace. As Charles Kettering stated it: "A problem is not solved in a laboratory. It is solved in some fellow's head, and all the apparatus is to get his head turned around so he can see the thing right."

This method should aid you in developing your intellectual and practical possessions to the fullest. It will help you to make the most progress and gain the greatest benefits from your alert, energetic new creative thinking processes and the resultant creative ideas you produce.

As a creative person, you keep going forward. A seasoned research man writes, "The creative people I have worked with don't spend the rest of their lives staring in admiration at what they have done. On the contrary, once the problem is solved, they move on to something else."

One of the most renowned novelists said in an interview that the creative individual "has something to wake up to, every morning of his life, another chance." And, I add, another opportunity.

In discussing the overwhelming importance of arousing the creative spirit, especially in college students, a leading educator told his audience most fervently, "We must keep search alive . . . we must allow sensitivity to new ideas . . . we must not develop critical abilities to the point that anything unproven is stupid . . . we must not insist on conformity, or we will end with traditionalists rather than with innovators."

Take this caution for yourself. Keep your sense of search alive. Seek the fresh, the new, always probing for something better, a better way, a better result.

I asked a young-minded creative man in his late seventies what he considered the greatest reward of being creative. "I've thought about that for a long time," he replied thoughtfully, "and I know the answer. For me it's the feeling that each problem is a new challenge, a new excitement—that it's always the beginning."

The surging and constantly rewarding joy of greater creativity is before you. As poet John Godfrey Saxe wrote in about 1850:

> " 'Tis wise to learn; 'Tis God-like to create."

May your future creative thinking bring gratifying rewards and greatly increased happiness to you always.

SOLUTIONS TO MENTAL-EXERCISE PRACTICE PUZZLERS

CHAPTER 1. SOLUTIONS TO AVOID-THE-OBVIOUS PUZZLERS

1. One-Line Puzzler. The first obstacle to solving this puzzler is to analyze whether it's permitted to go beyond the outlines of the diagram. Reread the challenge. You'll find that each line in each box must be crossed once, but nothing has been said about restricting where the pencil line goes.

As you cross each line once, you're usually stumped by the need to cross at least one line a second time. Without this second crossing, it seems impossible to solve the puzzler. Yet, by using your creative imagination, you can find a way.

Check back and you'll note that nothing was stated to prevent you from going *through* a line—that is, following along the length of a line. By finding and following this extra dimension, the puzzle is readily solved, as shown here:

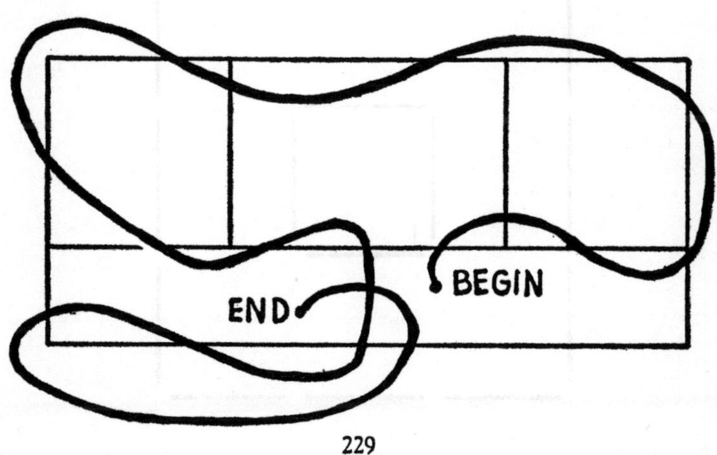

This puzzler makes a vital point: By studying and restudying a problem, noting the facts and then finding the hidden but permissible solution, you can solve many different problems in your normal activities—creatively. How to help find the hidden solution is made clear in the six-step method.

2. TANTALIZING-TOOTHPICKS PUZZLER. If you didn't solve this problem, don't be annoyed with yourself for not seeing one of the correct solutions, as shown here. The mind immediately leaps to the conclusion that the squares must be the same size, yet nothing was said about any such limitation. See how easily you form two squares, one large and one small, by removing eight matches.

If you limit yourself right at the start, with this and other problems, by accepting a mental block without question, you'll be passing up many creative solutions that are easily in your power.

Take the advice of a wit who suggested, "Beware of being like a blotter that soaks it all in, but gets it all backward."

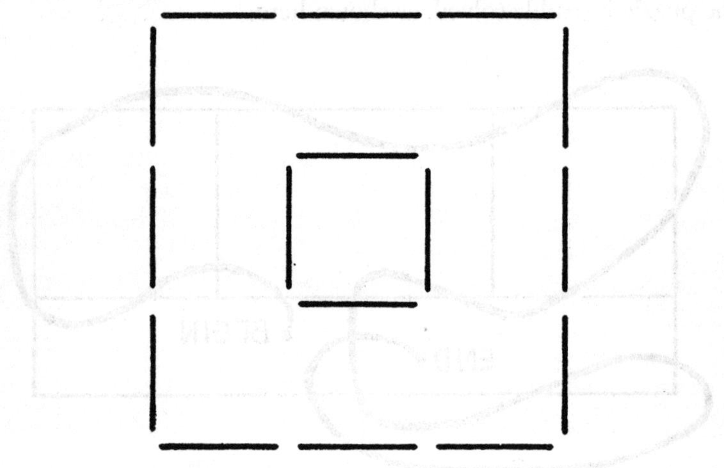

3. DIVIDE-AND-CONQUER. The shape is the clue to unlock this puzzler and reveal the answer. First, you must shrink the original shape to quarter-size. Then you can repeat it within the total area, using six of the matches, then adding two more, as shown. Thus, by repeating the same shape three more times within the boundaries, four equal areas are produced.

The obvious attempt by most people is to divide the space into squares or rectangles or triangles. The creative solution in this case is to study the unique shape and then visualize that it can be repeated four times within the allotted space.

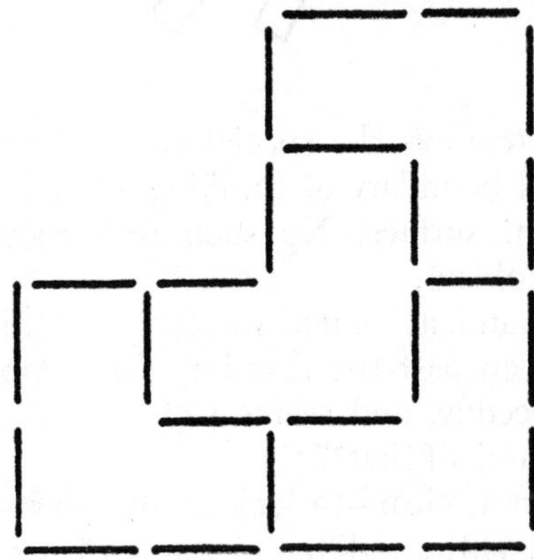

Here a combination of shrinking and then multiplying leads to the correct solution. You'll find that this can be an effective creative approach to help solve some problems in daily living. Instead of adding or expanding, it often pays to consider the military axiom "Divide and conquer."

You'll find applications of this approach as you learn the six-step method.

4. MATCH-MANEUVER PUZZLER. The solution seems so simple when you see it here. You just place three heads together as

shown, touching snugly. Then you pile the other three matches on *top* of those, with their heads meshed similarly. Thus, all six matches are touching every other match firmly.

The solution requires the special creative approach of going beyond the usual boundary of thinking—that the matches must all rest on a flat surface. No such restriction was stated in presenting the problem.

On the other hand, as soon as you free your mind of automatic restrictions, and go past the first impulsive approach, the solution is found speedily, and seems very obvious. You'll wonder, "Why didn't I think of that?"

The lesson here is clear—to seek a solution in another dimension, perhaps an entirely different angle of approach from the obvious one.

For instance, in simple comparative terms, it might well be that the first tunnel was created by an imaginative thinker who realized that he had to get to the other side of a mountain. He couldn't go over the mountain, as it was too steep. He couldn't go around the mountain because of distance and other obstacles. Instead of giving up, he found the creative solution—by tunneling through the mountain.

Simple? Elementary? Perhaps. But the tunneling solution was no less creative than the solution to this puzzler which stumps most people. Yet the answer involves nothing more than the imaginative approach of piling three of the matches on top of the others instead of keeping them all on the flat surface. It might be called a matter of *dimensional* thinking, which in itself is a tremendous creative advance.

Remember this creative approach in solving a problem. Seek out the extra dimension by trying to go above, below, around or through the physical or mental obstacles.

You'll find out in detail how to look for and find the extra dimension that often leads to the wanted solution as you study, learn and practice the six-step creative method.

5. IDENTIFY-THE-SHAPE. In the case described, only one creative man of all the executives at the meeting drew the correct round top within two minutes. Did you draw a circle, as shown here?

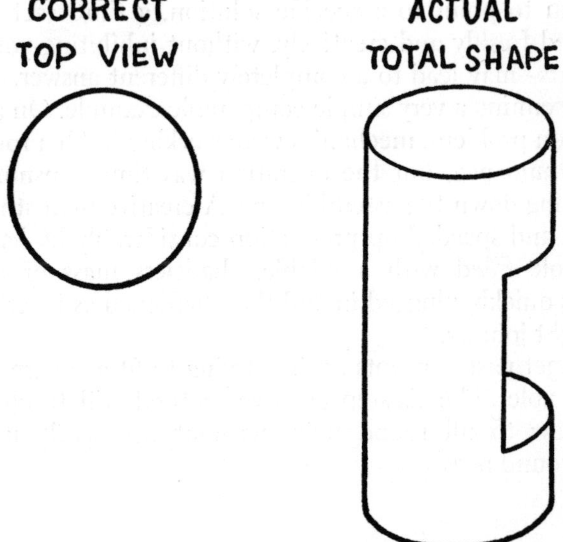

The important lesson to be learned in this instance is, once more, to keep your creative thinking from being blocked or led astray by preconceptions or nonexistent limitations. In this case, because the front and side diagrams of the shape are straight and sharp, the common reaction is that the top similarly must be square, rectangular or some other straight formation.

But, by freeing your thinking creatively, the solution that the object may well be a round, long, notched cylinder presents itself. All the clues were there in the presentation of the problem. The difficulty was to see them in their correct relationship.

As the chairman of the meeting then told his associates, in this example, "Let's free our minds of seeming limitations or obvious but incorrect blocks, and tackle the problem before us with open, inquiring, uninhibited minds."

It's worth remembering this as you seek creative solutions and ideas. In this problem, what may have looked square in two dimensions was actually round in another dimension. In solving a personal or business problem, realize that though two factors may seem to point to a specific solution, a third factor—to be considered freshly and creatively, without inhibiting yourself by precedents—may lead to a completely different answer.

Let's examine a very simple comparable example. On a factory production problem, mechanics were working to fill a round hole with a round peg, but the operation was time consuming and was slowing down the assembly line. A creative man studied the situation and speeded up production considerably by having the round hole filled with a pliable, shapeless mass of material. This was quickly plugged in and then hardened as it set by itself into a tight joining.

So, forget past concepts against trying to fit a square peg into a round hole. The six-step creative method will teach you, in effect, how to fill round holes without necessarily using the obvious round pegs.

CHAPTER 2. SOLUTIONS TO FILL-THE-NEED PRACTICE PROBLEMS

1. Provided storage racks on the inside of the refrigerator door. This extra storage space seems such an obvious idea now, doesn't it? Yet for many years, no one was creative enough to suggest and build door racks.

2. Offered more decorative and appealing sheets in solid colors, patterns and lovely floral designs. Plain white sheets were the only type generally available for decades. New twists are being added annually—appliqués, fitted corners, trim-it-yourself lengths. Will your creative idea be the next big hit?

3. Mix peas, carrots, lima or string beans and other vegetables with bits of bacon, frankfurters, almonds, onion, leftover rice and other items that add eye-appeal and sparkle up the flavor. In other words, apply creative cooking to transform a commonplace dish into an inviting treat.

Here's a specific application of creative thinking and ideas to something as usual and recurrent as daily family meals.

Applying this to the principle illustrated by the rooms in the brain early in this chapter, the woman doesn't just stand in the front room stolidly, dishing out the same plain vegetables meal after meal. Instead, she opens the combination lock, enters the "thinking room," and sets her creative machinery in motion. Then she serves forth a whole series of inviting and satisfying dishes seasoned with creative imagination and application.

4. With creative ingenuity, manufacturers produced a small desk with collapsible leaves that open up in seconds to form a large-size serving table.

5. A creative-minded company provided strong magnetic hooks which cling to metal shelves and firmly hold even heavy cups, utensils, tools, etc.

6. Creative plastics manufacturers produced thin, inexpensive gloves that could be thrown away after just a few uses. Also, being so thin and skin tight, the gloves increased efficiency for kitchen and garden chores, as well as for changing tires and working around greasy machinery and tools.

7. A creative manufacturer produced an efficient grater which fits as a lid over a plastic container. The compartment catches and holds all the scrapings like a safe-deposit box, with no mess or loss.

8. This woman applied her creative thinking. She called other women who might have the same need. Five of them formed a book club. Each one contributed only twenty percent of the price of each book, and they all were able to read the latest books soon after publication. And then each one became the permanent owner of one out of every five new books.

Other alert, creative women have formed even larger book clubs right at home. They've established money-making businesses by providing book-rental service, charging a membership fee, then selling each book after a specified period to the highest bidder. Note in this case how creative thinking produced a money-making idea.

9. Creative people designed intriguing shapes of macaroni that were easily manufactured and delighted children. They produced pinwheels, space rockets, even shapes that looked like popular comic strip characters. They filled the need, and sales went up.

10. As with so many excellent creative ideas, the solution now seems simple and incredibly obvious.

Yet it was quite a while before makers provided vitamin capsules in decorative little jars so attractive that they took their place next to the salt and pepper shakers on the dining table. Of course the presence of the capsules right on the table reminded the family to take their vitamins with their meals.

Although very simple, this bright creative idea helped boost vitamin sales annually by millions of dollars. When you learn how to produce practical creative ideas that "fill the need," you'll certainly profit, too.

11. Ingenious creative people produced the mending tape in many lovely colors and decorative designs, as well as plain white. They also created an instructions booklet which showed how to cut out the tape in appealing shapes like stars, crescents, letters and numbers.

When the colorful and shapely pieces of mending tape were applied, they performed their utilitarian function very decoratively. Because of this ingenious creative thinking, the mending tape was transformed from a small item into a big business.

A valuable lesson to learn here is that other firms had gone along for years producing plain mending tape and scoring very limited sales. Bright creative thinking made the magical difference that sparked skyrocketing volume and profits.

12. The inventive cosmetic maker simply but cleverly combined six different shades into one long stack of lipsticks. One little lipstick screwed into another so that a woman could carry six different colors in her purse, in one stack about the same size as an ordinary ball pen.

Here's further proof that the world of opportunity is wide open to the creative person. Every time a lipstick maker feels that "everything's been done that possibly can be done," a creative innovator comes along with something new. Then the originator profits by producing a new oval-shaped lipstick, one with a mirror, with a jeweled case, an intriguing square shape, the six-in-one stack described here, or another variation.

What's going to be the next big hit? After you learn the six-step method, perhaps you'll be the inventor to profit from a new variation, improvement and success in anything from appliances to lipsticks to zithers.

And, of course, more to the point, you'll produce ideas for your own business or other activities.

CHAPTER 3. SOLUTIONS TO CONCENTRATION PUZZLERS

1. The Elevator Mystery. The first name of the elevator operator is your first name. By concentrating on the wording of the puzzle, as stated, you'd have noted that "*You're* on the job eight hours a day . . . *you* start at the basement," etc. Clearly, you are the elevator operator. The correct name is your first name.

I used this puzzler myself on nationwide quiz shows three different times. In each case, the contestants gave up and lost the prize because they had listened only to the figures involved. They hadn't concentrated enough to catch the fact that "*You're* on the job eight hours a day."

The naturally alert or trained creative mind concentrates on each pertinent point and should solve this puzzler instantly.

2. The Secret of Driving. The usual answer from those who answer impulsively is wrong. Instead, they should first concentrate on each step of what they actually do after getting into the car.

The answer almost always is, "I place the key in the ignition slot," or, "I step on the starter," or, "I check to see whether the gear is in neutral position," or some other second step.

The first thing you do actually is to *sit down*. But, unless you concentrate clearly on exactly what you do once you open the door and enter the car by stepping in, you miss the inevitable act of sitting down.

3. Penetrate the Smoke Screen. The obvious answer is that if the man had thirty-six butts, and could make a whole cigarette with each six butts, he could smoke six more cigarettes.

But, by concentrating, you'd realize that each time he smoked one of those six cigarettes, he had another butt left over. Thus, he accumulated six more butts. He was able to form another whole cigarette—and he thus could smoke *seven* more cigarettes during the balance of the night.

4. UNCORK YOUR THINKING. The usual quick answer—proved dozens of times when I've tried this puzzler on men, women and youngsters—is that the cork cost ten cents out of the $1.10. Most people figure hurriedly that ten cents for the cork and one dollar for the bottle add up to the correct $1.10 total.

But those who give that answer haven't concentrated on the key fact that the bottle costs a dollar *more* than the cork.

By focusing on that fact, it becomes clear that the cork only costs five cents and the bottle $1.05. For when the five cents is deducted from $1.05, the bottle costs a dollar more than the cork.

5. A MATTER OF CORRECT TIMING. Most people say very quickly and emphatically that the correct answer is sixty seconds, because if it takes a clock thirty seconds to strike six, it will take twice as long to strike twelve.

But when you concentrate on the actual sequence of the clock-striking, you add thirty seconds for strokes 1, 2, 3, 4, 5, 6 to thirty seconds for strokes 7, 8, 9, 10, 11, 12. Then you finally realize that there's a six-second interval after each of the six strokes, or five intervals after each of the six strokes, or five intervals of six seconds each. So you must add the six-second interval between strokes 6 and 7, for a total of sixty-six seconds.

You may have to concentrate on the answer to understand this solution thoroughly. It will help for you to look at a watch face and note the intervals *between* the numbers, rather than consider the actual numbers themselves.

CHAPTER 4. SOLUTIONS TO WAKE-UP PRACTICE PUZZLERS

1. Name the City. In this puzzler, you must focus not only on the general wording, but also on the actual words. Thus, you would detect that the name of the city is half "gol*den*" and half "sil*ver*." Combining the half-words, the name of the city is Denver.

The solution to this puzzler spotlights the importance of being wide awake to many aspects and possible different meanings in any problem.

2. The "Nothing" Problem. In attacking this problem, you solved it swiftly if you were alert to two clues. First, that "slanguage" could help. Second, that the solution is "nothing." By placing the matches in position as shown in the illustration, you produce the word "nix." The dictionary will tell you that "nix" is slang for "nothing." You can also produce the word "nil," which has the same meaning.

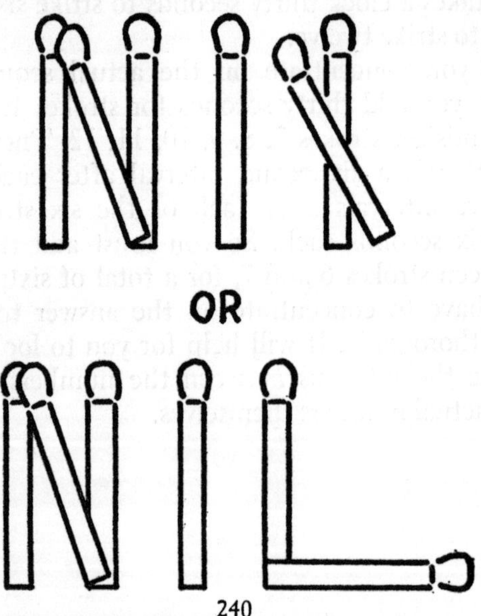

Were you wide awake to these clearly presented clues? If not, you certainly will be on other problems in the future. That alertness is a vital aid in the creative approach.

3. DETECT THE DEVICE. This is about as simple as a problem can be, yet has been proved one of the most difficult to solve for most people. The reason is that the person challenged is usually not looking for the most commonplace answer. Instead, the tendency is to think about some obscure or unusual scientific item.

Of course you need simply look, with eyes wide open and discerning, at most any brick wall. You'll note that the device used to look through the wall is surprisingly evident—a window.

4. PROBLEM OF GRAVITY. What is the center of gravity, in no more than three words? Again, if you're alert, you not only look at the all-over question but also at the word itself—gravity.

So, what's the center of the word "gravity" in no more than three words? The answer is clear (once you see it): The letter V.

It becomes simple when you look at every aspect of a question in the wide-awake creative way, doesn't it?

5. A QUESTION OF DOLLARS. If you look at the front of the dollar bill alertly and intensively, the answer to the problem becomes just as clear as the nose on Mr. Washington's face.

In the sentence at the left of the portrait, you'll find the precise description of "a delicate, secluded type of woman . . . even considering slang."

Note, as in the illustration:

GAL TENDER
AND PRIVATE

All the clues were plainly there—all you had to do was to focus on them. As the dictionary states, "gal" is slang for "woman," "delicate" is a synonym for "tender" and "secluded" is included as a definition for "private." And you were permitted to break words apart, namely, "legal."

As noted previously, there's a world of difference between merely looking and really seeing. Learning the difference can be a great step in advancing your creative thinking and idea-producing powers.

CHAPTER 5. SOLUTIONS TO MYSTERY PRACTICE PUZZLERS

1. THE CASE OF THE THREATENING DAGGER. In trying to solve this mystery, most people miss the main point: Why did Oscar threaten Carl with the dagger? Why did Carl (and the police) accept his explanation so readily?

The first question leads you to examine the action preceding the dagger threat. Why was Carl sipping water all day? Answer that, relate it to the threatening action, and you have the solution.

Oscar explained to Carl, and then to the police, that he pretended to threaten him with the dagger to scare him out of the hiccups; Carl had been sipping water repeatedly to try to cure his hiccups. His sudden death the next evening was due to causes related to the severe hiccups.

2. THE CASE OF THE SCOT-FREE SHOPLIFTER. Many wrong answers are given to this classic mystery puzzler. Some say that the man owned the store, or that he had some special diplomatic immunity, and so forth. But, to arrive at the one correct solu-

tion, you must penetrate to a realization of what "particular, unusual physical condition" could keep a thief or a murderer from being jailed.

The answer is that the man was a Siamese twin. He couldn't be jailed because this would involve jailing his twin, who had to be permitted to go free because he was innocent.

3. THE CASE OF THE INEFFICIENT OPERATOR. In many instances people study this puzzler for several minutes but can't find the solution. The answer lies in focusing on the *purpose* for giving a word for each initial. The reason was not to understand the word but to clarify the initial.

Thus, "B for Bratwurst" explained the B, not the related word. So when the operator asked, after "O for osculation," "O for what?" she was asking an unnecessary question, as she already knew the "O," and it was absolutely unnecessary to know the word related to it.

In this case, the target was the initial, not the word. Focusing on the word would never provide the solution.

4. THE CASE OF THE MYSTERIOUS LETTER. It has surprised me how often people try to find an explanation in the possibility that the police chief had written the letter himself, or that the envelope was transparent and that the address was visible on a sheet inside, and so forth.

The objective is clearly to analyze why the three words were placed in the peculiar formation. This leads to searching questions as to why "JOHN" was under "WOOD" and over "MASS."

The name, city and state thus become painfully clear:

JOHN UNDERWOOD
ANDOVER, MASS.

5. THE CASE OF THE DASTARDLY DREAM. If you were trying to find in the dream itself the reasons why Frank was fired, you were looking toward the wrong objective. The reason why the

boss would fire his employee would be logically because he didn't perform his job well.

The clues revealed that Frank arrived "at eight o'clock on Tuesday morning . . . on his way home from work." If you focused on the fact that Frank did dream, instead of what he dreamed (the mistake most people make), you'd probably arrive quickly at the correct solution.

Unfortunately, Frank was not such a "faithful" employee. He was the night watchman and shouldn't have been dreaming on the job.

Keep this example, like the others, clearly in mind when you're seeking a creative solution. Here, you had to focus on the relationship of the fact of dreaming to the problem, not on the content of the dream.

Don't be fooled by the magician's trick of fixing your attention on his right hand while he slips a card from his sleeve into his left hand. Misdirection leads to mistakes that prevent the creation of well-directed, successful creative ideas.

In other words, in approaching a problem, beware of sleight-of mind which may cause you to lead yourself astray and away from the true objective.

CHAPTER 6. SOLUTIONS TO FACT-FINDING PUZZLERS

1. The Baffled Nonworker. This puzzler makes the pertinent point that you must consider *all* the facts, not just a mass of seeming facts and figures. The important clue here is what the boss left out.

Instead of deducting full Saturdays, Sundays and other non-working days—in terms of a basis of twenty-four-hour days—he should only have taken off one-third of each of those days, or eight hours each. Thus, Herman actually worked 81⅓ full days of twenty-four-hours each out of the 366 twenty-four-hour days in a year.

Don't you agree that the fakery and distortions of facts alone entitled Herman to be given a raise?

2. Chained to a Dilemma. The facts in this case are the

links of the chain. The restriction is that the landlady must receive no more and no less than one added link each day for seven days. Also, Charlie could only cut out one link of the chain. So, picture and study the links above.

Charlie solved the problem, as you could, by cutting out only the third link of the chain. Thus, he had three separate sections with one, two and four links each, as shown here:

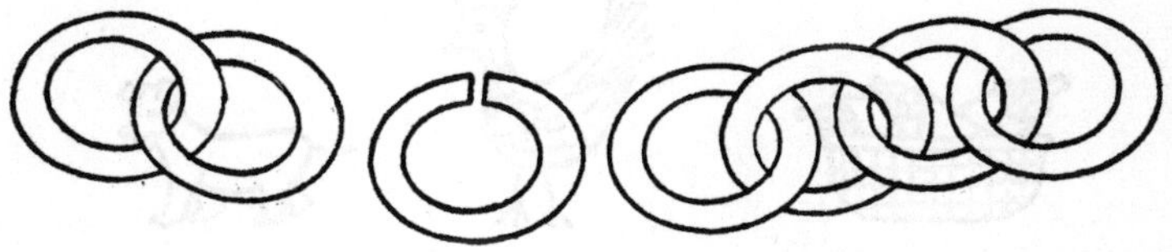

Having separated the facts, in effect, the seemingly complicated solution becomes simple, as follows:

Monday: Gave landlady the one separated link.
Tuesday: Took back the one, and gave her the two links.
Wednesday: Gave her the single link.
Thursday: Gave her the four links, took back the one and two.
Friday: Gave her the one link.
Saturday: Took back the one, gave her the two links.
Sunday: Gave her the one link, and both were happy.

Thank goodness, Charlie's allowance arrived the next day, as he was all out of links and would have been out of luck. That's a fact!

3. HOW FAR FLIES THE HUMMINGBIRD? In all the confusion caused by the hummingbird's gyrations, you must nail down the actual clear facts. Then figure out the answer from there.

1. The motorcycles start 50 miles apart.
2. One travels 30 miles an hour, the other 20 miles an hour.
3. The combined speed of the motorcycles is 50 miles an hour.
4. Therefore, together they cover the 50-mile distance in one hour.
5. The hopped-up hummingbird speeds 100 miles an hour.
6. By traveling back and forth at top speed during the period of one hour, the hummingbird flies 100 miles.

It's so simple—isn't it?—once you put down the facts and follow through accordingly.

4. THE CHICKEN AND THE CHICKEN-EATING DOG. First, face the facts of the problem, lay them out and examine them, thus:

The solution becomes simple when you fix on one basic fact, that there's no prohibition against the farmer's *bringing back* anything on his return trips across the river. Thus, his routine can be figured out in a minute or so.

1. He takes across the chicken, leaving the corn with the non-corn-eating dog. He returns alone, leaving the chicken alone, pecking happily at a worm.
2. He brings the dog across, but takes back the chicken, leaving the frustrated dog sulking alone.
3. He takes over the corn, leaving the chicken alone. Returning by himself, he leaves the dog and corn.
4. He brings over the chicken and takes them all to his customer.

Let's hope that since the farmer was smart enough to solve his dilemma, he'll be too wise to stop at a tavern on the way back and drink up the profits from his complicated maneuvering. Or, the fact may be that he has earned a liquid reward. Skoal!

5. Profit and Loss Puzzler. Assemble and analyze the facts of the case, and it quickly becomes clear who made the profit and who suffered the loss.

1. Wilbur broke even, since he was given back the $20 he had loaned to Pete in the first place.
2. Pete made a profit (as of this moment, anyhow), since he started with $14 and wound up with $20, which he paid back to Wilbur. Thus, he had borrowed $20 originally, spent $6, and yet was able to pay back $20. In effect, he had a $6 profit on the original $20.
3. Ernest had thought he was a smart cookie to buy a pawn ticket worth $10 for a payment of only $8. However, when Ernest went to the pawnbroker to get the $10, he found that, of course, he had to repay the proprietor the $8 which Pete had borrowed on the ticket, in order to get back the $10. So, the $10 at the pawn shop cost Ernest the original $8 he'd given to Pete, plus $8 more to the pawnbroker—adding up to $16 paid

out and $10 return, for a loss of $6—the same $6 that had been Pete's "profit." (Let's not be concerned about any interest on the loan.)

Yet Ernest could have foreseen the fact of his loss, just as clearly as you can now, if he'd looked at all the facts in the first place. As noted, you can profit if you'll "seek out and fill your mind with facts."

CHAPTER 7. SOLUTIONS TO MATCH-THE-FACTS PUZZLERS

1. Four-Square Problem. Just as you'll sift and shift the facts in forming ideas in step four, you'll probably have to shift the matches a number of times until you produce four squares out of five, as shown here in one solution, by moving only two of the matches.

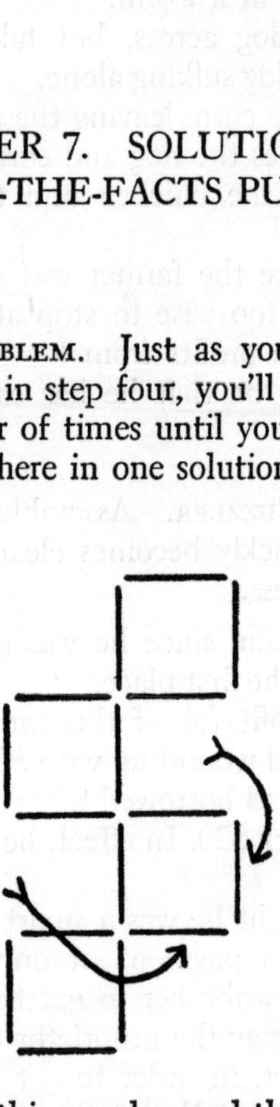

If you wish to use this puzzler, and the others in this group, as party stunts, start several people tackling the problems at the same time. Check which one can solve the puzzlers in the shortest interval.

2. FORM-A-SQUARE PUZZLER. In rare instances, just a short, quick, clever move can solve a problem.

That's the case here. Simply move down match D, as shown in the diagram, and you form a square in the center of the four matches.

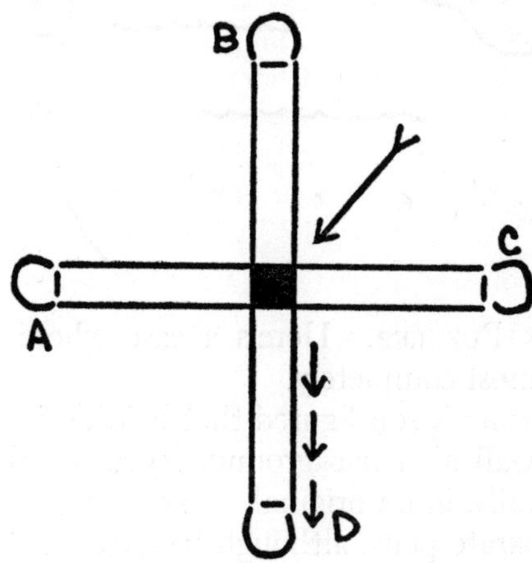

3. REACH-THE-ISLAND PROBLEM. Sometimes you can solve a problem by juggling the facts at cross-purposes, as you'll learn later.

In this instance, you place one plank across the two ends of the pond. Then you cross the other one *over* it so it reaches to the island.

It's a cinch then to wheel the load of bricks from shore to where X marks the spot, as shown in the drawing.

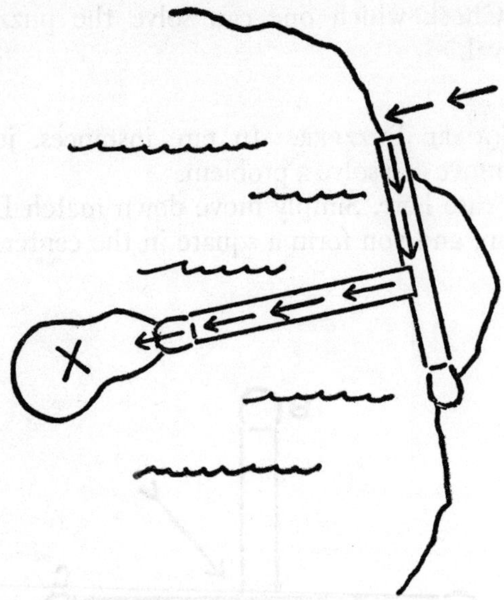

4. The Pigpen Puzzler. Here's a case where you leave the original plan almost completely.

The bright farmer's son figured that he'd do just as well without the stone wall as a background. By using the "facts," his six remaining walls, in an original, creative, pinwheel formation, he provided separate pens, although in a different shape, for all six pigs.

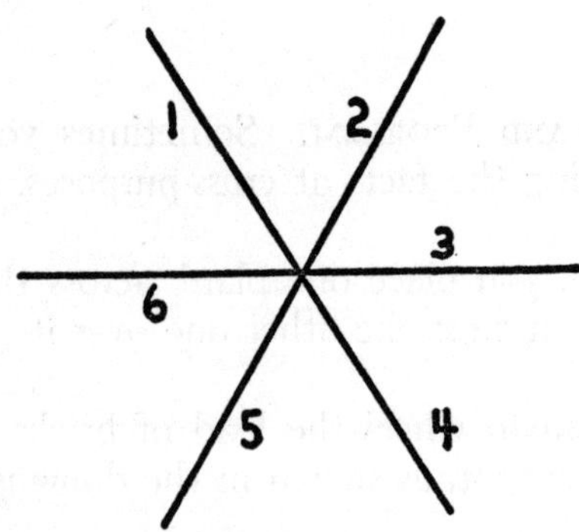

Obviously, sometimes it pays to go around in circles to arrive at the wanted creative solution.

5. NINE-INTO-THREE TRANSFORMATION. Like so many creative ideas, the solution to this puzzler looks simple once it's concluded.

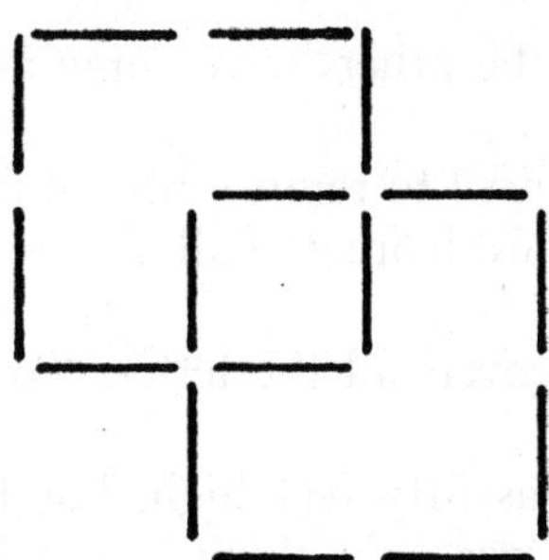

In this case, a special twist did the trick. The fact that even though one square is smaller than the other two, the formation still "leaves three squares," as specified in the challenge.

Note later on in this chapter how importantly "larger" and "smaller" play a part in clarifying the specific lessons on how to create ideas in step four, "after the facts."

CHAPTER 8. SOLUTIONS TO MENTAL-RELAXATION RIDDLES

1. Just one. All the others were going away from St. Ives.
2. A rainbow.
3. A man is required to remove his hat for his barber (unless he wants the unkindest haircut of all).
4. Holes.
5. Alphabet. It covers all the letters from A to Z, a total of twenty-six.
6. The ladder was fifty feet high, but the man fell off the lowest rung, which was only about a foot from the ground.
7. Baby tigers.
8. Neither candle burns longer. Like candles of any color, width, height or shape, they'll both burn shorter.
9. A baseball team. Nine players, eighteen legs, and with any skill at all the team certainly catches flies hit by opposing batters.
10. In the dictionary—where Saturday also comes before Thursday each week.
11. Fast. (Did you err?)
12. Your photograph.
13. Only one egg, because, after that, his stomach isn't empty any more.
14. The side of an apple that you haven't eaten is the side that's left.
15. The ladies don't get wet because it isn't raining.
16. A very clear echo.
17. "California" has always begun with a "C" . . . and "end" has always begun with an "E." Reread the question before you throw this book at me.
18. Silence. (As Shakespeare wrote, "The rest is silence.")

19. Because there's not a *single* person in the room.
20. Your lap.
21. No one could possibly own such an egg, as peacocks don't lay eggs—peahens handle that for the species.
22. Just one day of the year for sure—the shortest day (not counting the longest night!).
23. A sponge. You may wish to soak your head if you missed that one.
24. Wrong!
25. Too wise you are,
Too wise you be.
I see you are
Too wise for me.

And so to bed, to let your mind simmer and create the ultimate ideas.

CHAPTER 9. SOLUTIONS TO "HOWDUNIT" PRACTICE PUZZLERS

1. WHAT'S HER NAME? The tricky answer is astonishingly simple, like many very successful creative solutions and ideas. The stated facts reveal that Herbert had known his friend for many years. When the little girl explained that her name was the same as her mother's, Herbert knew that she was Gwendolyn, because his "friend" was the child's mother.

Most people, seeking the "how" of this puzzler, assume readily that Herbert's friend is a man, since he himself is a man. But an assessment of the facts, stated or possible, leads to the correct "how" explanation.

2. HOW THE GRAY MUSTACHE? You don't have to be a dermatologist or a barber or a bearded lady to figure this out. The

man's hair on his scalp is fifteen to twenty years older than his mustache.

3. Speedier Than Light? Here's another puzzler that reveals its tricky answer readily when you assess and recheck all the facts.

Nothing was stated about the time of day. George (or anyone) can turn out the lamp and get into bed "before the room is dark," when he goes to bed in the bright daytime.

4. Penetrate the Proverb. Assess the meaning of each word separately—"unseen" and "idiot." By evaluating the sense of each, you penetrate to the famous proverb: "Out of sight (unseen), out of mind (idiot)."

5. How to Win the Race? You should dash out to the autos and drive your brother's car to Chicago as fast as you can possibly do it (legally, of course) so that you arrive before he does.

Examination of the terms of the will reveals that the prize will go to the brother "whose *car* comes in last." If you can bring your brother's car in first, your car will come in last.

Yes, here's a specific instance where bright creative thinking can be worth a million dollars.

CHAPTER 12. SOLUTIONS TO BRAIN-PROD PUZZLERS

1. How Start a Fire? You could use the round glass from the top of the flashlight as a burning glass to concentrate the sun's rays on dry leaves or twigs. (You could use the tutti-frutti ice cream to cool off after you started the fire.)

2. How Cut the Pie? First make a circular cut within the pie, then two cuts across, as shown. Nothing was said about cutting equal pieces. (Find four people who don't like crust, then four others will have plenty of crust—like the creator of this puzzler.)

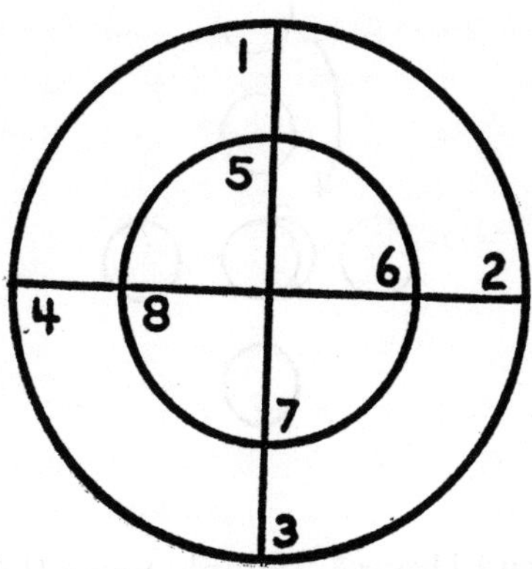

3. How Arrange the Diamonds? As arranged in the diagram, you can count the diamonds in any straight row or at right angles. The total is always nine.

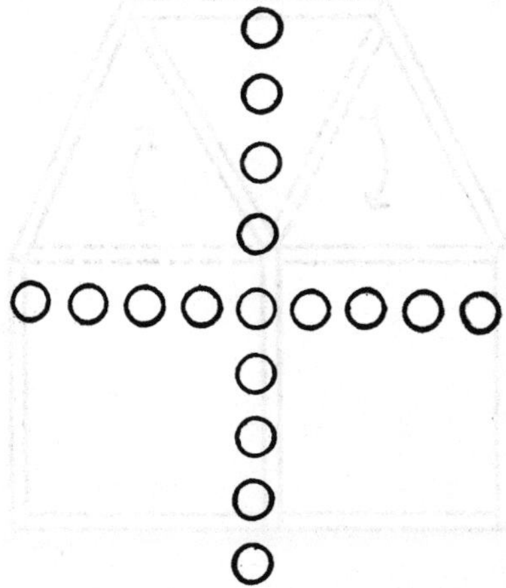

4. HOW WIN THE COINS? Just move the top coin down and place it on top of the center coin. Now the coins add up to four, counted horizontally or vertically. Cash in!

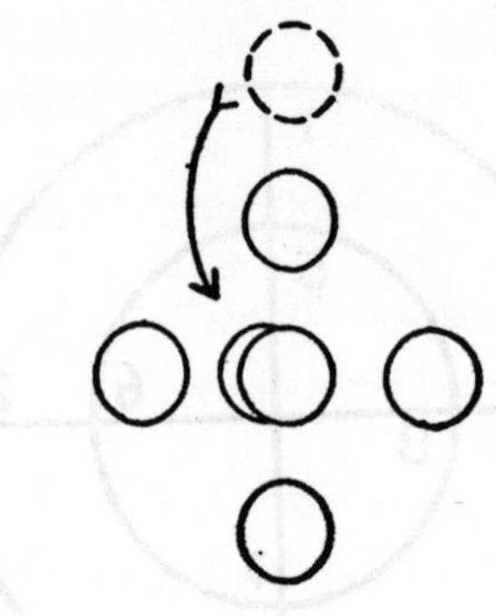

5. HOW ALTER THE HOUSE? Simply move the two matches as shown, and the house faces to the right instead of to the left. (If you accomplished this in the first two quick moves, congratulate yourself—very few people can solve this rapidly.)

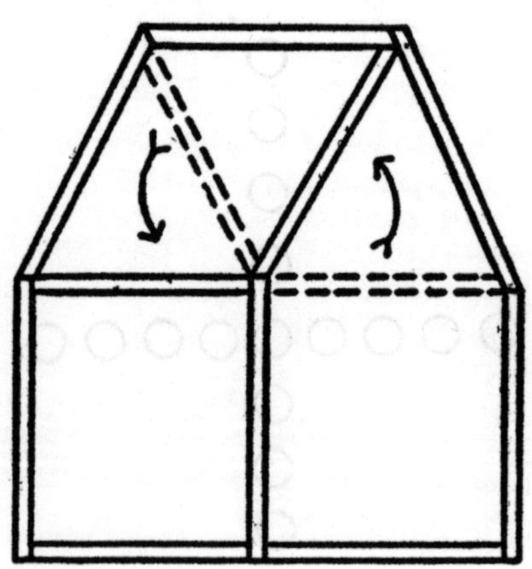

CHAPTER 13. SOLUTIONS TO FUN-WITH-WORDS PUZZLERS

1. THE HIDDEN WORD. The hidden three-syllable word is "continue." It works out this way: C-on-T-in-U.

2. CLIMB THE WORD LADDER. Here's how you can climb from *Seed* to *Crop* in seven rungs. It's fun, and excellent vocabulary exercise, to make up your own word ladders. Here are a few more where you can work out the answers: *Colt* to *Mare* in six. *Cold* to *Heat* in six. *Safe* to *Hurt* in eight.

When you're relaxing for a half-hour, see how many original word ladders you can create, extending between related or opposite words.

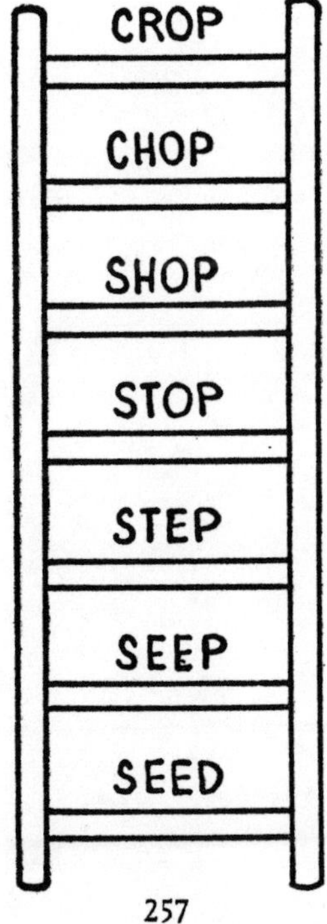

3. Find the Phrase. "*Wether*" is "a bad spell of *Weather.*"

4. Place the Punctuation. Here's how a few marks make a perfectly clear sentence out of the unintelligible string of words:

"It was 'and,' " I said, "not 'are,' and 'and' and 'are' are different."

5. Make a Word Grow. "Digging" into this puzzler helps. By adding to "ERGRO" the three letters "und" in front, and the same three letters in back, you produce the word "undERGROund."